Building
Real Estate Wealth

by Jay Butler and
Dr. Robert Hagopian

AssetProtectionServices.com

ISBN 978-0-9914644-1-8

BUILDING REAL ESTATE WEALTH

HOW TO BUY, FLIP, HOLD OR SELL REAL PROPERTY

Table of **Contents**

Disclaimer

The publication is copyrighted © 2016 by Asset Protection Services of America (hereinafter "APSA") with all rights reserved. No part of this publication may be reproduced, retransmitted or rebroadcast in any form or by any means without the express prior written consent of the copyright holder.

Information contained in this publication has been prepared for continuing research and, although these materials may be technical in nature, carries no weight other than being educational in purpose. The materials are provided only as a starting point in order for the reader to undertake his or her own investigation of the subject matter contained herein.

This publication has been garnered from sources deemed reliable at the time of rendering. Since laws, rules, rulings, regulations, statutes and codes are constantly changing and evolving, the information may not be current and APSA takes no responsibility for updating, omitting or correcting any information in this publication.

APSA offers no guarantees the information in this book as being comprehensive, exhaustive, accurate or complete and furthers the information provided is on an "AS IS" basis. Any guidance or reliance on the content found in this publication is at the sole risk of the user. APSA offers no assurances as to the suitability of any particular service or strategy meeting any stated aims, goals or objectives. APSA strongly recommends the reader seek independent accounting, financial, investing, legal, tax or other professional advice.

No representations or warranties are given or implied to render any accounting, financial, investing, legal, tax or other professional advice. No accounting, financial, investing, legal, tax or other professional advice is intended, approved or authorized by APSA. If any accounting, financial, investing, legal, tax or other professional advice is required, then a competent professional should be sought.

APSA and any APSA advisors, directors, employees, members, officers, partners, professional agencies, professional intermediaries, shareholders, staff, ultimate beneficial owners and any other affiliated firms or third-parties wherever situated, take no responsibility whatsoever, whether individually or collectively, for the manner in which the reader may choose to interpret or use the information presented in this publication. APSA shall not be held liable for any civil or criminal liability or damages whether direct, indirect, special or consequential resulting from any interpretations or use of the information provided in this publication.

This publication shall not be taken as sanctioning or advocating any unlawful act or for any improper use of any entity structure, asset protection, tax strategy or estate planning activity, nor for any illegal or fraudulent purposes.

Asset Protection Services of America

The inverted "V" displayed on our shield is the uppercase letter "L" in ancient Greek identifying the people of Lacedaemonia, which in historical times was the proper name for the Spartan state. The Greek cry "Molõn Labé" means "Come and Get Them" as spoken by King Leonidas in response to the Persian army's demand for the outnumbered Spartans (300 against 300,000) to surrender their weapons during battle in the narrow pass or 'hot gates' of Thermopylae in 480 B.C. The iconic expression has become a symbol of courage to defend that which belongs to you, even if faced against overwhelming or insurmountable odds.

Author

Jay Butler is the Managing Director of Asset Protection Services of America, the former Managing Director of Asset Protection Services International, Ltd and the former Vice-President of Sales and Marketing for Corporate Support Services of Nevada Inc. Mr. Butler holds a Bachelor's Degree of Fine Arts from Boston University.

Jay has provided customized business entity structuring for clients in all 50 states along with some of the most respected names in the industry including the Jay Mitton organization "the father of asset protection" and Real Estate Investor Association seminars.

While working with Wealth Protection Concepts, LLC under the tutelage of the former Las Vegas and North Las Vegas city attorney Carl E. Lovell Jr. (now deceased from Leukemia), Mr. Butler was bestowed the title of "Asset Protection Planner" for his competency and experience. He also co-authored the first edition of his book "Cover Your Assets: Legal Authorities on Asset Protection, Tax Strategies and Estate Planning" © 2006 with Dr. Lovell.

While residing in Switzerland, Mr. Butler was the Associate Director of "CO-Handelszentrum GmbH" providing Swiss company formation and administration services and executed a full-range of fiduciary responsibilities including sales, client support and international corporate compliance services (KYC, FATCA, AML, FATF and Swiss Code of Obligations).

Jay builds his relationships through consistent attention to detail and reliable support. He has traveled extensively throughout the United States (having visited 49 of the 50 states), explored 36 nations worldwide, and has lived in a total of 7 countries throughout North America, Central America, the Middle East, North Africa and Europe.

Dr Robert Hagopian is semi-retired and the former CEO of Nevada Trustee Services Group Inc, which has provided trustee services to attorneys and law firms throughout the United States since 2005, and the former CEO of the Commerce Bank Ltd in Hong Kong.

Since 1968, Robert has traveled extensively throughout Asia and lived in Japan, Hong Kong and the Philippines with current residency and offices in Manilla.

Dr. Hagopian holds a Bachelor of Science (BS) degree in business administration, an MsD (doctorate) in philosophy and a "jure Dignitatis" Bachelor of Laws degree.

Since 1984, Dr. Hagopian has been structuring business entities for optimum wealth preservation, profitability, asset protection and limiting personal liability through the use of domestic corporations, limited liability companies and various trust vehicles.

Robert has developed innovative processes for the acquisition, holding and marketing of real property. In 2008, Dr. Hagopian applied for the patent-pending "Equity Recovery Program". Based on IRC 351 rules for the transference of real estate to a corporation, the program lawfully avoids capital gains tax, self-employment and state taxes upon the sale of real property.

Contact Us

Please browse our website at www.AssetProtectionServices.com and contact us to schedule your free private asset protection consultation. We welcome the opportunity to hold a 3-way conference call with your tax advisor and/or legal counsel to address any specific questions or concerns you may have. Experience has demonstrated it favorable to have all related parties "on the same page" when creating your structure.

Asset Protection Services of America
701 South Carson Street (Suite #200)
Carson City, Nevada 89701-5239
Office   (775) 461-5255
Skype   Jay_Butler
E-Mail   info@AssetProtectionServices.com
Website www.AssetProtectionServices.com

Books by Jay Butler and Dr. Robert Hagopian

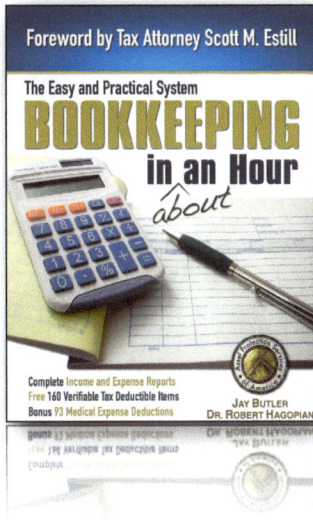

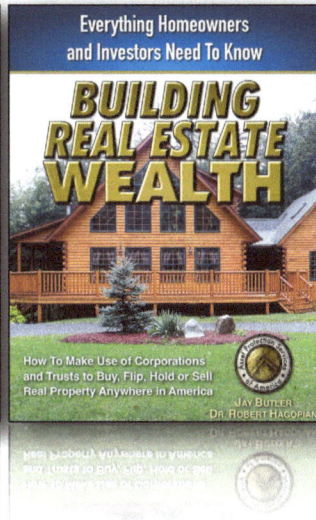

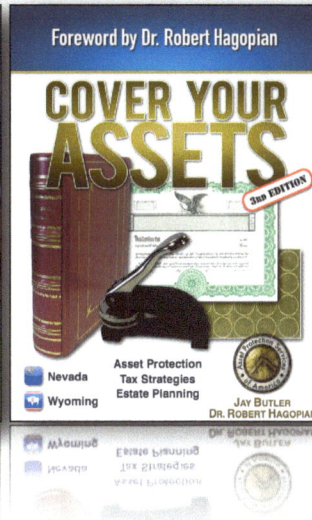

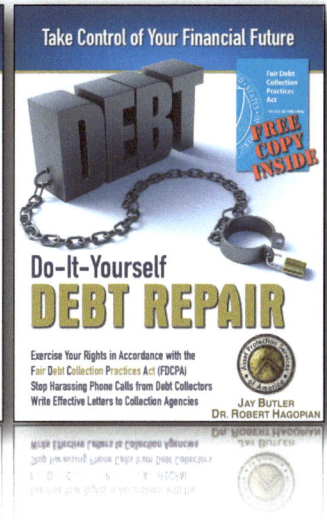

Bookkeeping in About an Hour	ISBN 978-0-9914644-0-1	
Building Real Estate Wealth	ISBN 978-0-9914644-1-8	
Cover Your Assets *(3rd Edition)*	ISBN 978-0-9914644-2-5	
Do-It-Yourself Debt Repair	ISBN 978-0-9914644-7-0	

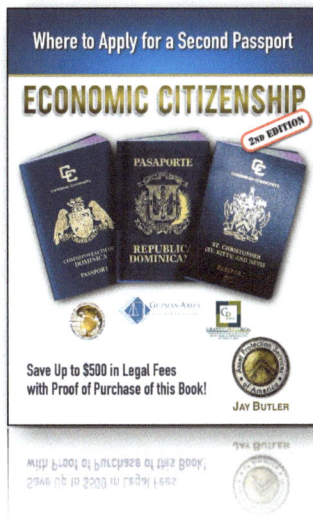

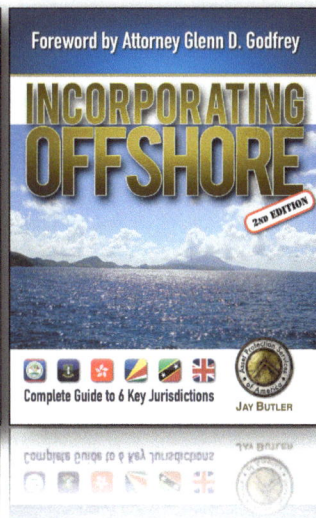

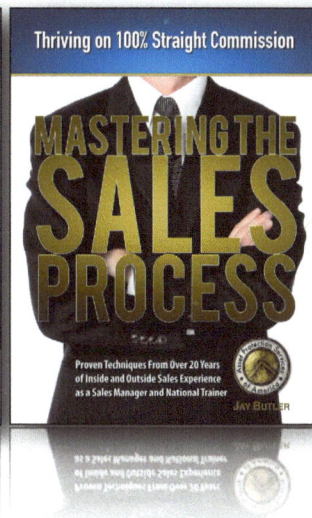

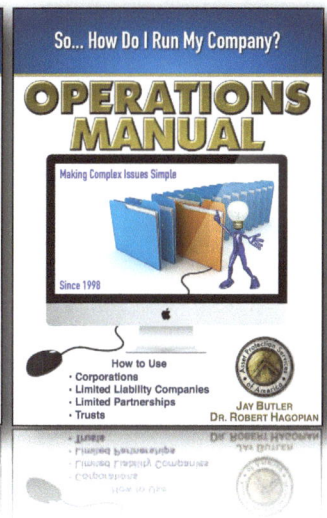

Economic Citizenship *(2nd Edition)*	ISBN 978-0-9914644-4-9
Incorporating Offshore *(2nd Edition)*	ISBN 978-0-9914644-5-6
Mastering the Sales Process	ISBN 978-0-9914644-6-3
Operations Manual	ISBN 978-0-9914644-3-2

Asset Protection Services of America

**Everything Homeowners
Need to Know**

AssetProtectionServices.com

Fair Market Value

Fair Market Value (FMV) is the price at which a property changes hands between a willing buyer and seller. Sales of similar or 'comparable' properties (comp's) are helpful in figuring the most current value (or estimated price) for a property. However, **opinions** of such value differ greatly and are largely dependent on who has the most to gain financially.

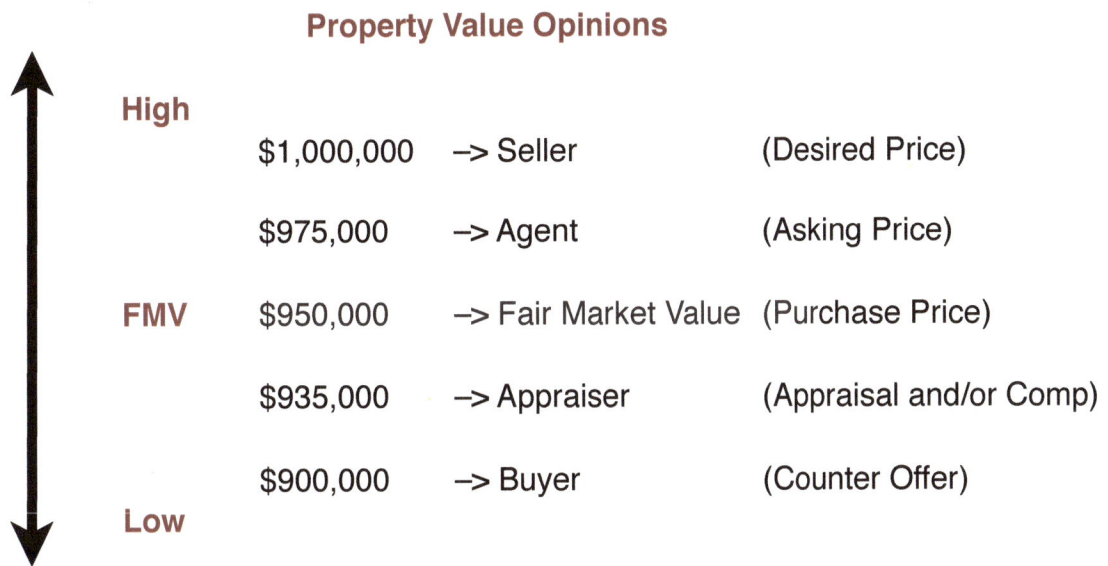

Property Value Opinions

High			
	$1,000,000	–> Seller	(Desired Price)
	$975,000	–> Agent	(Asking Price)
FMV	$950,000	–> Fair Market Value	(Purchase Price)
	$935,000	–> Appraiser	(Appraisal and/or Comp)
	$900,000	–> Buyer	(Counter Offer)
Low			

At the end-of-the-day, regardless of the amount for which the seller *wants* to sell the property, or what the (real estate) agent *thinks* the property is worth, or what value the appraiser *believes* the property to be worth, or what the *estimated* value of the property is (based on comparable properties that have already sold), **the buyer decides** the current property value with his or her purchase price. **Buyers determine** the Fair Market Value (FMV) of a property.

Original Value

Under the rules of private mortgage insurance, 'original value' means the lesser of the contract sales price of the property or the appraised value of the property at the time the loan was closed. If a new loan refinances an existing loan secured by the property, the refinanced loan amount becomes the new cost basis. The 'cost basis' becomes the base cost for figuring gains and/or loses for tax purposes.

Capital Improvements

If you are considering updating or improving your home to make it 'more sellable', be aware that not all capital improvements are tax deductible and may not give you a return on your investment. When trying to decide which things to repair or replace prior to selling your home, focus on items which are of most importance and will help you sell your property.

Capital improvements are costs related to making changes to improve or increase their useful life, productivity and/or add to the value of these assets. Such changes, which must be capitalized, are distinguished from deductible repairs which are more minor in nature. A capital improvement increases your home's value, while a non-eligible repair just returns something to its original condition. According to the IRS, capital improvements have to last for more than one year and add value to your home, prolong its life, or adapt it to new uses.

Capital improvements can include everything from a new bathroom or deck to a new water heater or furnace. The improvements must still be evident when you sell. So if you put in wall-to-wall carpeting 10 years ago and then replaced it with hardwood floors five years ago, you can't count the carpeting as a capital improvement. Repairs, like painting your house or fixing sagging gutters, don't count. The IRS describes repairs as things that are done to maintain a home's good condition without adding value or prolonging its life.

There can be a fine line between a capital improvement and a repair. If you replace a few shingles on your roof, it's a repair. If you replace the entire roof, it's a capital improvement. Same goes for windows. If you replace a broken window pane - repair. Put in a new window, capital improvement.

Keeping track of the cost of capital improvements to your home can really pay off on your tax return when it comes time to sell. (See Real Estate Forms for the Capital Gains Worksheet) You cannot claim the deduction until you sell your home when the cost of additions and other improvements are added to the cost basis of your property. A higher cost basis lowers the total profit and its associated capital gain which you're required to pay taxes on.

Selling Your Own Home

✔ Clean-Out Your Home

As soon as you decide to sell your home, thoroughly clean it from top to bottom. Don't forget rarely-cleaned areas such as baseboards, roof gutters and window wells. A clean home will help an appraiser see your home in a better light and will be more appealing to buyers. Trim the trees, wash the windows, get rid of big heavy draperies. Things which help bring the light in make a home warm, more inviting and spacious.

Because of familiarity, you're likely to overlook some aspects of cleaning that scrutinizing potential buyers won't. If you want to make the best possible impression, shell out some cash and hire a professional cleaning service, at least for an initial deep clean. Don't underestimate the power of a spotless home. Once you get it that way, keep it that way, even if you have to hire the professional cleaner once a week to keep your home clean.

✓ Clear-Up Any Clutter

Make your home look more spacious by getting rid of any unnecessary junk. You'll see a big difference in how your closets look, as well as your garage, porch and bathrooms. Buyers want to feel like they're purchasing sufficient space, and clearing out more of your stuff helps them see themselves in your home. Limit furniture in your home to the absolute essentials. If you haven't used it in three months, store it, sell it or give it away as the rooms will appear larger. Freshen up the house with air freshener, fresh flowers and/or bowls of fruit.

If you can't bear to part with something, consider moving the item(s) to a storage unit temporarily. Remember you want a buyer to see 'space' and not 'stuff'. The buyer needs to envision his or her things in the home and will not be able to do so if your home is filled-up.

✓ Critically Look-Over Your Home

Paint scuffed or brightly colored walls in soothing neutral colors (beige or white). Check the carpets and drapes to ensure they are clean and odor free. Replace faded or stained carpeting and refinish or re-polish floors. Make sure that your home is cosmetically clean and as perfect as you can afford. Then turn to the functional things and see if they need to be repaired or replaced. Ruthlessly inspect appliances, heating and air conditioning, roofing, sidewalks and driveways. If they are nearing the end of their lifespan, repair or replace them.

Finally, take a look at things that you can't change about your home. Is it on a busy road, adjacent to a smelly restaurant, on a funny shaped lot or facing train tracks? You may need to adjust or lower the price to entice buyers if it suffers any of these or other types of 'detractions'.

Home Appraisals

As much as you'd like to set the price of your home as high as possible, you have to be realistic. Many home listings fail to sell because owners persist in thinking their home is worth more than the market will pay, or because they have already settled on a set amount of money that they want and refuse to budge. Having a professional, third-party appraisal of your home's worth will help you get comfortable with a price range and provides you with a solid reference point if a buyer or realtor says that you have set your price too high.

Appraisers

A certified residential appraiser will come to your home, measure the property, take notes and photos, research information about any land parcels and assemble a list of comparable sales in your neighborhood to determine an estimated value of your home. An appraiser will cost about $300 to $500 but the value the appraiser sets for your home will be more accurate than any other process you might employ. Many banks keep a list of reputable appraisers they contact for refinancing or mortgage loans; ask your local branch manager to refer you to an honest, qualified professional. Once you receive your copy of the appraisal, make a second copy and store it in a secure location. Keep a copy on-hand to go over with serious buyers.

Comparisons

The number one mistake owners make is pricing their home too high. Price it too high and you will scare off potential buyers. It will sit on the market and get stale. Buyers will start to wonder what's wrong and pricing effectively helps a home sell faster. Home comparisons (also known as comparables or comps) are what other similar homes in your area are selling for, or have sold for, and often determine (for better or worse) what price range your home will fall in. Always use comps when arriving at a realistic assessment of your home's value.

Inspections

Most real estate contracts are going to give the home buyer the right to inspect the property, so be prepared. Have your home inspected before you advertise it for sale or contract with a realtor. Under a general inspection you might find that you will need to make repairs to appliances, plumbing, septic, electrical and heating or air conditioning systems, etc. You can expect your home's roof and foundations will definitely need to be inspected as well. Follow the recommendations and make the necessary repairs. Any additional inspections that are requested by the buyer are customarily paid by the buyer. As much as possible, get your home to 'move-in condition' before you put it on the market. Buyers are lazy. If they feel like they'll need to do extra landscaping, plumbing, appliance and electrical work before they can enjoy a trouble free home, they'll balk when it comes to buying, even if the rest of your home is an absolute steal. So make it easy for them. Hire a handyman or general contractor to get the home as close to 'move-in ready' as possible.

Timing Your Sale

Be aware that the real estate sector sees a noticeable uptick in business over the summer — people prefer to move when it's warm, and they're reluctant to have their children change schools in the middle of the school year. Start trying to sell your home in April or May and continue to promote it throughout the summer. If you haven't sold it by late fall, think about taking it off the market until the weather warms up again.

Another thing to be aware of is the trend your neighborhood is going through. If your neighborhood is undergoing a mini boom of strong residential sales, those transactions will increase the value of your home. Conversely, if your neighborhood has seen a lot of short sales or foreclosures, your home's value will be decreased. Try to time your listing so that you're not affected by distressed sales. For instance, in most areas, a comparable sale can only weigh against the value of your home for 90 days after the sale date. It might be worth it to wait a few months to list your home if you can do it at a higher price.

Staging Your Home

Staging is a term used to express putting your home on a 'stage' and preparing it for sale, and is an especially important part of selling your home. During the 'staging', potential buyers begin mentally imagining their own items (personal possessions) in the home what their lives would be like in your home. If they can't make the imaginative leap because the home is too cluttered, dirty, overly colorful or quirky, the potential buyers will politely say 'no thank you'. The best approach is to 'stage' a home so as to be as spacious, clean and welcoming.

Selling Points

Know your selling points in order to attract interested buyers. Before you start 'marketing' your home or hiring a realtor, write a list of special selling points you think will attract the kind of buyers who would be interested in your property. Potential items include school districts, recent renovations, benefits that have been built into the property, energy-saving windows or doors, added insulation and new appliances. Highlight these items in your ads and be sure to mention them when you talk to people about your home or while you're showing it.

Do Your Research

The first order of business in preparing for a home sale is to become familiar with real estate transactions. Since you've been through the experience at least once, pull out your old paperwork from when you purchased the home and review them. Learn the language of real estate and/or read a book or two about how to help you sell your home.

If you are selling your home yourself (not through a realtor) you will need to gather all the paperwork and forms for the home sales process and closing, including copies of property records for the appraisers, title company and insurance documents, disclosures and legal instruments. You should also line up people who will help you in the selling and closing process, including a title company, real estate attorney and/or an appraiser, if you plan to use one. Finally, consider how you want to structure the deal. Will you want to offer such incentives as owner-financing, selling 'subject-to' the mortgage or a lease-option (rent to own) to attract buyers? Although this publication gives you a good overview of these subjects, continue studying the advantages and disadvantages of how these arrangements work.

Marketing Your Home

The internet has taken away what used to be a real estate agent's ace-in-the-hole, which is the MLS or Multiple Listing Service. For a small fee owners can list their home for-sale-by-owner in the MLS and websites geared exclusively to real estate sales, giving them similar exposure to the market just like a realtor. Whatever online avenues you use to market your home, make sure the method draw a lot of unique visitors. For example, you don't want to waste your time and money on a website that doesn't get a lot of traffic.

You can also spread the word on social networking sites, forums and blogs you frequent and traditional media outlets like local newspapers. To entice agents with buyers, offer a commission, one comparable to one they'd receive in a normal sale. Many first-time buyers use an agent and it can pay to offer a 'co-broker' fee to help reach a buyer/agent market.

Networking

Even if you are selling your home through a Realtor, you might want to consider telling your friends, family and business associates that you're selling your home. You can also call local bank managers and school principals to tell them you have a great home for sale if they know a family who's looking. If you know that a nearby company often relocates workers to your area, contact their recruiting or human resources department and tell them you have a home you're ready to sell. Do whatever you can to get the word out. You may even offer them a referral fee if they send you a buyer.

Showing Your Home

When potential buyers or their realtors contact you and want to see the home, try to be as available and flexible as possible. Be aware that many people will want to see the home in the middle of the day, when you might be working. If you can't be home for appointments, try to arrange for a close friend or family member to be there. However, you can show your home at your convenience. To avoid the headache of having to straighten up your house and show it at a moment's notice, decide which days and times of the week you want buyers to view your home and take appointments. When potential buyers come one-at-a-time, your free time may be consumed and the process could be unnecessarily elongated. This is not acceptable for many people. Tell buyers and/or realtors that you would love to show them your home on Saturday at 1 p.m. and 3 p.m. and ask, 'Which time is best for you'?

Setting the Mood

Be sure your home is clean and free of any clutter. Put away food on the counters, put dishes into the dishwasher and gather up laundry. Light a scented candle if you have one, or put a few drops of vanilla on a cookie sheet at put it in the oven at around 250 degrees Fahrenheit (120 Celsius). Turn on some lights and play soft classical music in the background. If the weather is nice, open a few windows. If the weather is cold and wet, light a fire or turn the heater up a bit. These extra little steps will make your home inviting and relaxing.

Be a Good Host

This might seem like obvious advice, but some people are so anxious about selling their home that they forget basic etiquette. When your potential buyers arrive, greet them with a smile, firm handshake and look them in the eye. Introduce yourself and do your best to remember their names. As they step inside your home, ask if you can provide them with a glass of water, cup of coffee or light refreshment. Inquire about *their* interests! An effective tool to sell your **HOME** is to ask about their **H**obby, **O**ccupation, **M**otivation and **E**ntertainment. Do they have kids or animals? Talk about the home in those terms. Lead them from room to room without rushing. At the end of the tour, ask if they have any questions or if they'd like to see anything again. Have your contact information ready to give them on a notepad or card. Coming off as polite and prepared will make you seem like someone with whom they could enter a real estate transaction with minimal hassle.

Keep it Positive

Be honest, but do not dwell on the home's flaws or offer apologies like "Sorry it's so messy in here." If you're selling your home because of a divorce, lost job or other personal tragedy, do not discuss these issues with your buyers, even in jest. Make your entire interaction with them as positive as possible. You want them to leave your home feeling happy and excited at the possibilities of living there.

Secure Your Valuables

Lock up anything truly expensive or irreplaceable in a safe location before you open your home to strangers. Don't let your buyers walk around unsupervised; if they ask for a moment alone, try to give them some privacy in the back yard or kitchen.

Getting a Bid

Give yourself a timeline to lower the asking price if no serious bids have come through. Many sellers price their homes too high, and then they keep them too high for too long all while paying for maintenance, mortgages and property taxes. Before you start in earnest, set a timeline for how you'll lower the price of your home if you're not getting any bids: say within two months, try lowering the price by $20,000. And if you still haven't gotten a bid within six months, try lowering your price by as much as another $50,000. Having a pre-determined outline of how you'll lower the price in the absence of bids will help take emotion out of the decision and ultimately help you sell you home more quickly.

The Buyer's Shoes

Take a walk around the neighborhood if you aren't getting any bids. Put yourself in the buyers' shoes and ask yourself, 'Would I want to buy my home or another home given the prices'? You need to be as honest with yourself as you can. If you come to the conclusion that other homes around the neighborhood might be better options for your potential buyers, it's time to lower your asking price in order to make your home more appealing.

Offering Incentives

Find a way to sweeten the deal a bit. Don't underestimate the power of a small rebate, a 'security blanket' or even a kind gesture. Here are some things that you can do to make a deal more attractive:

✓ Offer a credit on the closing costs, or offer to pay them entirely. Closing costs can get expensive quickly (sometimes thousands dollars), so this becomes a great incentive.

✓ Give a transferable home warranty to cover home appliance malfunction. These typically only cost $300 to $500 to purchase, but give the potential buyer peace of mind.

The Closing

Most sellers assume that the buyer has been through the process and know the stages of buying a home. The fact is that this is one of the many valuable services a realtor would normally provide. But now it is left to you, as the seller, to walk the buyer through choosing a mortgage broker and getting to the closing table. By aligning yourself with a local mortgage company first, you are giving the loan officer leads in return for assisting you with the transaction, a virtual win-win. The broker should also estimate the closing costs for your home and give you strategic financing tips for marketing (zero-down, buy-down and interest-only options, etc). Financing can sell a home just as quickly as good staging.

Pre-Approval Letter

Hopefully, your buyer will have already shown you a lender's pre-approval letter and you will sail through the closing process, but be prepared for snags or delays along the way and add some cushion to the closing date. Schedule your move and the turnover so that it's somewhat flexible should the mortgage approval process be delayed. Be prepared for unexpected results from home inspections and/or appraisals. Be familiar with the required closing paperwork for a home sale in your state and come to the closing table with everything mandated by state and federal law.

Be Prepared to Negotiate

If a buyer says he or she likes your home but is not sure about buying it, again, this is your opportunity to sweeten the deal. Did you notice the buyer looking longingly at your new barbecue? Throw it in. Did they seem dismayed that the patio hadn't been surfaced for awhile? Say you'll come down $500 to cover the cost of resurfacing the patio. Giving up an appliance or making a small concession for home improvements could cost you less than continuing to pay a mortgage on a home you don't want.

Be prepared for the offer and the counteroffer on your home sale. If you have a firm bottom-line in mind, make sure it's justified with research and weigh the cost of continuing to market the home. If you are squeamish about haggling, consider bringing in someone to assist with negotiations.

Close the Deal

Once the buyer is making offers and negotiating, try to close the transaction as quickly as you can. Make sure you've provided all the necessary disclosure documents required by your state. If you don't like the buyer's offer, do not just say 'no' and walk away; make a counter offer. Try to accommodate the buyer wherever you can afford to do so and finish the sale.

Sellers Beware!

If you have been trying to sell your home for any length of time, you've most likely seen "We Pay Cash For Homes" signs around town, on the internet or you might have received a letter, postcard or flyer in the mail that promises that an investor can buy your home regardless of its condition and best of all for cash almost immediately.

So what's the real story here? If this was true then how come these investors don't contacted realtors and work exclusively through them? The reason is very simple, investors are buying homes to resell them and won't pay 'retail' for any home. By necessity and training, investors are always looking for home sellers who are distressed and must sell quickly. In the trade, these homeowners are known as 'motivated sellers'.

While some real estate investors are sincere and genuine people who do not take advantage of others, some do. If you are unable to sell a property at your leisure, where you can select a buyer and/or program that best meets your needs, you could be setting yourself up for a very big financial fall. Here are some ways to help you distinguish real estate investing wolves disguised in sheep's clothing.

Home Buying Programs

Dealing with investors who want to buy your home may appear to offer many benefits, but their approaches cannot guarantee you will be happy with the end results as most programs which offer cash incentives involve varying degrees of risk. Here are a few examples of how 'creative' and 'non-traditional' methods are employed by many real estate investors.

Investors may tell you that they buy homes for cash within a very short time period, but their purchase will not be a 'traditional' purchase because they want to 'help you' close in a few days or weeks. Traditional closings usually take a month or more to get to the closing table. Investors often use some sort of 'creative process' in order to take control of your property and pay far below your asking price for the property, which generally translates into 50% to 70% of Fair Market Value (FMV).

Investors may try and convince you that they can buy your home by taking over your mortgage payments through an assignment of the mortgage or 'subject-to' the mortgage. They often want you to sign over your deed to them and may even give you some money 'now' and promise 'more money' after they re-sell the home or at some future date. Buying a property 'subject-to' the existing mortgage means that the title to the property is transferred to the new buyer, but the loan remains in the original borrower's name. The buyer takes over making the payments on the loan, but does not formally assume the loan. However, you are still liable to repay the loan until such time as the home is sold or otherwise paid-off in full. So you had better be sure to protect yourself before you accept any 'subject-to' the mortgage offers as such 'great deals' could excite a due-on-sale clause accelerating the mortgage and calling it due and payable in full.

Most investors really don't believe the lender's due on sale ability is a real problem because they feel most lenders would rather have a monthly payment from *anyone* instead of calling the mortgage due. While this might be somewhat true, the clause is none-the-less in the mortgage and the lender can 'accelerate' the mortgage if the property is transferred to anyone other than the individual(s) currently listed on the mortgage.

Rules for Protecting Yourself

If you *do* need to sell your home fast, here are a few rules for protecting yourself.

✓ Get All Agreements in Writing
If a disagreement arises about a verbal understanding, the issue becomes your word against theirs and often must go to a court to be settled. Don't risk that! Always demand that all terms be in writing and do not agree to anything that is not in writing.

✓ Always Understand What You're Signing
Not asking questions because you are afraid of looking stupid could end up costing you thousands of dollars or more if you end up in a deal that wasn't what you thought it was. Seek a lawyer can help you or professional advice from a third-party.

✓ Be Willing to Walk Away
If you have any doubts about the buyer or the contract, or if it just doesn't feel right to your instincts, be willing to walk away. You can always revisit the deal again later. Also remember that for every motivated home seller there are most likely 5-10 investors wanting to work a deal with each seller. It's never worth the months (and maybe years) of headaches to sell your home a few days sooner than you would otherwise.

Seller Options

Today's home sellers have many options from which to choose. They can list their home with a realtor, **F**or **S**ale **B**y **O**wner (FSBO) or they can sell their home to or through an investor. No one of these choices is inherently 'better' than the others, the questions is which option is best for you at the time when you are prepared to sell your property?

Most sellers want to sell for all cash, but this is not the only option and for some deals it is not possible because there may not be enough equity in the property to warrant it. In such cases, 'carrying back' (commonly referred to as seller financing) some of the financing is an option a seller may need to consider. A cash offer may be what you think you want, but it is not always your best option. A cash offer from an investor usually means that you must accept a heavily discounted offer, whereas if you were to take back a note for several months (or even a year or more), you may be able to get a higher immediate offer for the property.

Little to No Equity

Having little to no equity in a property is more common than you might think. When you purchased your home, most likely a considerable amount of financing and closing costs were rolled into the loan. So even if the home was purchased with a 10% down payment, it doesn't mean there is any equity in the property to speak of at this point. And if you are selling your home using a realtor and there is not enough equity in your home to cover the average selling costs of 8%-15% for realtor fees, inspections, closing costs and associated fees, you will be left 'upside-down' when you go to sell.

The scenario of little to no equity, or negative equity, is the most common problem homeowners face today. When homeowners attempt to sell their home, they usually try to list it through a realtor without realizing that in order to cover the realtor's commissions and closing costs, if they (the seller) don't have enough equity in the property they might have to bring their own cash to the closing table or dramatically increase the asking price. Increasing the asking price to cover the Realtor fees and other costs of selling will reduce the likelihood of selling the home even further. If you need to sell your home with no, low or negative equity left in it, there are two 'main stream' options you can undertake to get out from under the home. But there are other viable options available to you as well.

Short Sale

The lesser of two evils is to attempt a short sale. In a short sale, a seller may be able to sell their home for less than (or short) of the balance of debts secured by the property. Banks are not forthcoming in their willingness to accept short sales as they must agree to release their lien on the real estate and accept less than the amount owed on the debt. Not too mention there is no guarantee the property will sell at the reduced price and the short sale process itself is very time consuming and stressful.

Foreclosure

The evil itself is to walk away from the property and accept a foreclosure. In a foreclosure, a seller chooses to walk away from their home and the lender generally sells the property and keeps the proceeds to pay off the mortgage debt and any incurred legal costs. The seller's credit is normally damaged, if not ruined, and in some cases the debt from the home may follow the seller even after the home was sold in foreclosure.

Mortgage Takeover

A 'mortgage takeover' plan, often referred to as a 'subject to' financing plan, is where the mortgage stays in place and the new owner (buyer) begins making the payments. Have you ever heard of people taking over the payments to buy a car? It's basically the same thing, but with real property and not an automobile. Mortgage takeovers work should a seller allow a buyer to take over the payments of a home. However lenders will generally not agree to this, so this process needs to remain the private business of the seller and buyer. But it may be a preferable option to get out from under your home mortgage payment than a short sale or foreclosure.

The downside to a mortgage takeover plan is that you will most likely get much less cash from the sale of your home. However, if the home had very little or no equity in it - you weren't likely to get cash anyway. In fact, if your goal was to get out of the home and not have to pay money in order sell it, then the mortgage assumption strategy can accomplishes that.

Lease to Purchase

Another option a seller has is to sell the home through a 'lease to purchase' plan, often referred to as a 'rent to own' plan. A lease to purchase is outstanding should a seller not need immediate cash from the sale of the property. A lease with an option to buy is also known as a 'rent to own', 'lease option', 'rent to purchase' or 'lease to purchase'. It is generally two contracts and not a single contract as the name(s) might imply. One contract is basically a normal lease while the other is the option to purchase.

Leases

The lease works the same way as any other lease or rental agreement would. The seller is obligated to pay the taxes and insurance on the home and the person who leased the home makes lease (rental) payments each month. If you (as the seller) have a mortgage, you continue to make those payments as well. You're generally responsible for maintenance over a fixed amount (generally as low as $100 to as much as $500) during the lease period.

The advantage for buyers is that with a rent to own - lease option, they have the opportunity during the term of the lease to accumulate the needed 10% to 20% down payment and, if needed, to fix credit problems they may have in order to qualify for conventional financing.

For Sellers whether you're a homeowner who is '*stuck*' with a home that isn't selling, your home is about to go in (or is in) foreclosure, or you must move for your job, a rent to own / lease option is a viable option for you and worthy of consideration.

For Buyers lease options are viable whether you've previously lost a home to foreclosure, have credit problems, or just don't have enough money for a down payment.

Lease Option Agreements

Lease Term Any time during the term of the rent to own / lease contract the person leasing the home generally has the right to purchase the home by exercising their option to purchase. The most beneficial length of the lease with an option to purchase for both parties is 2 to 3 years.

Down Payment Down payments on rent to own / lease options can vary tremendously. The most common practice is for the tenant / buyer to pay between $4,000 and $10,000 down. Most, if not all, is applied to the selling price or down payment of the home. These funds are normally non-refundable should the person undertaking the lease / purchase decide not to exercise his or her option to buy the home.

Selling Price With the rent to own / lease option process, the future selling price is established up front and is seldom negotiated by buyers because of the terms of the option. The way the option process is structured generally makes the selling price irrelevant unless it is an unreasonable price. The selling price must benefit both the buyer and the seller if both parties are to agree to the terms and conditions of the lease / purchase.

Rent Credits   Rent credits are a percentage of the monthly lease payment (over and above the normal market rent) applied to the purchase price or down payment of the home. The range is generally between 10% to 100% *in excess* of the rent payment. Common practice is 30% to 50% of the lease payment is allocated by the landlord (seller) to reduce the home's price or act as an added down payment. This is not money set aside by the seller, it is a book entry allocation. These allocated funds are non-refundable and are not applied for the tenant / buyer if the option to buy the home is not exercised.

Generally, in order to receive a rent credit the tenant / buyer must pay the rent on or before the due date each month. Any payment received after the due date would result in the tenant / buyer receiving no rent credit for that month. Rent credits build up over the life of the lease reduce the final purchase price. These credits are stipulated in the lease / purchase contract and are fully documented so that when the tenant / buyer goes to the bank to apply for a mortgage the rent credits can be applied as part of a down payment or toward the purchase price of the home.

Normally rents do not qualify as any proof of a person's credit worthiness. However, rent credits will help to show credit worthiness of the tenant / buyer with many banks and lenders. In other words rent credits help a tenant / buyer to qualify for a home mortgage.

Maintenance   Another difference between a rent to own / lease option and a normal lease agreement is evident with maintenance issues. Rent to own / lease options require the buyer to assume more responsibility when it comes to repairs and maintenance. But once again, both parties must come together and agree on limits. Generally, the buyer is responsible for all repairs and maintenance for the duration of the lease above a given amount, which is generally $100-$500 per repair.

Purchasing 'Subject-To'

When a buyer purchases property 'subject-to' the existing mortgage, if the loan is in default, the buyer can bring the loan current and take over making the monthly payments. The seller's credit only shows late payments, but no foreclosure. The seller's credit will improve once the buyer brings the loan back in good standing and continues to make monthly payments. This is a big benefit for the seller, especially if they are considering buying another home in the future. One of the most important things to a seller in difficulty is the speed with which the buyer can close the deal and solve their problems. Once the seller has agreed to the 'subject-to' deal, the buyer will still need a few days to do a home inspection and title search, but buyers can usually close within 1 to 3 weeks.

Buyer's Market

A Buyer's Market is a weak market, where the real estate market is not moving very quickly. There tends to be little or no appreciation, or even depreciation. And until a buyer's market turns into a seller's market, sellers need to be more open-minded to new and creative ways to sell their homes.

Conventional Selling

Conventional selling is generally conducted through realtors, where the realtor runs the ads, put up signs, creates and distributes flyers, and puts the home on the local realtor's MLS (Multi Listing Service) for all realtors in the area to view. A realtor will be able to show the property to prospective buyers, one of whom will hopefully buy your home. This requires an incredible amount of work for a Realtor who only has the time allowed by the terms of the contract to sell the home. If the home sells, the seller will need to compensate the realtor by paying a fee of somewhere around 6% of the selling price of the home. However, according to the National Association of Realtors, 40% of homes on the MLS are or will become 'expired' listings. Depending on the conditions of your property and the circumstances surrounding your need to sell, those figures may or may not be to your advantage.

Loan Modifications

According to HUD (Housing and Urban Development), a loan modification *"is a permanent change in one or more of the terms of a mortgagor's loan, that allows the loan to be reinstated and results in a payment the homeowner can afford."* Loan modifications can lower monthly payments by extending the loan term or by reducing the interest rate or the mortgage's outstanding balance, or by a combination of both. Cutting the amount of principal owed, an option that could be of more help to borrowers, is rare because it means homeowners pay less money back to the bank over time. Banks have to write off the principle reduction amount immediately. And although the government launched its 'Making Home Affordable' program to stabilize the housing market by incentivizing banks to approve loan modifications, the program focuses on making loans affordable through lower interest rates but delinquent amounts and late fees are typically added onto the mortgage balance.

If at all possible, avoid the loan modification trap offered by lenders. Most loan modification programs focus on making payments affordable for the short term instead of reducing the borrower's principal to eliminate the burden of negative equity, when what is owed on the home is often more than its value. Banks may reduce payments using gimmicks similar to sub-prime loans, such as an ARM (Adjustable Rate Mortgage), or temporary rate reductions that defer principal, such as setting new adjustable rates for 2 years. These rate reductions will lead to balloon payments in as little as two years as interest rates reset. Moreover, in many cases, salaries and property values would have to move dramatically higher in that same time frame to make the new adjustments affordable. All the while homeowners making payments on the loan modification will be unable to refinance the mortgage or sell the home because far too much is owed on the property. Should a home need to be sold because of life changes (job loss, transfer, illness, death or divorce), borrowers will find themselves unable to sell. Basically, the reality is that borrowers who opt for a loan modification will be trapped in a prison of debt and may be forced to foreclosure within 12 - 24 months.

Traditional modifications only add the delinquent payment to the unpaid principal without changing other terms of the loan. The amount of debt increases and often results in higher monthly payments. This type of modification is likely to lead to higher re-default risks in the long run, especially if higher debt burdens are accompanied by declining home prices.

Most modifications do not bring mortgage debt in-line with declining home values or reduce mortgage payments to an affordable or sustainable level. To bring debt into line with declining home values, lenders need to reduce the principal owed so that the home is affordable for the long term. Few lenders are willing to do this because it reduces the income they receive from their borrowers. A high debt burden (credit cards for example), increased unemployment and/or a decline in property values continue to add to the growing default rates. So steering away from loan modifications will benefit the seller in the long run.

Resources

FSBO	http://www.forsalebyowner.com/
AOL Real Estate	http://realestate.aol.com/blog/homes-for-sale/
InstaComps.com	https://www.instacomps.com/
Redfin	http://www.redfin.com/
Eppraisal	http://www.eppraisal.com/
Trulia	http://www.trulia.com/
Zillow	http://www.zillow.com/homes/for_sale/
HomeGain	http://www.homegain.com/
Realtor.com	http://www.realtor.com/

Free Classifieds

Craigslist Sites	http://www.craigslist.org/about/sites
BackPage	http://www.backpage.com/
Free Classifieds Ads	http://ebayclassifieds.com/
30 BEST USA Classifieds Sites	http://adsolist.com/usa-best-classifieds-sites-list/
Us Free Ads - Free Classified	http://www.usnetads.com/

Resources for Comparables (Comps)

1. DataQuick: Real Estate Solutions & Data
2. Home Value Estimator
3. United States Property Records Search – Realtor.com
4. Homeseekers – Southern California Real Estate Search
5. Homesteps – We VALUE Your Neighborhood
6. homevaluehunt.com
7. HomeFindingInfo – Home Value Requests
8. Appraiser Suite
9. netronline.com
10. octitle.com
11. Homes for Sales by OWNERS
12. REAL-COMP
13. realestate.com
14. Real Estate ABC – Home Value & Sales Comps
15. Home Values & Comparable Home Valuations @ Yahoo.com
16. Listingbook

Asset Protection Services of America

**Everything Investors
Need to Know**

Introduction

As a real estate investor you undoubtedly have spent many hours pouring over books, CDs and attending seminars in order to learn the 'secrets' of making a profit in real estate. I am sure you have diligently employed all those techniques to the best of your ability in your search for properties from which you can enjoy a profit. However, to truly benefit from your real estate investments, you must learn the fundamentals to buying, flipping, holding and selling property. In this publication you will learn the strategies and how best to use them for profiting from real estate investing.

How to 'Hold' Real Estate

The first and biggest mistake you can make as an investor is holding title to real estate in your own name. It is fine to 'take' title in your personal name as long as you transfer the title to a 'controlled' entity at your first opportunity. All deeds are public record and free for prying eyes to see. Having property in your own name makes you an easy target for tenants, creditors and attorneys. If a liability is created on your property, then the owner is liable (i.e. you).

Sole Proprietorship

A Sole Proprietorship is the same as you owning the real estate. This means that the title to the property is held in your name. Individual (Sole Proprietorship) ownership is **_not_** recommended, but includes property held as:

Community Property — Also called 'Tenancy by the Entirety' in non-community property states, and is a typical form of holding equal interests in real property by a husband and wife. Even though title is in the community, each spouse's interest is separate. But if your spouse is sued, you will likely end up being named in the suit as a co-conspirator, etc.

Joint Tenants — Another typical form of holding equal interests in real property by two or more persons. If one joint tenant dies, his or her share generally passes automatically to the other joint tenant by right of survivorship.

Sole and Separate — The default for someone buying property on his or her own.

Tenants in Common — The other typical way two or more individuals acquire an equal (or unequal) interest in real property. Each co-owner's interest is separate property. Again, if your spouse (or partner) is sued, you will likely end up being named in the suit too.

Sole Proprietorship Advantages

The greatest advantage to individual ownership is its simplicity. The cost of operations and record keeping requirements associated with such ownership are minimal.

Sole Proprietorship Disadvantages

The most notable drawback is the unlimited personal liability for the owner(s) of the property. Liability is unlimited for debts arising out of its operation and for any potential tort liability associated with property ownership and operation. Additional disadvantages include:

1. **Capital Gains Taxes**
   When you sell property owned in your own name, you will pay a minimum of 0% to a maximum of 39.6% capital gains tax on the income you receive. Notwithstanding the forgoing, should you wish to claim the personal $250,000 to $500,000 federal capital gain tax exclusion, you must keep the property in your personal name and live in the property for at least 2 years.

2. **Dealer Status**
   Starting in the 2013 tax year, the IRS (and many states have started to follow suit) is now attacking individuals by arbitrarily tagging them with a "Dealer" status. A dealer is an individual who regularly buys, sells and holds real estate as a business. If an individual is tagged as a "dealer," the income from his or her sales of property is subject to self-employment tax. Notwithstanding the forgoing, buying and selling real estate through an entity, can completely avoid the "dealer" status, which is explained herein.

3. **Income Taxes Reported on a 1040 Tax Return**
   The tax effect of holding investment property as an individual, is that losses from the operation of the property are deducted from the individual's income (assuming the losses are not limited by the passive loss rules) and profits are added to it.

4. **Self-Employment Taxes**
   All income you receive from the sale of property will be hit with a federal 15.3% self-employment tax up to $113,700 while income above that amount is taxed at 2.9% and these taxes must be paid quarterly.
   (See IRS Code Section 1402 and/or IRS Publication 533)

   Note: The Social Security Administration anticipates future cut-offs shall be moved to:
   $115,500 in 2014
   $118,500 in 2015
   $123,600 in 2106

IRS Definitions for Real Estate 'Investors', 'Dealers' and 'Professionals'

Unfortunately, real estate investors are not all created equal in the eyes of the IRS. If you're an investor, there are three different types of real estate investors defined by the IRS, namely real estate 'investor', 'dealer' and/or 'professional'.

Determining Status

The IRS determines status based on the 'intent' of the taxpayer buying, flipping, holding or selling the property. The characterization of gain or loss on the sale or exchange of the property hinges on whether the property was held 'primarily' for sale or for investment. The Courts have come up with fifteen items that they look for in determining status:

1.) Amount of advertising
2.) Amount of income from sales as compared with the taxpayer's other sources of income
3.) Duration of ownership
4.) Extent and nature of the transactions involved
5.) Extent and value of the taxpayer's real estate holdings
6.) Extent of improvements and subdivision made to facilitate sales
7.) Number, frequency and continuity of sales
8.) Ordinary business of the taxpayer
9.) Taxpayer's control over any sales representatives
10.) Taxpayer's desire to liquidate landholdings unexpectedly obtained
11.) Taxpayer's overall reluctance to sell the property
12.) Taxpayer's purpose for acquiring, holding and selling the property
13.) Taxpayer's use of brokers
14.) Time and effort expended by the taxpayer in promoting sales
15.) Use of a business office for sales

The most important issues appear to be the number, frequency and continuity of sales. Thus, if you sell a multitude of properties, you may be considered a 'dealer' based solely on the type of real estate 'investing' being conducted. None-the-less, it is also possible to be treated as a 'dealer' on one property and an 'investor' on another.

Real Estate 'Dealer'

Real estate dealer status is defined as *"an individual, or 'pass-through entity' such as a partnership or LLC, engaged in the business of selling real estate with a view to the gains and profits that may be derived from such sales"*. Under IRC Section 1221(a)(1), real property will not be deemed a capital asset if it is *"held by the taxpayer primarily for sale to customers in the ordinary course of his trade or business"* (hereinafter referred to as "for sale"). Thus gains or losses on real property held 'for sale' will be ordinary in character. If the property is not deemed 'for sale', the gains or losses will be capital or, in the case of depreciable rental property, a

Section 1231 gain or loss. By contrast, dealers can offset their losses against ordinary income with fewer restrictions than capital losses. Property held for sale is not subject to Section 163(d) 'investment interest' limits; only property held for investment are subject to Section 163(d).

Real Estate 'Investor'

If you buy and hold properties for long-term appreciation, then you are normally considered an 'investor' by the IRS. However, if you start to dabble in a few flips to generate income, then the IRS may peg you as a real estate 'dealer' and ALL your real estate income may be subjected to 'dealer tax' treatment where your rental income is treated as 'ordinary income' and subject to self-employment tax. If this happens you would lose the benefits of depreciation and the ability to have income from these properties taxed using long-term capital gains rates, even in situations when the investor's true intent is to keep a particular property as a long-term investment and can demonstrate profits were collected for more than 20 or 30 years! In short, you would get taxed upfront on the 'paper profits' regardless of whether you actually realize those gains. This is also known as 'phantom income'.

Tax Planning for Real Estate 'Dealers'

At the end of the day, if you are considered a real estate dealer by the IRS then the income you make will be subject to self-employment tax. Therefore you might want to strongly consider holding the real estate in an entity which files an 1120 tax election such as a "C" Corporation or an LLC (whether directly or indirectly via a land trust). Since a real estate dealer is being treated as a business, you need to plan for the appropriate business structure accordingly. If you are concerned that a portion of your real estate portfolio may be considered under 'dealer' status, a good strategy may be to have separate business structures for the two portions of your real estate.

Problems can occur when you are deemed a real estate dealer and you carry back a note. If you are a dealer, you cannot defer your gain from the sale until you receive money. In this case, the best strategy is to be forearmed. Instead of doing an installment sale, consider doing a "rent-to-own" type of lease-option program. The difference between these two types of programs (installment sale and rent to own) is the constructive ownership. When does the sale occur? If it occurs later, after you are paid in full, then you have no problem with this particular taxing issue. However, if the sale is considered to occur immediately you may have a very large and unexpected tax liability on your hands. But you cannot engage in this strategy 'after the fact', so the proper agreements must be set up ahead of time.

Real Estate 'Professional'

One of the benefits to investing in real estate is the ability to offset the real estate paper losses (primarily caused by depreciation) against your other income. If you can qualify as a real estate professional, by spending more than 750 hours per year or 51% of your total work on real estate work, then 100% of your paper real estate losses can be used to offset your other income. However, this real estate paper loss is limited to $25,000 if your income is under $100,000. The $25,000 phases out as your income exceeds $100,000 and is completed disallowed by the time you reach $150,000. The loss doesn't actually go away, instead it is 'suspended' to be allowed at the time that the property sells.

One way around the paper loss limitation is if you or your spouse (if filing jointly) can qualify as a real estate professional. The real estate professional status is based on hours that are performed in real estate functions. You must spend more time in real estate activities than in any other activity for which you are compensated. If you are in a real estate activity type profession, such as a real estate agent, then you will qualify as long as you own 5% or more of the business that is paying you. If you are a real estate agent, as most agents are paid as an independent contractor, your independent contractor income IS your business.

If you are paid as an employee of a real estate agency and do not own a minimum of 5% of the company, then you will not qualify under this provision. A qualified real estate activity is any thing in which you 'develop, re-develop, construct, re-construct, acquire, convert, rent, operate, manage, lease, or sell' real estate. The key is that you perform personal services in these activities, but you don't necessarily have to be the one performing the work. You can be supervising, meeting, planning all the activities that go into truly running the business.

If Not You, Then Who?

Just like Francis Ford Coppola's film character 'The Godfather', make sure that you have a 'buffer' between you and your properties to keep your ownership private. Using a different entity for each property will allow you to own, manage and transfer property with anonymity. However this can get quite expensive. Therefore, you should at least separate your 'flipping' properties and your 'rental' property into at least two separate entities.

Keeping a low profile is very important for investors who don't want prying eyes to have access to their business affairs or money. The solution is to create an entity or structure that has limited liability protection and/or veils ownership. Choices include Corporations (C or S), Limited Liability Companies (Single-Member, Multi-Member or Series), Limited Partnerships and Land Trusts. Which structure will work best for you depends on a variety of factors.

But if you hold real estate in your name, you will pay the maximum amount in capital gains tax and self-employment taxes upon selling. Additionally, most of your 'business expenses' are not be deductible when you file a 1040 tax return at the end of the year and your silent partner (the state and federal governments) will absolutely love being in business with you because they will collectively take the lions share of your hard work by taxing your Return On Investment (ROI). Don't forget that only *you* put up the risk-capital and sweat-equity to make your deals happen, so don't be generous in giving these silent partners all your money.

The secret to 'holding' property is in utilizing a legal entity controlled by you, one that will afford you deduction capabilities, asset protection and flexibility while reducing or eliminating taxes associated with holding and selling real property. The entities we recommend to accomplish these goals are a "C" Corporation, Limited Liability Company (LLC), Limited Partnership (LP) and/or Land Trust (which is an agreement and not an entity), or any combination thereof (hereinafter referred to altogether as an 'entity').

Once the process has been completed to transfer the ownership of your property, your 'entity' will be paying the mortgage payments and all other expenses associated with the property and not you. Naturally, these payments are tax deductible for the entity and, when executed correctly, will not a be taxable event for you. Because you are the beneficial interest holder (owner) of the entity, you will still 'control' the real estate. When you transfer a property from your name to the name of an entity (owned and controlled by you), your ownership of the property can become virtually invisible (at least extremely difficult) to the prying eyes of predatory attorneys seeking to find assets in your name. Generally speaking, lawsuits work like this:

If you have assets titled in your name, you get sued
if you have no assets titled in your name, you do not get sued

Selling Property Through an Entity Filing an 1120 Tax Return

Contrary to conventional thinking, the tried and true Nevada "C"-Corporation and/or Limited Liability Company filing an 1120 tax return will afford you exceptional business 'write-off' capabilities, maximum asset protection and flexibility, all while dramatically reducing the taxes associated with holding and selling real estate. (See our publication "Cover Your Assets" for full details on Corporations, Limited Liability Companies, Limited Partnerships and Trusts.)

Entity Taxation	1040 Individual	1065 LLC / LP	1120-S "S" Corp	1120 LLC / "C" Corp
Capital Gains Taxes	Yes	Yes	Yes	No
Self-Employment Taxes	Yes	Yes	Yes	No
Dealer Status Applies	Yes	Yes	Yes	No
Can Zero Out Tax Liability	No	No	No	Yes

Entities filing an 1120 (whose business purpose is real estate) are not subject to any capital gains tax liability from the sale of real estate. Instead, corporate gains are included with the rest of the corporate income and therefore become part of the ordinary income of the Corporation (or LLC filing an 1120). The IRS Code makes no distinction between short-term or long-term gains either. [See Ordinary or Capital Gain or Loss in IRS Publication 544]

Owning Real Estate with a Nevada "C" Corporation

Nevada Corporations can own real estate in most states in the country without having to register with that particular state (save Florida, New York and Texas), as long as the corporation is not buying and selling properties frequently. Real estate may be bought and sold through a Corporation without too many restrictions and save lots of money doing so.

If you are purchasing a home and want to 'write off' the mortgage payments, the mortgage must be in the name of the corporation or an agreement needs to be drafted between you and the corporation which transfers ALL your equity and future income from the property to the corporation. Once this agreement has been executed, you formally transfer your interest in the property to the corporation. In many states, this can be accomplished by using an un-recorded grant deed or quit claim deed (in some states a warranty deed). So that you don't spark the due-on-sale clause of most mortgages, or have the property re-assessed, you should have the deed notarized, but do not file it unless you absolutely must.

Whether buying, leasing or renting real estate, your utilities should be placed (or transferred) to your corporation and made to the 'care of' your name. In doing so, the corporation can pay and deduct these expenses. These expenses are deductible only if the lease or mortgage on your home / office is in the name of the corporation. Otherwise, only the portion of the premises that your corporation actually occupies and/or uses can be written off on your taxes.

To Rent or Not To Rent

This is a very sensitive issue with the IRS. Because you previously resided in the property, and should you desire to remain living in the home after you transfer it to your entity, the IRS will require you to pay a fair market rent (the rental that 'like homes' in your area rent for) to meet the IRS 'no free ride' test. However, should you wish to remain in the home and 'write off'' the mortgage payments, maintenance and utilities, you should put the property up for sale at fair market value. You need not place a for sale sign in the front yard but the home must at least be listed on the local realtor MLS listings. In this way, as long as the property is for sale you simply become a 'caretaker' and live in the property rent-free. When the home sells, the proceeds are paid to the corporation and not to you. When the corporation buys the next home, this requirement is not applicable if the new mortgage is in the name of the entity.

Exchanging Cash, Assets or Services for Shares

In most states, the exchanging of stock can be done for cash, vehicles, boats, planes, real estate, equipment and even services. A few rules to remember is that when making an exchange, you must first decide on the value of your stock (If you have a Nevada Corporation, most likely your corporation came with no-par value stock). That is stock that has not been valued. (No-par value stock is not valued until you decide on what the stock is worth). Once you establish the value of your stock, you then establish the exchange based solely on the 'Fair Market Value' or FMV of the item or service exchanged. The stock exchanged for the item or service must be recorded in the stock ledger of your corporate minute book. This includes the name and address of the person receiving the stock.

California Revenue and Taxation Code
Part 6.7 Documentary Transfer Tax Act
Chapter 3 Exemption
Section 11925(d)

"No levy shall be imposed pursuant to this part by reason of any transfer between an individual or individuals and a legal entity or between legal entities that results solely in a change in the method of holding title to the realty and in which proportional ownership interests in the realty, whether represented by stock, membership interest, partnership interest, co-tenancy interest, or otherwise, directly or indirectly, remain the same immediately after the transfer."

Interest Rates

There is no magic in interest rates unless you are planning to hold your real estate forever. Most people hold real estate for an average of 5 years or less, or are buying to 'flip' their property (buying with the intent to resell within 12 months). Consider Adjustable Rate Mortgages (ARM) because while ARM rates are low, it could take 4-5 years of increases in property value to bring investors to the same rates offered for 30-year mortgages.

Refinancing

It is recommended that you refinance your property prior to transferring it to an entity. You can use some of the cash to "fix it up" if you decide to hold the property, as investment capital for your real estate business, or to buy more property, etc. To refinance a property it must be in your personal name. Some lenders will refinance a property in the name of an entity, but not the majority of them. If you have already transferred your property to an entity, you will likely have to transfer the title back to your individual name before refinancing. Once the refinance is accomplished, most lenders will allow you to transfer the property back into the name of the entity without issue.

The primary reason for refinancing is because when you transfer the property to your controlled entity it must compensate you for the equity you had in the property, and this equity could be quite substantial. The money the entity pays to you for the equity would be taxable to you unless you handled the transfer correctly as described.

Refinancing will effectively lower your capital gains tax exposure. For example, $200,000 minus $200,000 = $0 in capital gains as pulled out any 'liquid' equity when you refinanced. That money just seems to 'slip through the cracks' as refinanced proceeds are not generally tracked by any government agency. Therefore, it may make good sense to refinance several times to change the 'cost basis' of the property in order to liquefy as much equity as possible. If most or all of the equity is pulled out by refinancing, the property could be transferred to your controlled entity with little or no equity. This reduces the amount that the entity must pay to you for the transfer, as well as the amount that you must pay in taxes.

This newly adjusted 'cost basis' would be the amount owed (or financed) for future sales tax gain or loss computations. Cost, as basis, is defined as the purchase price, including certain settlement or closing costs. Cost includes the cash down payment and any mortgage debt taken on the property, such as a first or second mortgage or notes and any capital improvements you made to the property.

Three Ways to be Compensated for the Equity Transferred to a Controlled Entity

✔ Reimbursement

The entity can reimburse you the amount paid for the down payment, fix-up, remodeling capital improvements, sale preparation, advertising the property for sale, inspections and closing costs to consummate the sale including escrow and realtor fees. Reimbursements are paid upon presentment of receipts for such expenses and are therefore non-taxable to you. Should the entity **not** have the money to pay you outright, you might consider opting for a promissory note method of repayment. (See the 'Real Estate Purchase Agreement' in our publication entitled 'Operations Manual' for this document.)

✔ Exchange of Stock

If you are holding title in the name of a corporation, the corporation can exchange its stock for the equity (See the 'Bill of Sale Agreement' in our publication entitled 'Operations Manual' for this document.) This process is known as a 351 transfer of property into a "C" Corporation for at least 80% of its stock.

✔ Promissory Note

The entity can give you a promissory note in the amount of (and secured by) the equity at the time of the transfer. This note would be due and payable with a fair and reasonable interest rate upon the sale of the property. The promissory note would be placed in the escrow as an escrow payment instruction when the property is sold. (See the 'Promissory Note' in our publication entitled 'Operations Manual' for this document.)

> **Note:** You will have taxable income unless it is stated in the Promissory Note and/or Agreement that this payment is a 'reimbursement' for money you 'advanced' on behalf of the entity for the needed down-payment or other tax deductible expenses.

To Record or Not To Record a Transfer

After refinancing your debt to as close to the full-amount of the equity as possible, you can execute an unrecorded but *notarized* deed. States vary between the use of a warranty deed, grant deed and bargain-and-sale deed, however most every state accepts a quitclaim deed.

The deed transfers title from you (as held in its current method) into the name of the entity. Take great care to ensure the legal property description is entered exactly as it is on the current deed. The transfer is complete when the notarized documents are handed to the entity and a copy is retained in your personal records, even without recordation at your county recorder's office.

An assignment can also be employed wherein you have pulled out all the equity (by refinancing) or where the price is such that there is no equity in the property when the property is transferred to the entity. In this case, you are 'assigning' the future debt to be paid and the future income to be received to your entity when the property is sold. (See the 'Assignment' form in our publication entitled 'Operations Manual' for this document.)

Why Unrecorded?

Even though the 'beneficial interest' (ownership) remains the same before and after transferring the property to an entity, not all lenders will accept the transfer (unless it is a land trust, which again is not an entity) even though they will gladly take the check each month from the entity. Lenders may still want to spark the due on sale clause or 'acceleration clause' contained in most mortgages when the property is transferred.

Recording a Transfer

Some counties are demanding a copy of a corporate stock certificate issued in the personal name of the transferring party or other absolute proof that *you* are the sole owner(s) of the corporation and/or prove that you own the majority interest owner before the County will allow a tax-free transfer. The reason for this is that all you are transferring is your future equity and income from the property and they wish to ensure you are still the sole 'borrower of record' for the mortgage. Should you attempt this process and both the lender and the county agree to the transfer, then by all means record the transfer.

If for some reason you can't record the transfer right away, then be sure to do so at the time of the escrow when you sell the property. This will be recorded, but the lender and county recorder will not have the opportunity to object to it or reassess the transfer. In addition, should you anticipate any legal action be sure to record it immediately. The date of the transfer of the property will be fixed by the date the notary signed the transferring instrument and not the date you recorded it.

Proper Documentation

You *must* carefully document the transfer of the property into your controlled entity by completing the proper state forms and through corporate resolutions, declarations and contracts as found in this publication and our 'Operations Manual'.

Multiple Properties

You can hold several pieces of real property in your controlled entity, provided the following safety precautions are undertaken:

1. Separate rental properties from those properties that you intend to 'flip' (sell within 12 months) into separate entities. At least one entity is to hold all rental properties and another entity can hold your 'flipping' property.

2. You should purchase an umbrella insurance policy in the amount of 3-5 times the fair market value (FMV) of all properties in each entity. The reason for this is that should you be sued while multiple properties are contained inside one entity, they will ALL be subject to the lawsuit and frozen until the suit is concluded. For as long as you are in litigation you may not sell, transfer or give away any of the properties held by the entity being sued. By purchasing an umbrella policy 3-5 times the FMV, your insurance company should be able to handle any claims someone might bring against you.

Insurance

All property subject to a mortgage must be insured. Here are some guidelines concerning how to handle the insurance that you carry on a property.

A transfer of title to real estate will usually void a hazard insurance policy. Thus, a claim for loss may be denied by the insurance company if the person(s) that is insured no longer has an 'insurable interest' and the titled owner (the corporation or LLC - but not a land trust) is not a party to the insurance contract. Immediately after transferring title, notify your insurance company to name the entity as the primary insured and yourself as an additional insured on the policy. Remember, you are still on the mortgage as the 'borrower of record' and therefore you still have an 'insurable interest' in the property. (See 'Real Estate Forms' for this letter.)

Hazard Insurance

A transfer of title to real estate will usually void a hazard insurance policy too, since you no longer have an ' insurable interest' in the property. As the title to your property will no longer be in your name when you transfer it to your entity you cannot technically be the beneficiary of your hazard insurance policy. Thus, a claim for loss may be denied by the insurance company, since the name insured no longer has a 'direct' interest, and the titled owner (your entity) is not a party to the insurance contract. However, the manner in which we suggest you transfer the property to your entity should enable you to retain an 'insurable interest'.

A hazard insurance policy on a property has two parts of coverage:

Loss Loss coverage is to reimburse the insured for damage, fire or destruction of the property. The check is made payable to the primary insured and the lender (the *loss payee)* to the extent there is an outstanding balance on the mortgage note.

Liability Liability coverage gives protection to the insured in case of a lawsuit or other claim. The insurance company will *indemnify* (pay for any claims or court judgments against the insured) and *defense* costs incurred such defending claims (namely the attorney fees). A policy can also name *additional insured* for liability coverage. The additional insured do not receive a check in the event of loss, they are merely covered for liability claims. Thus, if the property is held in an entity's name rather than your name make sure that you are named as an additional insured.

Hazard Insurance Change of Beneficiary

A change on the hazard insurance is the most common way a lender discovers a transfer of interest in the borrower's property. If you notify your insurance carrier of a change in insurance beneficiary (not to be confused with the *beneficiary* of the Land Trust) the lender, who is also a named insurance beneficiary, receives a copy of the change. But if you transfer title into a Land

Trust, the named insurance beneficiary will most likely be the trustee of the Land Trust. If you then sell the property by transferring the beneficial interest in the trust, the lender will not be notified since the insurance beneficiary (the trustee) has not changed.

Any transfer of beneficial interest is the same as a transfer of title to real property as far as the IRS is concerned. You cannot take depreciation or mortgage interest deductions on property you no longer own. Thus, if you transfer title of your rental property into a land trust, then assign the beneficial interest to your Corporation or LLC, your Corporation or LLC would now file its tax reporting as though it owned the property. On the other hand, a transfer of a beneficial interest with any reservation of control or the right to revoke the transfer may not be considered a transfer at all. *[See, Estate of Bowgren v. Commissioner 105 F.3d 1156.]*

<h2 style="text-align:center">Tax Considerations</h2>

Accounting Method

In order to take maximum advantage of the tax considerations discussed here, you should have your entity operate using cash basis accounting principals.

Depreciation

Depreciating property of any kind is a deferred tax trap, as all the depreciation you 'take' must be paid back when you sell the property.

Recaptured Depreciation

Real property that has been depreciated is subject to a special depreciation recapture tax. A special 25% tax rate applies to the amount of gain that is related to depreciation deductions that were claimed or could have been claimed on a property. The remainder of the gain will be taxed at ordinary rates or long-term gain rates, depending on how long the property was held. For more details on depreciation recapture, refer to: IRS Publication 544, Sales and Other Dispositions of Assets, Chapter 3, Depreciation Recapture.

IRC Section 351

Transferring property into your wholly owned entity is known as a Section 351 (IRS code section) transfer and is a contribution of property to your controlled entity on a tax-free basis, as no sale to an outside party has occurred.

✓ A corporation does not recognize gain or loss when it issues stock in exchange for cash or property.

✓ A shareholder does not recognize gain or loss upon contribution of cash in exchange for corporation stock. A shareholder may recognize gain or loss upon exchange of property for corporation stock.

✓ When services are performed in exchange for corporation stock, the FMV (Fair Market Value) of the service is taxable compensation. The amount included in income is the shareholder's basis in the corporate stock received.

Capital Gains Tax

When you sell real estate owned in your name, you will pay capital gains taxes. When an entity (in the real estate business) sells property, no matter how much equity (income) is realized, there are **no capital gains taxes** to pay as the sale is an 'ordinary' part of the entity's business activities. This is considered 'ordinary business income' by state and federal taxing agencies. Furthermore, the IRS Code makes no distinction between short-term or long-term capital gains. Best of all, corporations pay only a 15% tax on its **net** income (after all expenses are paid) up to $50,000 and fewer taxes than most individuals would pay federally all the way up to $250,000.

Self-Employment Taxes
(IRS Code Section 1402 and Publication 533)

Most people who pay into Social Security work for an employer. Their employer deducts Social Security taxes from their paycheck, matches that contribution and sends taxes to the IRS and reports wages to Social Security. But self-employed people must report their earnings and pay their taxes directly to the IRS on a quarterly basis.

If you are a sole proprietor (where you own an unincorporated business by yourself and/or your spouse as a sole proprietor), or if you provide services for your tenants (such as managing your properties), or if you are deemed to be a real estate investor, then you are 'self-employed' and are subject to employment taxes.

You **are** self-employed for this purpose if you are a sole proprietor (including an independent contractor), a partner in a partnership (including a member of a multi-member limited liability company (LLC)), or are otherwise in business for yourself. (A sole proprietor also includes the member of a single member LLC that is disregarded for federal income tax purposes and members of a qualified joint venture).

You usually must pay self-employment tax if you had net earnings from self-employment of $400 or more. [*See: IRS Code §1402 and IRS Publication 334 and 554*]

IRS Publication 533 states *"You are self-employed if any of the following apply to you"*:

1. *You carry on a trade or business as a sole proprietor or an independent contractor.*
2. *You are a member of a partnership that carries on a trade or business.*
3. *You are otherwise in business for yourself.*

Only "C" Corporations are exempt from self-employment taxes. Technically, "S" Corporations are also exempt from self-employment taxes unless the individual is determined or otherwise recognized by the IRS as a Real Estate Dealer. All Members in a Limited Liability Company (save passive members) and General Partners in a Limited Partnership are almost always liable to pay Self-Employment taxes, unless the managing member / partner is a Corporation.

Profits or losses flow through to each member at the end of the year and are not subject to self-employment taxes under Section 1402. Under Section 1402(a) there are three exceptions concerning distributions of LLC income to members, which are not subject to self-employment taxes as they relate to the business of buying, holding, flipping and selling of real estate. They are income derived from:

1. Rental income
2. Interest and dividends
3. Capital gains and losses

Calculating Self-Employment Taxes

Tot fill out the Schedule SE to calculate how much SE tax you owe, take your bottom-line net business income from Schedule C (if you're a sole proprietor), or Schedule E (if you're a self-employed business that's treated as a partnership for tax purposes) and multiply that bottom-line number by a factor of .9235. The result is your Self-Employment (SE) income for tax purposes. The first $113,700 of your 2013 SE income is taxed at 15.3%, while any remaining SE income will be taxed at either 2.9% or 3.8% if the new 0.9% extra Medicare tax applies.

Rental income from real estate is not included in earnings subject to SE tax unless you provide services for your tenants (such as you personally managing your properties) or you are a real estate dealer. *Only* entities filing an 1120 tax return can be exempt from self-employment taxes. Technically, all partners / members in partnerships and LLCs must pay Self-Employment taxes. Should a husband and wife be 'in business' together (individually receive income from their business) they are both subject to SE taxes on their individual income.

Self-Employment Taxes for "S" Corporations

For "S" Corporations, rules on self-employment taxes are well established. Shareholders of an "S" Corporation pay self-employment taxes on monies received as compensation for services,

but not on profits that automatically pass through to the shareholder. For example, if an "S" Corporation has $100,000 of income and the shareholder performs reasonable services for the corporation worth $65,000 at fair market value prices, the shareholder would owe 15.3% self-employment taxes on the $65,000 but not on the remaining $35,000.
[See IRS Publication 542 and 583]

Real Estate Rental Income

Rental income from real estate is not included in earnings subject to SE tax unless either of the following applies to you.

1. **You are a Real Estate 'Dealer'** if you are personally engaged in the business of selling real estate with the purpose of making a profit from those sales. Rent you receive from real estate held for sale is subject to SE tax. However, rent you receive from real estate held for speculation or investment is not subject to SE tax. (This would *not* apply to you if you are operating your business through a 'controlled' entity.)

2. **You Provide Services for Your Tenants** when you personally manage your properties.

Trade or Business

A trade or business is generally an activity carried on for a livelihood or in good faith to make a profit. The facts and circumstances of each case determine whether or not an activity is a trade or business. The regularity of activities and transactions and the production of income are important elements. You do not need to actually make a profit to be in a trade or business as long as you have a demonstrable profit motive. You do need, however, to make ongoing efforts to further the interests of your business.

MORTGAGE CONTRACT

Appendix to Order No. XC/44/34/22

Avoiding the Due on Sale Clause

AssetProtectionServices.com

Due on Sale Clause

Land trusts help avoid a 'due-on-sale clause' or 'loan acceleration' invoked by a lender. A due on sale clause is when a bank intends to accelerate your loan payments by calling the loan due. Banks loan money to *you* for the purchase of a property, should you quitclaim deed that property (transfer ownership) to an entity, even if you are sole owner of that entity (Corp, LLC or LP), that is a transfer to a *different person* and lenders may consider that a sale.

Brief History

Lenders began including 'due-on-sale' clauses in their loans back in the 1970's during a time when interest rates were rapidly increasing. Instead of taking out new loans, people were assuming the existing loans on other people's homes because the interest rates of those older loans were much lower than new loans. Because of this pervasive practice, Lenders started to insert the 'due-on-sale' clause in their loans citing that they needed this clause to protect their collateral by staying abreast of who was actually living in such properties.

Lenders did not like creating a loan for a home only to find someone else lives there, especially when the new occupants have very poor credit and/or really have little invested in the home, at least as far as the lender is concerned. Additionally, lenders don't want to make loans to one person only to find that the mortgage is being passed onto a subsequent buyer (by assignment of the loan) without being asked first. Ironically, lenders do this very thing without first notifying their borrowers about who possesses their loan while borrowers face potential problems should they take the same action.

Garn-St. Germain Act

During the Ronald Reagan administration, an federal act was created called the 'Garn-St. Germain Depository Institutions Act', which was intended to revitalize the housing industry by ensuring the availability of home loans. However, within the Act there was a significant consumer benefit that allowed a mortgage holder to place real estate in a land trust without the lender being able to trigger their "due on sale" clause.

By utilizing a land trust you take advantage of the Garn-St. Germain Depository Institutions Act, 1982 and can avoid the invocation of a due-on-sale clause.

United States Public Laws
97th Congress - Second Session Convening January 25, 1982
PL 97-320 (HR 6267) October 15, 1982
Part C Preemption of Due-on-Sale Prohibitions
Due On Sale Clauses
Sec. 341. // 12 USC 1701j-3. //

(d) A lender may not exercise its option pursuant to a due-on-sale clause upon--,

   (1)   the creation of a lien or other encumbrance subordinate to the lender's security instrument which does not relate to a transfer of rights of occupancy in the property;

   (2)   the creation of a purchase money security interest for household appliances;

   (3)   a transfer by devise, descent, or operation of law on the death of a joint tenant or tenant by the entirety;

   (4)   the granting of a leasehold interest of three years or less not containing an option to purchase;

   (5)   a transfer to a relative resulting from the death of a borrower;

   (6)   a transfer where the spouse or children of the borrower become an owner of the property;

   (7)   a transfer resulting from a decree of a dissolution of marriage, legal separation agreement, or from an incidental property settlement agreement, by which the spouse of the borrower becomes an owner of the property;

   (8)   a transfer into an inter vivos trust in which the borrower is and remains a beneficiary and which does not relate to a transfer of rights of occupancy in the property; or

   (9)   any other transfer or disposition described in regulations prescribed by the Federal Home Loan Bank Board. (Emphasis Added)

The Garn-St. Germain Act permits the transfer of a property into a land trust without the lender's ability to invoke the due on sale clause. Land trust agreements are private documents, only the filing of title made with the county recorder's office is public (which may disclose the name of the trustee. However the land trust document itself remains private, as no public record of the agreement is filed, providing excellent anonymity for the beneficiary.

Borrower of Record

Only transfers of a home to an *inter vivos* trust (i.e. revocable living trusts and land trusts) owned by the original mortgage 'borrower of record' are the transfers excluded from the due-on-sale acceleration clauses contained in most mortgage contracts.

Therefore, transfers of property into a land trust structure employing an entity, wherein the entity is in fact owned by the original mortgage 'borrower of record', the lender is clearly unable to enforce the due-on-sale acceleration clause contained in most mortgage contracts. However, should the property be transferred into and entity not owned by the original mortgage 'borrower of record', to an offshore entity (not accessible in the US courts) or to a person other than the original mortgage 'borrower of record', the transfer may **not** be excluded from the due-on-sale or acceleration clauses contained in most mortgage contracts.

If all or any part of the property, or an interest therein, is sold or transferred by a borrower without the lender's prior written consent, a lender may (at the lender's sole and exclusive option) declare all the sums secured by the mortgage to be immediately payable and due in full.

Lease Options

Many people are mistaken, or misled by real estate investor 'gurus', in believing they can get around the due-on-sale clause by executing a lease option instead of a sale. No true! Subsection (4) articulates, as shown above, that a due-on-sale clause *is triggered* by any lease longer than three years *or* by any lease that contains an option to purchase the property, regardless of the length of the lease.

Another gimmick is for the current property owner to transfer the property to a land trust and *then* sell the beneficiary interest of the land trust to the person who wants to take over the mortgage by an assignment of the mortgage or other method. Not true! Although subsection (8), as shown above, and the Code of Federal Regulations [Title 12, Volume 591.5(b)(vi)] stipulate that the transfer of a home into an inter-vivos trust does not trigger the due-on-sale clause, the regulations do not cover (or rather did not intend) for the beneficial interest of the inter-vivos trust to subsequently be sold or assigned to a third-party.

Only the transfer of a home to an inter-vivos (land) trust, owned by the same people as the original mortgage borrowers, are acceptable. The purpose of the regulation was definitely not intended to create a 'loophole' for avoiding a due-on-sale clause when selling or assigning a property to a third-party. The exception to the due-on-sale clause only applies to owner-occupied homes, not investment (rental) properties. Be aware that if you place a property into a land trust then sell or assign the beneficial interest in the trust and move out, you have likely violated your mortgage contract and risk invoking a lender's due-on-sale clause rights.

Not Just Sales, But Transfers of Any Interest

To understand the avoidance of the due-on-sale clause fully, you have to break it down into smaller parts. When you do, you immediately find that the 'due-on-sale' clause is a misnomer and would be better-named the *'due-on-transfer-of-any-interest'* clause. The list of actions covered by the actual clause is far broader than just 'sales'. Federal Regulation 12 C.F.R. 591.2 states *"The due-on-sale clause is triggered by just about every creative way of transferring property"*, to wit:

> *"Transfers of real property subject to a real property loan by assumptions, installment land sales contracts, wraparound loans, and contracts for deed, transfers subject to the mortgage or similar lien, and other like transfers."*

A great many people as well as real estate investors think that all you have to do to get around a due-on-"sale" clause is a transaction that is not a sale 'per se'. As the regulations show, this simply is not true.

Code of Federal Regulations

It is important, however, to reiterate where under the Code of Federal Regulations Title 12, Volume 591.5 (Revised January 1, 2013) lenders may **not** enforce the due-on-sale clause under the following circumstances:

1. *A transfer where the spouse or children of the borrower will become an owner of the property;*
2. *A transfer to a relative resulting from the death of a borrower;*
3. *A transfer by operation of law on the death of a joint tenant or tenant by the entirety;*
4. *A transfer resulting from a decree of dissolution of marriage, legal separation agreement, or from an incidental property settlement agreement, by which the spouse of the borrower becomes an owner of the property;*
5. *A transfer into an inter vivos trust in which the borrower is and remains a beneficiary and which does not relate to a transfer of rights of occupancy in the property;*
6. *The creation of a purchase money security interest for household appliances;*
7. *The granting of a leasehold interest of three years or less not containing an option to purchase;*
8. *A subordinate lien which does not involve a transfer of rights of occupancy in the property, and,*
9. *Any other transfer or disposition described in regulations prescribed by the Federal Home Loan Bank Board.*

Notifying Your Lender

Under Federal law, you are required to notify your lender when you transfer the property into the name of any other person, entity or trust. For this reason, the following information and suggested letters to your insurance agent and lender were drafted (See 'Real Estate Forms'). The process of moving your property into a controlled entity or a land trust usually requires several steps. You should notify your lender after you have completed the transfer and the property is titled in the name of the entity or trust.

Your lender will likely inquire about the transfer and may require additional supporting documentation to validate the consistency of ownership. You should regard such process as 'normal' and the lenders request should be respected. While this information was originally drafted for use when transferring real estate to a Land Trust, it has also been effective in every case when transferring property to a Corporation where the entity remains 100% owned by the same 'borrowers of record'.

Transferring Future Financial Interests

Assume that you have obtained a loan from a mortgage lender and the loan is separately guaranteed by you and your spouse (or partner). While loan agreements prohibit *'any change in ownership interest in the property'* and each guarantor ('borrower of record') has individually agreed *'not to transfer any ownership interests in the property'*, most often the language drafted into these agreements will not prohibit the transfer of some or all of the 'borrower of record's' **rights to receive** in the share of profits, losses and/or distributions that may be derived from the property.

The lender may have problems enforcing its due-on-sale clause if the clause only prohibits a 'borrower of record' from transferring any 'ownership interests' and says nothing about the 'assignment' of **lesser rights to share** in any future income, profits and/or distributions that may be derived from the property.

With the advent of securitized financing, individuals and 'borrowing entities' (such as a Corporation, Limited Liability Company or Limited Partnership), it has become more common for mortgage due-on-sale clauses to contain a 'change of control' provision. (i.e. a prohibition against certain direct or indirect changes in the equity ownership, control or management structure of the mortgagee).

Such provisions usually provide that at anytime certain principal individuals or entities, which own less than a specified percentage of the management or ownership ('borrower of record'), sells, conveys or assigns more than a specified percentage of interest, a default will have occurred under the mortgage and the mortgagor may accelerate the loan and call it due.

If the lender does not draft the due-on-sale clause specifically to include these types of equity and/or control transfers, a court will likely determine that such a transfer do not constitute a violation of the due-on-sale clause and the lender may not accelerate the mortgage.

Fidelity Trust Co. v. BVD Associates

For example, in *Fidelity Trust Co. v. BVD Associates, 196 Conn. 270, 491 A.2d 180 (1985)*, the court held that a change of membership occasioned by the withdrawal of general partners of a limited partnership, which was a distinct legal entity and remained so after the change in the general partnership interests, was not sufficient to constitute a 'sale or conveyance' under the applicable due-on-sale clause.

Hodges v. DMS Co.

Another example is in *Hodges v. DMS Co., 652 S.W. 2d 762 (Tenn. App. 1982)*, wherein the court held that in the absence of express language covering such a transfer (the withdrawal of two of the partners of the partnership mortgagor), while the business was continued in lieu of liquidation it did not amount to a 'sale or transfer' of the secured property even though the entity had changed by operation of law and thus did not activate the due-on-sale clause.

The court held that even though the entity had changed by operation of law, this could include transfers from you (as an individual) to your wholly-owned entity and should not activate the due-on-sale clause.

Reasonable Deductions

It is therefore reasonable to deduce from the Garn-St. Germain Act itself, and the aforementioned cases, that when you transfer a property wherein you are the 'borrower of record' to an entity (which you wholly-own), there is no transfer upon whom the lender could accelerate the mortgage and thus no sale, conveyance or transfer has taken place (because you are still the official 'borrower of record'). However, should you substantially change your percentage of 'ownership' in the property (or in the entities intended to 'hold title' to the property), then it may be possible for the lender to accelerate the mortgage and call the loan payable and due in full.

Transferring Property Into an Entity

Therefore, it would be prudent to explain the most common process undertaken when transferring property into an entity without invoking the due-on-sale clause.

1. You purchase the property in your personal name on behalf of a Nevada "C" Corporation that you 'wholly-own' (because a corporation on its own may not qualify for a mortgage).

2. You transfer the property to the name of the entity (where the ownership is the same throughout the entire structure) after signing and executing a 'Service Provider Agreement'. (The 'Service Provider Agreement' and supporting entity resolution can be found in our 'Operations Manual' publication available through My Biz Publishing at at AssetProtectionServices.com.) This transfer entitles the entity (Corp, LLC or LP) to all of the future income and losses and/or profits, but requires you to stay on the mortgage as the 'borrower of record'. The agreement states you are entitled to a full 'reimbursement' of all funds that you may have expended, or will expend, to maintain and/or fix-up the property.

3. Once all this has been accomplished, you need to provide your lender with a proper notice of the transfer of property into the entity, which you have chosen to hold title to the property. Such a transfer should be exempt under the Garn-St. Germain Act and drafting a letter to your insurance company and lender afterwards will assist in reminding them of this (See 'Real Estate Forms').

Asset Protection Services of America

Land Trust

Introduction

Land Trusts are sometimes referred to as Florida or Illinois 'type' trusts because of their favorable state laws and years of case history. Land Trusts are designed to hold title to real property and real property assets including real estate options, contracts and mortgages. Technically, a land trust is a form of *intervivos trust*. Intervivos means "among or between the living" and hence the term "living trust". Land Trust assets are considered personal property to the beneficiary, which is not subject to judgement creditors in some states. However, existing court precedence has held that, *"If a settlor has the right to revoke a trust, all of the assets are treated as owned by the settlor and is ignored for creditor purposes, just as it is ignored for tax purposes."* Land Trusts can be revocable or irrevocable. If created as revocable, the Land Trust serves primarily as a means of lawful tax avoidance and an excellent veil of anonymity. Even if a judge were to call you into a debtor's examination requiring you to provide ownership information under criminal penalty (wherein you may not plead your 5th amendment rights), if the beneficial interest owner of the Land Trust is an entity, such a structure can provide outstanding asset protection under scrutiny.

History of Land Trusts

The history of Land Trusts can be traced back four hundred years to the times of Feudal England. During the reign of King Henry VIII owning real estate as a citizen was considered somewhat of a liability. If you owned land in your name, you had two major obligations. One was to pay handsome taxes to the King and two was to serve in the King's army. Of course, wherever there are burdensome laws there are creative lawyers.

The people of that time saw opportunity in hiding or masking ownership of property. People began transferring title to relatives and friends to remove their name from the public records. When the King got wind of these arrangements, he enacted the 'Statute of Uses' under 27 Henry VIII, Chapter 10. The 'statute of uses' basically outlawed the use of trusts by declaring that such arrangements vested all title in the real estate in the *cestui que trust* (Latin for "he for whose use land is held by another"). Thus, the King would remain in control of his citizens through their ownership interest in real property. The English Courts modified this rule by stating that a trust was valid so long as the trustee has some duties to perform and was not a mere "nominee" titleholder.

The English court system made its mark in American Law by way of 'Common Law'. The 'statute of uses' is, in one form or another, still part of Common Law in America today. It has been applied to cases in which a trustee's duties are so nominal as to create a 'dry', 'passive' or 'inactive' trust. In America, most states expressly recognize the use of trusts. A handful of states also specifically recognize the Land Trust by statute. The first state in which Land Trusts were used was Illinois, hence the nickname "Illinois Land Trust." Most states have at least implicitly recognized the validity of Land Trusts by way of court rulings (or precedent). No state has enacted any laws making it 'illegal' (civilly or criminally) to use a Land Trust.

What is a Land Trust?

A Land Trust is an agreement (and *not* an entity), which is a simple and inexpensive method for handling the ownership of real estate. A land trust is a contractual arrangement by which a trust holds the recorded title to the real estate. All the rights and conveniences of ownership are exercised by the beneficial owner (beneficiary) whose interest holdings are not disclosed and where the beneficiaries of the trust retain management, control and the right to receive profits from the property. This method of owning real estate eliminates many of the difficulties that otherwise may be encountered in acquiring, owning or selling real estate.

The beneficiary of a Land Trust changes his or her interest in the property from real estate (title to the property) to personal property (ownership of the beneficial interest). Even though the beneficiary retains complete management and control over the property itself, he or she is not burdened with the legal characteristics of real estate when dealing with the property.

Since the beneficial interest is considered personal property, it is treated in much the same manner as a car, a savings account, or other tangible property. Consequently, the beneficial interest can be sold, pledged, or assigned in a simpler fashion than a conveyance of realty.

Legality of a Land Trust

This discussion of state laws regarding land trusts comes from several sources such as state statutes, common law, precedent and constitutional law. There is nothing in the United States Constitution about Land Trusts, but the Tenth Amendment of the Constitution reserves the laws affecting property to the respective states.

Within a state, the highest legal authority is provided by statute. A statute is a law enacted by state legislators. The next highest authority under state law is a decision by the state's highest court (State Supreme Court). If there is no decision on a particular area of law, then the law in that state is governed by the law of another state and/or the Common Law.

In the states where there is no state statute authorizing land trusts, then land trusts are governed by court cases and/or common law. As we will discover, some states have land trust statutes and/or court precedent, which specifically authorize land trusts while some states have statutes and/or court precedent which imply land trusts are authorized. In many states, the law is completely silent on the issue of land trusts. In such states, the use of land trusts is supported by general common law trust principles. ***There is no law in any state which makes it illegal to use a land trust.*** If a court determines your land trust to be invalid, you do not go to jail or pay a fine. Title to the trust property will simply vest as a matter of law in the name of the beneficiaries.

The general difference between the treatment of land trusts from state to state has to do with the 'statute of uses', which requires the trustee have some active duties to make a trust valid.

Some states require more duties of the trustee than others. Modern court decisions have eroded the strictness of the 'statute of uses', due to the growing popularity of living trusts. See: *McMahon v. Standard Bank & Trust, 550 N.W.2d 727 (1996)*

A properly drafted land trust agreement should cover all the powers of the trustee required by any state. These powers, however, are subject to the direction of the beneficiary. So, in states where the trustee is required to have active discretion in exercising his duties, the trust agreement may fail for lack of active duties if challenged in court.

If you wish to add additional duties of the trustee to satisfy the 'statute of uses' issue in such states, consider using our "Addendum to Trust Agreement (Co-Trustee with Power of Management)" as found in our publication 'Operations Manual' available through My Biz Publications at AssetProtectionServices.com.

Components of a Land Trust

Land Trusts requires the following components, if they are to operate legally and effectively. For more information on 'What is a Trust?' see 'Cover Your Assets' (3rd Edition) available through My Biz Publishing at AssetProtectionServices.com.

Grantor

The grantor (or settlor) is the person, whether an individual or entity, who is currently named on the property deed that transfers the property to the Land Trust.

Trustee

The trustee is the person, whether an individual or entity, who holds legal and equitable title to the real estate under a Land Trust agreement. The trustee has the full legal authority to transfer or convey the property as if they were the owner. However, the trustee has no authority to do any such acts with the title without the direction (i.e. written approval) of the beneficiaries. The trustee executes deeds and mortgages and deals with the property only as directed in writing by the beneficiary. Furthermore, the trustee generally has no right of possession, management or income from the property.

By law, a trustee can be any individual who is of legal age and sound mind, but could be a qualified trustee services company such as the Nevada Trustee Services Group, Inc. Some states may require a trustee to either reside or have a business address within the state where the property is located or the trust is domicilled. A trust 'situs' refers to the state under which laws the trust was created or is governed. In short, situs refers to as the 'venue', 'choice of law' and/or 'legal jurisdiction of the trust'.

Beneficiary

This is the person (individual or entity) that directs the trustee on what to do with the property. The beneficiary has the ultimate liability should there be a property related lawsuit. Also the beneficiary receives all the income derived from the property and thus the tax liability for same. One of the best beneficiary strategies is to create an LLC (or a Nevada "C" Corp) as the beneficiary. This LLC filing an 1120 (or Series LLC) may own 100% of the land trust's beneficial interest. Here you cannot be held personally responsible for any problems that may arise on the property (unless you personally are the cause of the problem), as members are not liable for the debts and obligations of an LLC.

Beneficiaries are not akin to 'tenants in common' on a deed, although their beneficial interests can specify them as such. Individuals who hold title to real estate as tenants in common have the right to file a lawsuit called 'partition'. In a partition lawsuit, a tenant in common can ask the court to force the sale of the property to liquidate their interest. This forced sale may be a financially disastrous situation to the other owners of the property because of capital gains tax implications. Furthermore, a forced sale usually means a lower sale price for the property.

Beneficiaries under a land trust cannot commence a partition action because they do not have an interest in the real estate. Their interest, like the other beneficiaries, is a personal property interest. Therefore a third party, such as a creditor, *can* force the sale of beneficial interest in the trust property to satisfy a judgment against one or more of the beneficiaries of the trust involved in the debt. This is an excellent reason why you should assign your beneficial interest to an entity.

Beneficiaries under a land trust cannot bind each other for trust obligations. The trustee must execute a contract for sale, deed of trust or other conveyance affecting title. Generally, the trustee cannot perform such an act without a letter of direction signed by a majority, if not all, of the beneficiaries. Thus, a trust agreement can be drafted to prevent less than all of the beneficiaries from gaining control of the property and will prevent a creditor who is cunning enough to attach one beneficiary's interest from taking control of the property.

A properly drafted land trust agreement will designate what happens to a beneficiary's interest upon his death, thus preventing any disruption in the affairs of the real estate. If one beneficiary dies, the trust agreement can specify who will be the successor of the beneficial interest. If there is no such designation, the beneficial interest will be included in the probate estate of the decedent. A successor-in-interest cannot force a partition of the real estate, which is often the case when an individual inherits an interest in realty (real estate).

Lastly, beneficiaries are obligated under the trust agreement to manage, maintain and preserve the trust property. A land trust agreement may specify which beneficiaries are to physically handle the responsibilities or may specify that a property manager should be hired by the trust to manage the property. Many variations can be spelled out in the land trust agreement, and the agreement can be amended at anytime.

Beneficiary Obligations to the Trustee

Under a typical land trust agreement, the beneficiaries agree to defend (pay for a lawyer) and indemnify (pay any claims against) the trustee for any lawsuits arising from the trustee's management of the trust property. The beneficiaries further agree to reimburse the trustee for any expenses incurred in administering the trust or the trust property. There also is usually a provision that any assignments of beneficial interest must be reported to the trustee for proper maintenance of the trust books and records.

Since the beneficiaries retain the rights and obligations of managing the trust property, these activities may create a duty to third parties. Under tort law principles, an owner or manager of a property may be liable to third parties if his conduct (or lack of conduct) creates a foreseeable risk to potentially injured parties. This potential for liability makes it critically important that you *have your insurance carrier name the beneficiaries as well as the trustee as additional insured for liability.* The beneficiaries, and not the trustee, are liable for the expenses related to the management and control of the property. Beneficiaries are also liable for income taxes (if any) and capital gains taxes when the property is sold.

Changing Beneficiaries

A beneficiary's interest under a Land Trust is personal property and thus it is freely transferable. A beneficiary can transfer their interest by executing an 'Assignment of Beneficial Interest'. This process is similar to transferring shares of stock in a corporation, although the beneficial interest under a Land Trust is personal property and not realty. This form does not need to be notarized absent specific trust legislation in your state requiring it. It is none-the-less recommended that all transfers of beneficial interest be notarized because it adds undebatable validity to the transfer. It also authenticates the date the transfer occurred which is of particular importance if you are involved in a lawsuit that alleges a fraudulent transfer to hinder creditors.

The Trust

The trust agreement wherein the grantor and beneficiary is one and the same person is called a 'self-settled' trust. A Corporation, Limited Liability Company, Limited Partnership or another trust can also create self-settled trusts. If you or your corporate entity already own a property, then create the land trust by executing the trust agreement with the trustee having the entity deed the property to the trust. If you want someone else to be the beneficiary of the trust (recommended), assign the beneficial interest to that entity when you set up the land trust agreement.

Administering the Trust Property

If the property you are placing into the land trust is an investment property, you might consider using a property management company to manage the rental property. The trustee signs a 'Property Management Agreement' (found in this publication under the section entitled 'Deeds for Transferring Real Property) with the management company to direct the management of the property on behalf of the trust. This strategy will also avoid revealing any beneficial interest ownership to your tenants. The beneficiaries of the Land Trust ought to issue a corresponding 'letter of direction' to the trustee to execute the said agreement with the property management company, which should be kept in the records book of the land trust.

The ideal situation would be to create your own property management company to manage your trust property. A real estate license is not usually required to manage properties in which you have an interest. Thus, you can contract with the trustee to manage the property on behalf of the trust.

If you use your own property management company to collect rents, you protect the anonymity of the beneficiaries. You also avoid the need for several bank accounts for the trust, since tenants enter into contracts with, and can make checks payable to, your property management company. The property management company can collect rents for all of your properties held in Land Trusts and disburse quietly the proceeds directly to the beneficiaries of the trusts. It is always wise to separate property management from property ownership!

In most states, a property management company can execute leases and file eviction proceedings in its own name on behalf of the owner. In states that don't permit management companies to execute leases, a stamp with the trustee's or co-trustee's signature may be required to approve such actions. The ability for a property management company to perform such activities is particularly advantageous with apartment buildings, which may have higher risks and/or require tenants to be evicted frequently.

Using your own property management company will help you negotiate more effectively with tenants, as you can inform the tenants that you 'just work' for the property management company who employs you to collect rents for the owner of some 'unknown trust'. This strategy gives you excellent negotiating power to deal with your tenants since you are not the 'owner of the property', but just a lowly 'manager' hired to collect rents. You can use the old 'higher authority' negotiating tactic effectively when your tenants believe that you are not the owner and just an employee.

Mechanics of Using a Land Trust

First, as an example, let us say that the property 'owners of record' are going to keep an existing loan on a piece of property in their names while creating a revocable inter-vivos land trust that they name the "123 Anywhere Street Land Trust" into which they title the property.

The owners establish themselves or an entity that they wholly own as the beneficiary of the trust. (Some lenders may require proof of the entity ownership.) When the property is transferred into the land trust by the 'owners of record' no sale of the property has been undertaken as the trust is still in the names of the owners of record as the beneficiaries. Even though the deed to the property has been transferred to the trust, it is no longer in the names of the 'owners of record' and therefore the lender's due-on-sale clause is not violated.

Should the 'owners of record' (beneficiaries) decide that they want to sell the property, they don't have to go through the traditional purchase / escrow / closing process. The sale can be undertaken through a purchase contract, as long as the buyer is paying cash or the owners are going to finance the sale. If the owners sell the property to a buyer through any process that doesn't pay off the existing mortgage, the lender could "call the note due" and accelerate the loan. Herein is a simple way to accomplish such a sale without the lender invoking a due-on-sale clause.

Because all land trusts require a trustee for the trust, the owners could set up a third-party buyer as the trustee (a trustee can not do anything without the written consent of the beneficiary). The buyer (now named as the trustee for the land trust) can take physical possession of the property without violating the lender's due on sale clause if a few simple rules are adhered. With *any transfer* of occupancy and/or possession in the property, the seller is *required* to notify the lender and the insurance company carrying the hazard insurance on the property of these changes. Most people ignore this and hope for the best.

Once the trust is set up as shown above, the trustee (the new buyer) can and should write a letter to the lender explaining that the owners of record have transferred the property into a Land Trust for which the buyer is the trustee. (Do not use the name as s buyer in the letter, show the person's name only as the trustee). Then the trustee (buyer) should instruct the lender to have all future correspondence and/or questions directed to the trustee (the buyer) at the properties address. This is also done with the insurance company insuring the property (See 'Real Estate Forms').

This is so simple and, to date, has worked 100% of the time. Plus, until the loan is paid off, owners are still the 'borrowers of record' on the mortgage even though the trustee (buyer) is now paying the monthly payments, as would be expected by the lender. When the loan gets paid off, the trustee (buyer) resigns as trustee and replaces himself or herself with a new trustee and becomes the sole beneficiary of the land trust.

An agreement for use and possession between the trustee (buyer) and the beneficiary is created whereupon the IRS (and most states) characterize the beneficiary as an owner of an "IRC -163 Qualified Property," even though the real estate has itself been converted by the land trust from real property to personalty. *See IRC – 163(h)4(D) pertinent to real property held in estates and certain trusts, in which ownership is characterized as personal property.*

Mechanics of Transferring Real Property with a Land Trust

When a land trust holds title to a property, **the deed is transferred to the trust not to the buyer**. One major reason for using the land trust is that there is no need to transfer the property through the escrow process or a closing attorney. The transfer is done at the county recorders office wherein the property is located. This saves a lot of hassles, money and best of all it secures the title to the property for the seller because it is *'held in trust'* and not transferred to the buyer prior to the mortgage being paid-off or getting a new loan for the property. To protect the buyer the beneficial interest in the property could be assigned by an unrecorded assignment from the seller to the buyer.

Should the buyer default on the contract with the owners, the trustee (buyer) resigns or is terminated as trustee by the beneficiaries who can replace them with a new trustee (a new buyer). Remember that the beneficiary of the land trust has 'absolute control' of everything the trustee does because they are the real owners of the trust property, not the trustee.

Accountants, Lawyers and Realtors

Many people with whom we discuss Land Trusts for the first time have failed to set them up in the past because their accountant, attorney or realtor had never heard of such a thing. Likewise, if attorneys where you live don't know about Land Trusts, then they also don't know how to sue them!

Age Requirements

A Land Trust may be created by anyone capable of entering into a contract (such as an individual 18 years of age or older), a group of persons or an entity (whether incorporated or unincorporated) who desires to purchase and own real estate.

Assignable Contracts

The ownership of a land trust (beneficial interest) is assignable, similar to the way stock in a corporation is assignable. Once property is titled 'in trust', the beneficiary or trustee of the trust can be changed, removed and/or replaced without changing title to the property. This can be very advantageous in the case of a real estate contract which would otherwise be non-assignable if not placed into a Land Trust. (i.e. Bank-owned or HUD properties.)

Avoidance of Probate

Probate is the process by which a will is officially proved and recognized by a court. This process is time consuming and costly. A Land Trust is one form of 'living trust', thus the Land Trust, if properly used as part of an estate plan, will be an effective tool for the orderly transfer of real estate upon the death of a beneficiary. A Land Trust agreement can specify that upon the death of a beneficiary, their interest will automatically be transferred to another person (individual or entity). This transfer is still subject to normal estate taxes (if any), but it bypasses the probate process.

Additionally, if the Land Trust is properly constructed, the decedent's beneficial interest will pass through (or around) his probate estate. The successor beneficiary will now inherit his or her interest without any public disclosure because there is no deed to be re-recorded to reflect the change of ownership.

Land Trusts also helps avoid 'ancillary probates'. An ancillary probate is required if the decedent (the person that died) owns property in another state. Partial administration of the estate is granted in the foreign state to collect the assets and settle all debts in the foreign state. The balance is then brought into the state in which the decedent's estate is being administered. Since a beneficial interest in a Land Trust is considered 'personalty', the 'personalty' goes where the decedent goes. Thus, the beneficial interest would remain in the state in which the beneficiary dies, not the state in which the real estate lies.

If there is a valid testamentary disposition in the trust, the decedent's interest should "pass through" probate. Thus, the interest in a Land Trust can be transferred to a person's heirs instantaneously, with little or no hassle.

Capital Gains Exemption

A transfer of property into a Land Trust for one's principle place of residency **does** affect the capital gains exemption rules as the trustee is the legal and equitable title holder of the property, thus placing you at risk of losing your capital gains exclusion after a period of three years.

Default without Recourse

A land trust allows a buyer to assume a loan **without** recourse, whereas a traditional assumption does not. Few people realize that an assumption is **with** recourse. Should a seller 'sell' a property to an investor who in turn 'sells' the property to a buyer who assumes and then defaults on the loan, the buyer, investor and the seller may all be held liable.

Discovery of Beneficial Interest

If the creditor knows you are the beneficiary, they can try to attach your interest under the trust. However, this difficult legal process may take a creditor months to carry out, giving you time to rearrange your affairs. Keep in mind, however, that any such transfers of your beneficial interest are subject to the rules prohibiting fraudulent transfers. In reality, it is unlikely that a creditor will discover that you are a beneficiary of a Land Trust. Unless you live in a state in which Land Trusts are widely used, a typical creditor's attorney would not even know enough to ask about beneficial interests under a Land Trust in a debtor's examination.

Doctrine of Equitable Conversion

What distinguishes a land trust from any other types of investment and asset management strategies is the Doctrine of Equitable Conversion. The Doctrine of Equitable Conversion enables people to convert real property to personal property. Once your property is placed in a land trust, and title is deeded to your trust, your transaction is no longer governed by mortgage law as the property is now governed by the Uniform Commercial Code, Article 9.

Equitable Conversion

In other states, the doctrine of 'equitable conversion' is recognized, wherein a contract for the sale of real estate converts the seller's interest from realty into personalty. The 'personalty' is essentially a right to the proceeds of the sale. The Land Trust agreement states that the trustee is to sell the property at the end of the term of the agreement. This agreement, even if not enforced, converts the grantor's interest under the trust from realty to personalty from the inception of the trust. Even without the sales provision, most courts will still respect the intentions of the creator of the trust that the beneficiary's interest be considered personal property. As an example:

"Whether the interest of a beneficiary is an interest in real property or in personal property depends on the provisions of the trust instrument. The interest of beneficiaries, who have under the terms of the trust agreement, no right title or interest in the realty as such, either legal or equitable, but only an interest in the earnings and proceeds with power to direct the trustee to deal with the title and manage and control the property, and the right to receive proceeds from rentals, which right is to be deemed personal property, is personal property only and not real estate." (90 C.J.S. Trusts – and – 76 Am. Jur. 2d. Sec. 12)

Employer Identification Number (EIN)

A land trust is considered a revocable grantor trust by the IRS and does not require the trust to obtain a separate tax Employer Identification Number or even file an income tax return.

Exempt from Due on Sale Clauses

Land Trusts are federally exempt from the due on sale clause found in almost all bank loans created within the last 20 to 25 years. Under the Garn-St. Germain Act, federal law emphatically prohibits lenders from taking exception to a borrower's right to place property into a revocable inter-vivos trust such as a Land Trust or Living Trust.

Few Disadvantages

A potential drawback, or disadvantage, to using a Land Trust properly is the highly recommended need to create and operate an LLC or "C" Corporation to act as the beneficial interest holder to the Land Trust. Although, in all fairness, the advantage to an entity being the beneficiary of a land trust is to protect you individually in the event of an inside lawsuit and to separate the amount of assets available to a potential judgement creditor in the event of losing a court case.

Financial Reporting

A Land Trust is a private agreement and requires no financial reporting whatsoever.

Flow-Chart

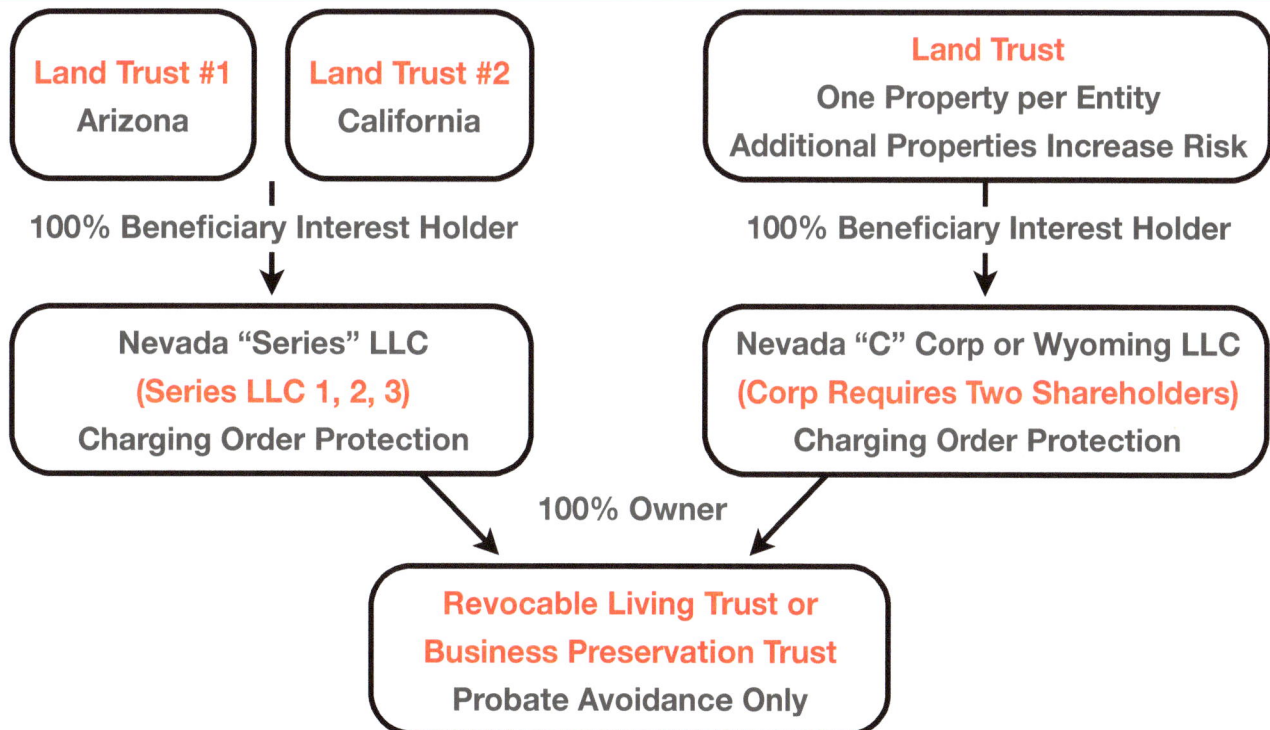

Land Trust #1
Arizona

Land Trust #2
California

Land Trust
One Property per Entity
Additional Properties Increase Risk

100% Beneficiary Interest Holder

100% Beneficiary Interest Holder

Nevada "Series" LLC
(Series LLC 1, 2, 3)
Charging Order Protection

Nevada "C" Corp or Wyoming LLC
(Corp Requires Two Shareholders)
Charging Order Protection

100% Owner

Revocable Living Trust or
Business Preservation Trust
Probate Avoidance Only

Homesteads

If you live in a state that does not have a homestead exemption, a judgment creditor can put your property up for sale at a sheriff's auction to the highest bidder. You can bet that the amount your house sells for will be less than fair market value.

Homestead Taxes

In certain parts of the country, property owners may claim their real estate as a 'homestead'. This designation affords them the benefit of lower property taxes, so long as they use the property as their principle place of residence. At least one state (Florida) has declared that an individual who has no legal or equitable title cannot claim a homestead exemption. Therefore it is best to contact your local taxing authority to decide how a transfer of your personal residence into a Land Trust may affect your property taxes and/or homestead exemption.

Ignorance of Land Trusts

Most banks, real estate brokers, title insurance companies and especially attorneys are ignorant about the nature of a Land Trust. You may hear comments like, *"I've never heard of that"*, or *"they are only valid in Illinois"*, or *"that isn't a valid trust"*, etc. This ignorance can make it difficult to implement and use Land Trusts to hold title. However, with a little patience (and education of your title company, lender and attorney about Land Trusts), you will see that using Land Trusts is worth the minor resistance you may encounter. As a practical matter, you may simply refer to your Land Trust as a "living trust" when dealing with real estate agents, lenders and title companies as you will likely receive less resistance that way. The fact that the Land Trust is not widely known or used makes it an effective tool for the individual who seeks to cloak the ownership of real estate. If Land Trusts were widely known or used, the protection of the Land Trust might not be as effective!

Income Tax Considerations

For income and estate tax purposes, the Internal Revenue Service considers a revocable living trust (and land trust) the same as if title is still in the name of the beneficiary (I.R.C. Code §~671-678) assuming the beneficiary and grantor created the trust for his or her own benefit and is still alive.

A Land Trust is treated for federal income tax purposes the same as if the property were owned outright in the beneficiary's name. There is no gift tax due upon the transfer of property into a Land Trust. The beneficiary of the trust continues to report the income and expenses relating to the property on a federal income tax return as if the property was owned outright by the individual. However, if the trust has many beneficiaries or centralized management and starts doing business as an entity, it may be treated as a corporation for federal income tax purposes. *(Outlaw v. U.S., 494 F.2d 1376 (1974).* A forty-one member Land Trust formed for the purchase, development and sale of crops from farmlands was considered a taxable association under I.R.C. Code 7701(a)(C). It is therefore advisable that you do not place multiple properties in one Land Trust and/or use your Land Trust as a business entity or corporation substitute.

There is no requirement that a Land Trust file for a tax identification number while the grantor is still alive. The IRS considers a traditional Land Trust to be, in essence, not a trust at all, since the trustee has no real duties with regard to the trust property. *(IRS Revenue Ruling No. 92-105).* However, since Land Trusts are not thoroughly tested in every state, it is possible that under *some* state laws, the IRS may consider a Land Trust to be the same as a living trust. If the land trust owner (beneficiary) makes the optional election to obtain an EIN for the land trust, they would be subject to reporting requirements on IRS form 1041.

The amount of duties a trustee is vested with is a double-edged sword. If a trustee has too few duties, the trust may fail because of the Statute of Uses. If the trustee has too many responsibilities (to satisfy the 'statute of uses), you may open another 'can of worms' as the IRS may require a fiduciary return be filed by the trustee where a blank 1041 return is filed with an attached summary of the income and expenses of all the trust properties. While creating some hassle and paperwork obligations, this requirement by the IRS does not add any additional tax liabilities since the same items are reported on the beneficiary's federal income tax return.

Interest Rates Rising

Lenders don't have spies at the clerk and recorder's office watching deed transfers. However, with recent leaps in technology, some counties have deed transfers on record that can be accessed for free from the Internet. A lender could also hire a local title company to search the records for any name changes. If interest rates rise substantially higher than rates on existing loans, lenders may start checking title on homes routinely.

Likewise, bank officers are far removed from the clerical workers who process mortgage payments. However, smaller banks have implemented systems for alerting bank officers of a change in payor name. If interest rates rise substantially higher than rates on existing loans, more lenders may implement a similar system to alert them of a different name on the check received for payment.

Invisible to Creditors

Land Trusts do not file tax returns nor are they required to obtain a tax Employer Identification Number (EIN) and, because of this, Land Trusts do not open bank accounts. Thus a Land Trust makes the true owners of any property in the trust truly invisible to creditors as it is 'transparent' to taxing authorities. The beneficiary of a Land Trust reports the income and expenses on their individual tax return just as if the Land Trust did not exist. And if a Corporation or LLC were the beneficiary of the Land Trust, the entity would report the income and expenses derived from the property held in the Land Trust on its tax return in the same manner. And since the Land Trust agreement is a private document, with no public record of it having ever been reported, Land Trusts make real property very much 'invisible to creditors'.

Land Trust Sales

When property held in a Land Trust is sold or refinanced, the property must first be transferred out of the Land Trust to the beneficiary (or grantor as a last resort) who can sell the property (i.e. Corporation, LLC or Individual). When sold, the money is paid to the beneficiary. For example, an LLC could pay 98% of the funds to a "C" corporation, who can then 'business expense' the money, and 2% to you, which would be taxable income.

Land Trust Transfers

Land Trust transfers are done by assignment not through an escrow.

Lawsuits

Everyday, thousands of lawsuits are filed in courts across America. Real estate owners are particularly vulnerable for two reasons. The first is that the real estate ownership is shown in the public records for anyone to find. The second is that any judgment against you immediately becomes a lien against all your real estate. What this means is that any lawsuit against you could potentially result in all your real estate being encumbered by a resulting judgment. These judgments will lien your properties until you either pay it off or win a later appeal. You will not be able to sell, mortgage or refinance your property until you pay the judgment in full.

A judgment of any size will tie up all your real estate until you deal with the judgment. If you appeal the decision, the judgment, will still lien the property. If you still lose after undertaking all available legal actions, then you must pay off the judgment. If you do not pay off the judgment, the judgment holder or creditor can execute on the judgment, giving the creditor the right to sell your real estate as they choose.

Legal and Equitable Title

With a Land Trust, the legal and equitable title is held by the trustee for and on behalf of the beneficiaries. The grantor, who generally becomes a beneficiary (in the form of a Corp, LLC or LP) under a Land Trust agreement no longer has any legal or equitable interest in the real estate itself. The beneficial interest under a Land Trust agreement is personal property, not real property as is the norm when real estate is held in your individual name.

This concept is difficult for some people to understand, because the beneficiary still has the right to possession, rents, profits, management and the like as if he still owned the property. The fact is a properly constructed Land Trust vests all legal and equitable title in the trustee, *not* the beneficiary. The beneficiary's interest is "personalty" not realty. States which have enacted land trust legislation specify that beneficial interests under a Land Trust are personal property and not real estate.

Lending Guidelines

Certain types of loans (i.e. HUD 203k Investor Loans) set forth guidelines which limit the number of units an individual can acquire using that loan program. If the individual transfers the properties into a Land Trust, there is no ownership interest in the property itself. Thus, an investor can avoid these restrictions by legitimately claiming there is no ownership interest in any other properties. If the properties are encumbered by assumable FHA or VA loans, you may consider having the trustee execute an assumption package on behalf of the trust; this will remove the liability from your credit report.

Multiple Properties

You can hold more than one property in each Land Trust, regardless of the state in which the property is situated, although it is not recommended. It is wiser to have one Land Trust for each rental property and at least one Land Trust for flipping properties.

No Annual Renewal Fees

Although you may elect to employ professional trustee services, a Land Trust itself does not require annual renewal fees to any state, saving you hundreds if not thousands of dollars annually.

No Registration Requirements

In most every state, the ownership of property through a land trust does not constitute the transaction of business, save the states of Texas and Florida. For that reason, a Land Trust formed for the sole purpose of owning real estate is not required to register in the state where the property is located.

Non-Recourse Financing

In some circumstances, a lender may be willing to offer financing without personal recourse against the borrower. In such a case, a default on the payment of the loan will leave the lender with the sole option of taking back the property through the process of foreclosure. If the property is sold at a public auction and the highest bid is less than the remaining balance due on the loan, there is a 'deficiency'. The lender may not hold the borrower personally liable for this deficiency on a non-recourse loan.

So why does it matter whether the trustee or the individual signs the loan papers and holds title? It matters because the borrower will have a foreclosure against his or her personal name and such foreclosure will be part of their permanent credit file. If the foreclosure is against the trustee (not personally, of course) the beneficiary's credit file remains pristine.

If an individual or investor is purchasing a property with an assumable FHA or VA loan, the trustee can sign the assumption package on behalf of the trust. If there is a default by the trust or subsequent purchasers, the trust (not the trustee or the beneficiaries) can be held liable.

Notifying Lenders

If the sellers of a property, who keep an existing loan in their names, vest a property into a revocable (inter-vivos) Land Trust which they name '123 Any Street Land Trust', the trust is directed solely by the sellers (as the beneficiaries). Since no sale of real estate has been undertaken with the deed being transferred to the trust, the lender's Due-on-Sale Clause is not violated. Along with the property's use, occupancy and possession, a trusteeship in the trust could be assigned to a third party buyer if the property was being sold by a loan assumption or any process not paying off the loan. The buyer can take physical possession of the property without violating the lender's due on sale clause if a few rules are undertaken.

With any transfer of occupancy and/or possession in the property, the seller is required to notify the lender and the insurance company carrying the hazard insurance on the property of these changes. Most borrowers ignore this procedure and simply hope for the best. This is a big mistake! Once a Land Trust has been established, the trustee can and should write a letter to the lender explaining the owners have transferred the property into a Land Trust (for which the buyer may also be the trustee). Then the trustee (buyer) should instruct the lender to have all future correspondence and/or questions directed to the trustee. A similar letter is also sent to the insurance company insuring the property.

This is so simple to do and it works 100% of the time. Plus, until the loan is paid off, the sellers of the property (the original borrowers of the loan) are still the 'borrowers of record' on the mortgage even though the trustee (the new buyer) is now paying the monthly payments, as would be expected by the lender. When the loan gets paid off, the trustee (buyer) resigns as trustee and replaces himself or herself with a new trustee and then becomes the sole beneficiary of the land trust taking ownership of the property.

An agreement for use and possession between the trustee (the buyer) and the beneficiary (the seller / owner) is created, whereupon the IRS and most states characterize the beneficiary as an owner of an 'IRC -163 Qualified Property'. Even though the real estate has itself been converted by the land trust from real property to personalty.

For more information on this, see IRC –163(h)4(D) pertinent to real property held in estates and certain trusts in which ownership is characterized as personal property.

Ownership Privacy

The primary purpose for keeping ownership private is for the proactive prevention of lawsuits. In every county in the United States, copies of all deeds to real estate are recorded in the public records. Anyone can go to the 'recorder of deeds' office to look up the owner of any property in that county. Under a Land Trust, the identity of the real owner (the beneficiaries) is not a matter of public record and therefore not discoverable.

A Land Trust agreement is *not* recorded. Only the deed and the name of the Trustee is recorded. Since the real estate is not titled in your name, only you and the Trustee know that you own it. A properly drafted Land Trust agreement should contain provisions explicitly preventing the Trustee from disclosing your ownership unless required to do so under court order or by state law. This is of the utmost importance, because if a person who wants to sue you cannot find any assets in your name they likely will not purse the matter further. And if an attorney takes the suit on a contingency basis, the attorney is unlikely to pursue the matter as they would see no means of getting paid.

Attorneys only 'win' a case when they are able to collect money from you. That is why attorneys don't sue poor people. In fact, attorneys have been known to fight amongst themselves just for the right to sue people with assets, especially easily accessible assets like real estate. If you hold title to real estate in your own name, you are begging to be sued.

Passive Loss Rules

A little trick to satisfy the 'statute of uses' and get around the IRS reporting rules are to use the 'co-trustee' method. If a co-trustee is vested with management responsibilities, the trustee is exempt from reporting requirements of 26 C.F.R. Sec. 1.671-4(b). In addition, the added responsibilities will satisfy the 'statute of uses' if the trust is challenged in court. While it is unlikely the IRS will ever make waves about the non-reporting issue (since they won't get any money except for some non-filing penalties), it isn't a bad idea to have the co-trustee addendum in your file for safekeeping.

The Internal Revenue Code requires that an individual be 'active' in the management of rental real estate to deduct passive losses of up to $25,000 against other active income. The beneficiary of a Land Trust, by the very terms of the Land Trust agreement, is involved in the management of the property and should easily satisfy the requirement of 'active participation'.

Property Tax Liabilities

The beneficiary of a Land Trust is held personally liable for any unpaid property taxes, the same as if title were held outright. This liability is not usually an issue as most taxing districts place a lien on the real estate and simply wait for the 'owner' to pay it off. The state may pursue the trustee in an effort to ascertain the identity of the land trust beneficial owner(s).

Property Transfer Taxes

Some states and localities impose an onerous transfer tax, also known as 'documentary stamps' in some states, on the transfer of real property - even into a Land Trust (i.e.

Pennsylvania). In most jurisdictions (except PA), a transfer into a trust with no change in beneficial ownership is exempt from transfer tax. The real property clerk (county recorder) or treasurer's office may require an affidavit or copy of the trust to prove that there is no change of beneficial ownership. It is best to contact your local taxing authority to determine the amount of taxes that may be due upon the transfer of property into a Land Trust of which you are the beneficiary. It has been our experience, under inconsistent circumstances, that the state has not charged any property transfer taxes when the property is transferred to an entity (Corp, LLC or LP) where the ownership is shown to be the same before and after the transfer.

Unless specified under state law, the transfer of a beneficial interest is not subject to real property transfer taxes, since the beneficial interest is not real property. However, there may be personal property or 'intangible property' taxes in your state or locality. For example Florida and Pennsylvania require the payment of transfer tax on the transfer of any beneficial interest in a Land Trust. It is best to contact your local taxing authority to determine the amount of taxes that may be due upon the transfer of any beneficial interest in a Land Trust.

Protection for the Owner

A Land Trust offers particular benefits in those cases where two or more persons hold the real estate. If two or more persons own the property, the title to the property might become faulty and unmerchantable because of death, legal disability, divorce, judgments, and many other types of litigation affecting one of the co-owners. When the property is held in a Land Trust, a judgment against one of the beneficiaries does not constitute a lien upon the real estate held in trust; neither do ordinary legal proceedings against any of the beneficiaries muddle the title.

Protection from Liens

Since the beneficial interest under a Land Trust is not an interest in real estate, a judgment against your personal name will not automatically attach to the real estate. Let's say, for example, you are involved in a lawsuit and a judgment is obtained against you personally. The creditor would normally take a 'transcript of judgment' and file it in the office of real estate records in the county in which you hold property. However, since title to your property is not in your name, the judgment does not attach as a lien to the real estate. You can sell it, refinance it, mortgage it or trade it without having to deal with the lien. If the liened property were titled in your name, you couldn't do anything with the property until you satisfied the lien.

Protecting Beneficial Interest

The proper use of land trusts allows for the avoidance of reassessment fees, transfer taxes and probate. Land trusts further allow you or a third-party buyer to assume non-assumable mortgages, ease transferring title, provide a veil of anonymity and will not invoke a bank due on sale clause. However, please be advised that land trusts are still a form of revocable trust and as such cannot protect beneficial interest owner assets from lawsuits or judgment creditors. It is imperative you properly assign the beneficial interest of a land trust to an entity to protect your personal assets (in the event of an inside lawsuit) or the assets held within the land trust (in the event of an outside lawsuit) depending on the circumstance of the suit.

Reassessment Fees

Reassessment fees may occur anytime there is a change in property ownership. In order to avoid reassessment fees when using a land trust, the percentage of ownership must remain unchanged and be the same the day after transfer of title as it was the day before the transfer. This includes continuity of ownership throughout the entities involved with the transfer. Should the ownership in the entities involved in the transfer differ from that of the property, you may be subject to reassessment fees. For people living in California, Proposition 13 allows immediate family members (father, mother, son or daughter) to be added to the title without invoking a change of ownership.

Refinancing

Most lenders are conservative and do not understand Land Trusts. The lender that holds your current mortgage will likely object if you try to refinance the property while it is held in a land trust and generally require that you first transfer the property out of the trust. The lender may or may not allow you to transfer the property into the name of the beneficiary (if an entity is the beneficiary) or the lender may require that you transfer the property back into your names (if the original grantors are the 'owners of record' on the current mortgage) and then have you apply for the refinancing.

In such cases, the beneficiaries would need to request that the trustee draft a quitclaim deed transferring the property to the beneficiary (if it is an entity) or back to you (if you are the beneficiary or grantor) so title is in an acceptable name for the refinance. In our experience, lenders generally will tell you that once the refinance is completed and the check has cleared the bank, you can put the property back into the trust again. You can then transfer the property back into trust by using another quitclaim deed, but this will leave a paper trail for potential creditors to follow. The only way to avoid such a paper trail back to you is to work with a lender who will allow for a loan to be in the name of an entity and not an individual.

Statute of Uses

Duties of a trustee under a Land Trust should vest enough 'active responsibility' in the trustee so as to satisfy the 'statute of uses'. In states where there are no specific statutes authorizing Land Trusts, we must rely on common law. Not every state applies the 'statute of uses' to trusts with the same scrutiny, some states require the trustee to have a more active role in the management of the property or the trust may be declared void.

If a court decides that your particular Land Trust or Land Trusts in general violate the 'statute of uses', you do not go to jail and you do not pay civil fines. If a court declares that your Land Trust is 'passive', the trust simply folds and title reverts to the beneficiaries. Thus, if you transferred title into a trust in which you are the beneficiary, and a creditor lawsuit resulted in the destruction of the trust, you would be in no worse of a position than when you started with title in your own name. If you assigned the beneficial interest holdings to an entity, then you would be in a far better position.

Title Companies

"But the title company says I have to disclose the beneficiaries on public record?" Only a few state laws require disclosure of the beneficiaries in a deed or reference to a recorded trust agreement. Title companies and attorneys often cite such state statutes as being a legal requirement for disclosing the beneficiaries on public record, but this interpretation is absolutely incorrect!

The purpose of such laws are to alert potential buyers for a property that certain beneficiaries exist who must be consulted before the trustee can sell the property. If the laws did not exist and a trustee sold a property without the permission of the beneficiaries, the transfer could later be voided (and the title company who insured the transaction would be liable for monetary damages). These laws usually state that third-parties can ignore the 'as trustee' designation if no beneficiary is named in the deed or no reference is made to a recorded trust agreement. The legal result of failing to disclose the beneficiaries is that a potential buyer can accept the trustee as the complete legal owner of the property. Thus, the buyer will have no legal duty to inquire further. This is exactly the intended result we want to protect our privacy!

Title Insurance

A question many people ask is whether obtaining title insurance is necessary when transferring a property into a Land Trust. The answer is, 'it depends'. When you purchase real estate the seller or the buyer (depending upon what state you live in) buys title insurance. The purpose of title insurance is to defend and indemnify the parties against any claims by third parties affecting the integrity of the title. If you transfer property into trust and remain the beneficiary, there is little risk of such a claim. When you sell the property, there will be what is known as a 'gap' in the title insurance coverage. That gap exists from the deed formerly in your name to the deed in trust. It does not create the type of gap that leads to uninsurable title, it simply means that when you sell the property you may have to pay a higher premium depending upon how much of a risk the title insurance company feels that the gap created.

Transacting Intrastate Business

In most states, outside of Florida Texas, the ownership of real estate does not constitute the transaction of intrastate business. For that reason, a Land Trust formed for the sole purpose of owning real estate is not required to register in the state where the real estate is located. Placing real property into a land trust, where the beneficial interest holder belongs to an entity formed in a foreign state, should not in-and-of-itself give cause for a state to claim the foreign entity holding the beneficial interest to be 'conducting intrastate business' within its borders.

California Corporations Code
(Limited Liability Companies) Section 17001

(ap) *"Transact intrastate business" means to enter into repeated and successive transactions of business in this state, other than in interstate or foreign commerce.*

(1) *Without excluding other activities which may not be considered to be transacting intrastate business, a foreign limited liability company shall not be considered to be transacting intrastate business merely because its subsidiary transacts intrastate business, or merely because of its status as any one or more of the following:*
   (A) *A shareholder of a domestic corporation.*
   (B) *A shareholder of a foreign corporation transacting intrastate business.*
   (C) *A limited partner of a foreign limited partnership transacting intrastate business.*
   (D) *A limited partner of a domestic limited partnership.*
   (E) *A member or manager of a foreign limited liability company transacting intrastate business.*
   (F) *A member or manager of a domestic limited liability company.*

(2) *Without excluding other activities which may not be considered to be transacting intrastate business, a foreign limited liability company shall not be considered to be transacting intrastate business within the meaning of this subdivision solely by reason of carrying on in this state any one or more of the following activities:*
   (A) *Maintaining or defending any action or suit or any administrative or arbitration proceeding, or effecting the settlement thereof, or the settlement of claims or disputes.*
   (B) *Holding meetings of its managers or members or carrying on any other activities concerning its internal affairs.*
   (C) *Maintaining bank accounts.*
   (D) *Maintaining offices or agencies for the transfer, exchange, and registration of the foreign limited liability company's securities or maintaining trustees or depositaries with respect to those securities.*
   (E) *Effecting sales through independent contractors.*
   (F) *Soliciting or procuring orders, whether by mail or through employees or agents or otherwise, where those orders require acceptance without this state before becoming binding contracts.*
   (G) *Creating or acquiring evidences of debt or mortgages, liens, or security interests in real or personal property.*
   (H) *Securing or collecting debts or enforcing mortgages and security interests in property securing the debts.*
   (I) *Conducting an isolated transaction that is completed within 180 days and not in the course of a number of repeated transactions of a like nature.*

The (above) California Corporations Code demonstrates in section (ap)(1)(A-F) that an out-of-state entity holding a share in a California domestic or foreign Corporation, or holding an interest in a Limited Partnership or Limited Liability Company, shall *not* be considered an act of 'conducting intrastate business' in the state of California. Thus, holding beneficial interest in a Land trust is no more an act of conducting business than is holding a certificate of stock in a California Corporation or a partner/member interest in a California Limited Partnership or Limited Liability Company. Be sure to check with your state statutes, but as it goes with California so goes it with the Union.

Transferring Property

When a land trust holds title to the property the deed is transferred to the trust not the buyer. One major reason for using the land trust is that there is no need to transfer the property through the escrow process or a closing attorney. The transfer is made at the county recorders office in the county wherein the property is located. This saves a lot of hassle, money and secures title to the property for the seller because it is 'held in trust' and not transferred to the buyer prior to the seller paying off the mortgage or getting a new loan for the property. To protect the buyer, the beneficial interest in the property could be assigned by an unrecorded assignment from the seller to the buyer.

Tax-Deferred Exchanges

Section 1031 of the Internal Revenue Code classifies certain 'like kind' exchanges of investment property as exempt from taxation. Thus, a beneficial interest in a *regular* trust cannot be exchanged for real estate. The IRS has ruled that a Land Trust is not a true trust for tax purposes, so that a beneficial interest in a Land Trust *can* be exchanged for another piece of real estate (See IRS Revenue Ruling No. 92-105). The beneficial interest in a land trust can be exchanged for another beneficial interest in a different Land Trust. This can be effective for 'swapping properties' without paying off or assuming the existing loans.

This ruling was limited to Land Trusts, which are not necessarily recognized in every state. If you add additional duties for the trustee, the same rules may not apply. If you are uncertain about whether the ruling will apply, you should 'step-out' of the trust first and have the trustee quitclaim the property to the beneficiary, then exchange the property and transfer the new property into trust. I.R.C. § 1031 Tax Deferred Exchanges are very precise and must be done 'by the book'. Do *not* attempt such an exchange without the advice of experienced and qualified exchanger.

Trustee and Title Issues

A beneficiary cannot personally sign any legal documents affecting title. The beneficiary must issue a 'letter of direction' to the trustee. This fact can create hassles if the trustee is not easily accessible. Real estate agents know the importance of catching a buyer while they're hot, so if the beneficiary cannot execute a sales contract there is the risk of losing a buyer before the trustee can be found for a signature. The solution is to insert a clause in the sales contract which states:

"Seller is signing this contract as beneficiary of a certain Land Trust dated _____,20__ that holds title to the property and hereby agrees to execute a letter of direction to the trustee to convey title at closing."

Since many real estate agents are unfamiliar with trusts, it is recommended that you make a purchase offer in your own name (or company name), reserving the right to assign by placing the words 'and/or assigns' next to the buyer's name in your contract or purchase offer. A few days before the closing, contact the title agent or attorney and tell him or her that you wish to take title in the name of a 'revocable land trust'.

The key to an effective Land Trust is an intelligent and reliable trustee. If you pick the wrong trustee, the Land Trust may create a royal nightmare for you. However, a properly drafted trust agreement will give the beneficiary the authority to promptly terminate the trustee's duties and appoint another one.

Title Seasoning

Due to recent loan fraud scams, some lenders are nervous about funding loans for flippers. Property flipping occurs when an investor buys and resells a property within a short period of time (generally recognized to be under one year). Suspicious of artificially inflated pricing on the part of the investors, these lenders require title seasoning, that is, the seller must own the property for 12 months. If the seller has not owned the property for the requisite time period, the lender won't fund the buyer's loan.

Let's say you are an investor that wants to buy a distressed property, fix it up and sell for a cash profit. If you own the property just a few months, the person who buys it from you may run into the *seasoning* issue with his lender. Rather than take title in your own name, take title through a land trust. When you sell, the buyer's lender will review the title report and see that the land trust has owned the property for three months. Before that, the owned the property for three years. The lender will likely presume that the seller transferred title to the land trust for estate planning purposes a few months ago and is now selling the property.

The truth is that Joe Seller sold the property to the land trust of which you are the beneficiary. This practice is not loan fraud, since neither you nor the buyer have made any false or misleading statements; the lender made his own conclusions of the trust.

Guidelines to Forming a Land Trust

Step 1   Find an appropriate trustee.

Step 2   Execute the Land Trust Agreement with trustee.

Step 3   Execute and record deed to trust. We recommend that the title is taken in the name of the trust itself, then execute and record "Trustee's Certification & Affidavit".

Step 4   Send letter to insurance company changing named insured.

Step 5   Execute "Co-Trustee Addendum" (optional). Complete the following Steps if you are using a "Trust Assignment."

Step 6   Execute "Assignment of Beneficial Interest" and "Bill of Sale."

Step 7   Have seller execute "Seller Disclosure" form and limited power of attorney.

Step 8   Have seller execute authorization to release loan information and a change of address for billing purposes.

10th Amendment

"The powers not delegated to the United States by the Constitution, nor prohibited by it to the States, are reserved to the States respectively, or to the people."

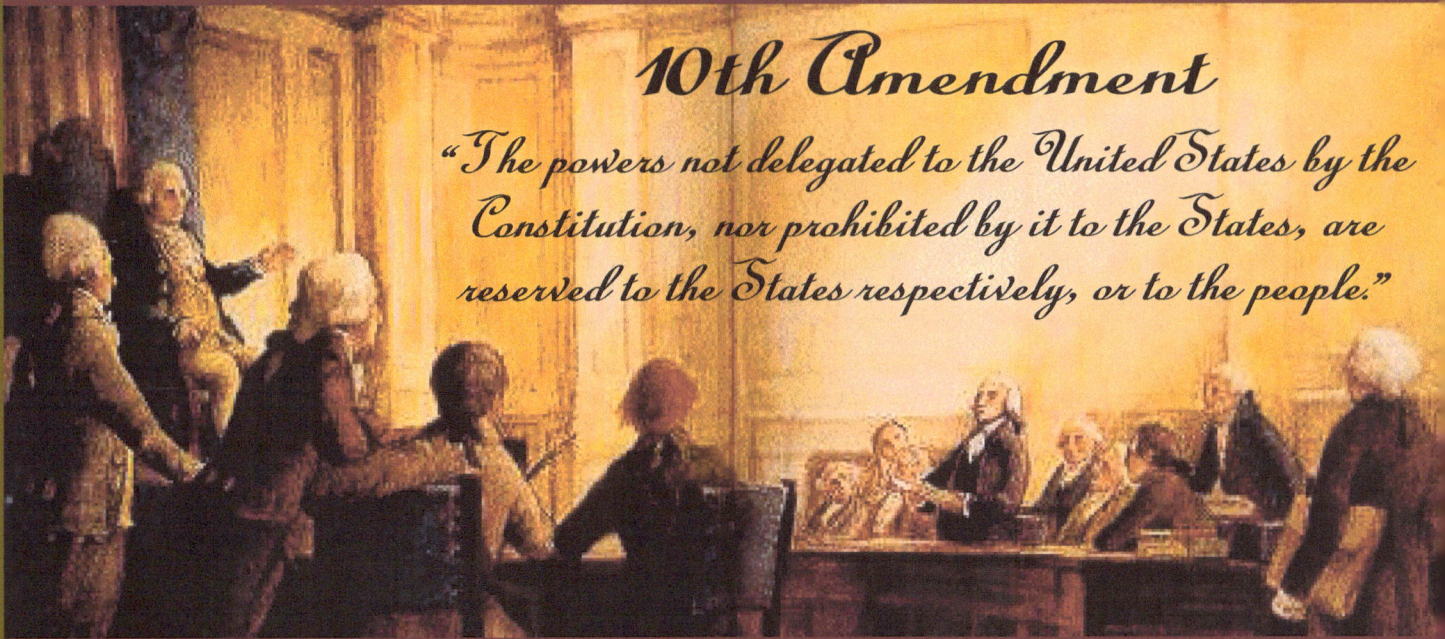

Land Trust State Laws

Land Trust State Laws

Alabama

Land trusts are specifically authorized by state statute in Alabama Code Sections 35-4-250 through 35-4-251. The trust is valid so long as the trustee has some active duties, such as collecting rents, exercising discretion in the management of the property and/or taking possession of the trust property. Trustee duties in case law:

Morgan County National Bank of Decatur v. Nelson, 244 Ala. 374, 13 So.2d 765 (1943); and
Nixon v. Nixon, 245 Ala. 43, 15 So.2d 561 (1943)

Alaska

There are no state statutes or cases dealing directly with land trusts. Therefore, it would be safer to error on the side of caution and use a land trust agreement with an addendum. Alaska law requires the registration of all living trusts and therefore, will most likely require the registration of all Land Trusts, but the penalty for not registering is inconsequential under Alaska Statutes Section 13.36.005.

Arizona

There is no land trust statute, but there is case law directly authorizing land trusts, so long as the trustee has some active duties. *Lane Title and Trust Co. V. Brennan, 440 P.2d 105 (1965).* Arizona law requires the disclosure of beneficiaries and any change of beneficiaries under Arizona Revised Statutes Section 33-404. Either party to the deed transfer (whether grantor or grantee) has two years to void the transaction. If you are transferring your own property into trust, there is no real issue since you control both grantor and grantee. If you are taking title from a third party to your trust, you can use an entity (such as a corporation) in the middle of the transaction so that the deed to the trust is from someone you control. For more information on Trustee duties in case law see:

Lane Title and Trust Co. v. Brannon, 103 Ariz. 272, 440 P.2d 105 (1968)

Arkansas

There is no land trust statute, but there is case law impliedly authorizing land trusts, so long as the trustee has some active duties, such as signing leases, paying taxes and distributing income.

Smith v. Wright, 779 SW2d 177 (1989); and
Murray v. Hale, 203 F. Supp. 583 (E.D. Arkansas, 1962)

In the absence of a statute to the contrary, the owner of property may create a trust therein for any lawful purpose for which he may deem wise or desirable and the trust may be created for his own benefit as well as for the benefit of another.

For more information on Trustee duties in case law see:

Randolph v. Read, 129 Ark. 485, 196 S.W. 133 (1917); and
Murray v. Hale, 203 F. Supp. 584 (E.D. W.D. 1962)

California

There is no land trust statute, but California does not follow the 'statute of uses'. At least two California court cases have expressly recognized the validity of land trusts in:

Walgren v. Dolan, 276 Cal. Rptr. 554 (1990); and

Re Tutules' Estate, 22 Cal. Rptr. 427 (1962)

Some title companies in California refer to a land trust as a 'Title Holding Trust'.

Colorado

There is no land trust statute. Support for land trusts are implied from:

Board of County Commissioners v. Howard, 640 P.2d 1128 (1982)

Conflicting decisions exist in Colorado regarding what duties of the trustee are necessary:

O'Reilly v. Balkwill, 297 P.2d 263 (1956)

A trust agreement, where the trustee's only duty was to quitclaim property to beneficiaries upon demand, is insufficient to create an 'active' trust.

Reed v. Munn, 148 F. 737 8th Cir. (1906)

Authority of trustee to sell or lease trust property at the direction of majority of the beneficiaries is sufficient to create an 'active' trust.

More recent cases have held that a revocable living trust is valid even though the grantor retains extensive control over the administration of the trust property.

Exchange National Bank v. Sparkman, 554 P.2d 1090 (1976)

A trust in Colorado may (and should) hold title to property in its own name, but must file a 'Statement of Authority' per Colorado Revised Statutes Section 38-30-172.

Connecticut

There is no state statute, but all trusts require active duties of the trustee to avoid the 'statute of uses'. The specific duties required of a trustee are not well defined by Connecticut law.

Goytizolo v. Moore, 27 Conn.App. 22 (1992)

However, Connecticut recognizes statute under Common Law:

Bryan v. Bradley, 16 Conn. 174

All Connecticut trusts must be active.

Delaware

There is no state statute. There is case law impliedly authorizing land trusts, so long as the trustee has some active duties. There is also a duty to manage the property.

Marvel v. Wilmington, 87 A. 1014 (1913); and

Houston v. Houston, 20 Cal. Ch. 1, 175 A. 51 (1922); and

25 Del. Code Ann. Deeds 101

For more information on trustee duties in case law see:

Doe v. Lank, Del. Super. 4 Houst. 649 (1874); and

Nickson v. Filtrol Corp., 262 A.2d 267 (Del. Ch. 1970); and

Marvel v. Wilmington Trust Co., 10 Del. Ch. 163, 87 A. 1014 (1913)

District of Columbia

There is no land trust statute. D.C. Code Annotated § 45-1101 implies support for the use of any trust so long as the trustee has "some power of actual disposition."
Liberty National Bank of Washington v. Smoot, 135 F. Supp 654 (Dist Ct. of D.C 1955)

Florida

The Florida legislature specifically authorizes land trusts under Florida Statutes Sections 689.07 through 689.071. Any active duties of the trustee are sufficient to validate a land trust.
Opinion of the Florida Attorney General 94-50, June 2, 1994
A property held in a land trust does not qualify for Ad Valorem tax treatment.
Two people must witness a deed to a land trust and a transfer of beneficial interest *is* subject to real property transfer tax. 'Statutes of uses' was adopted under Florida Statute 2.01 and applied to deeds under Section 689.09. But see protective provisions of Sections 689.071(1) and (4).
Gramer v. Ramos, 174 So. 2d 443 (Fla. 2d DCA 1965)

Georgia

Specifically authorized under the Official Code of Georgia Annotated, Sections 53-12-4 & 5 and 53-12-50 through 53-12-59. Any active duties of the trustee are sufficient to sustain the trust. Interest in a land trust may be evidenced by 'certificates', which are treated the same as corporate shares under Georgia law. For more information on trustee duties in case law implying active duties see:
Odum v. Henry, 254 Ga. 739, 334 S.E.2d 304 (1985)

Hawaii

Specifically authorized under the Hawaii Revised Statutes Section 558-4 (Land Trust Act). Any active duties of the trustee are sufficient to sustain the trust. The only 'glitch' with Hawaii law is that the names of the beneficiaries must be disclosed. If the property owned by the trust is in violation of any law or ordinance, the trustee is required to disclose the names of all beneficiaries and is not subject to civil liability for so doing under Hawaii Revised Statutes Section 558-8.

Idaho

There is no land trust statute. (Idaho Codes 68-1301 through 68-1322; and 68-104, 105, 106)
A trust is considered 'active' so long as the trustee's instructions at least imply an affirmative duty on the trustee to preserve and manage the trust property.
Garner v. Andersen, 527 P.2d 1264
Idaho requires the registration of all living trusts and therefore, will most likely require the registration of all Land Trusts as well.

Illinois

Specifically authorized under Illinois Revised Statutes Chapter 110, Section 15-1205 and Chapter 148, Sections 60-84. In addition, Illinois has a long body of case law to support the use of land trusts.

Robinson v. Chicago National Bank, 176 N.E.2d 659 (1961)

Trustee duties in case law provide expressed duty to sell and execute instruments.

Crow v. Crow, 348 Ill. 241, 180 N.E. 877 (1932); and

Chicago Title & Trust Co. v. Mercantile Trust & Savings Bank, 300 Ill. App. 329, 20 N.E.2d 992 (1939)

Indiana

Specifically authorized under Indiana Code Sections 30-4-2-7 through 30-4-2-14. The beneficiary may manage the property or give the power to manage to the trustee so long as the trustee has 'some power' related to the administration of the trust.

Iowa

No specific land trust statute. Trustee must have title, control and power to collect rents, receive profits and execute leases and mortgages to satisfy the statute of uses.

Olsen v. Youngerman, 113 N.W 938 (1907); and

Keck v. McKinstry, 221 N.W. 851 (1928)

Statute of uses is not violated if the grantor retains power of management while still alive.

Kansas

No land trust statute. Support implied by Kansas Statutes Annotated §58-2413:

"Trust considered 'active' if trustee has power of disposition and management."

Land Trusts - Adaptability to Kansas Real Estate Practice, 14 Kansas Law Review 97 (1965)

Kentucky

No land trust statute. Trust agreement requires a statement of active duties of property management.

Winn v. William, 165 S.W.2d 961 (1942)

It is not clear under Kentucky law what specific duties are required or if Kentucky recognizes lands trusts altogether.

Louisiana

Specifically authorized under Louisiana Trust Code 9-1721-2252; 1731, 9-2061-66; 9-2091 and 9-2118, with one caveat; Louisiana does not appear to recognize the designation of the beneficiary's interest as personalty.

St. Charles Land Trust v. St. Armant, 253 La. 243, 217 So.2d 385 (1968)

Since the interest under a land trust in Louisiana is considered realty and not personalty, a judgment against the beneficiary will attach to the realty.

Maine

No land trust statute. Trust agreement requires that trustee have some power of management, preservation, power of sale or duty to pay expenses.

Dixon v. Dixon, 124 A. 198 (1924)

Maine requires the registration of all living trusts and therefore, will most likely require the registration of all land trusts.

Maryland

No land trust statute. Real Property Law § 2-116 requires that the trustee have some express power of management or disposition.

Massachusetts

No land trust statute, but expressly recognized by case law.

New England Mutual Life v. Grant, 56 F. Supp. 192 (D. Mass 1944)

There is no duty required of trustee other than to convey the property to the beneficiary upon demand. Land trusts are referred to as 'Nominee Trusts' in Massachusetts. For more information on trustee duties in case law see:

Rothwell v. Rothwell, 283 Mass. 563, 186 N.E. 662 (1933)

Michigan

No land trust statute, but Michigan Complied Laws Annotated 555.4 requires some statement of powers and is expressly recognized under case law.

Rose v. Rose, 1 N.W.2d 458 (1942)

Minnesota

There is no land trust statute, but Minnesota Statutes § 501B.01 states that an active express trust may be created for 'any lawful purpose'. Section 501B.02 abolishes passive trusts. Any active duties of the trustee are sufficient to validate a trust in Minnesota.

Mississippi

No land trust statute, but all trusts, or transfers of beneficial interest in trust, must be registered to be effective under Mississippi Codes Annotated §91-9-1. Registration requires disclosing the name of the grantor, but not the beneficiary. Case law implies support for land trusts so long as trustee has some active duties such as managing, collecting rents, paying taxes, repair and upkeep.

Western Union v. Rhett, 50 So. 696 (1909); and
Leigh v. Harrison, 11 So. 604 (1892)

Missouri

No land trust statute. Any powers of management, sale, lease, mortgage or disposal are sufficient under Missouri Revised Statutes §456.020.

Maxwell v. Growney, 213 S.W. 427 (1948); and

Matthews v. Vancleve, 221 S.W. 34 (1949); and

Farkas v. Calamia, 373 S.W.2d 1 (Mo. 1963)

Montana

No land trust statute and the case law is also not clear. The Montana Probate Code, however (Montana Codes Annotated §~72-33-201 *et seq.*), is based on California's Probate Code, which permits trusts so long as the trustee has some active duties. Montana courts traditionally follow California law on trusts as seen under Montana Codes Annotated §~72-36-206, 101, et seq. - Trusts in Relation to Real Property.

In Re Strode's Estate, 167 P.2d 579

Nebraska

No land trust statute. Trusts are considered 'active' so long as the trustee has some affirmative duties such as control, management, leasing and sale.

Cahill v. Armatys, 177 N.W.2d 27 (1970); and

Jones v. Shrigley, 33 N.W.2d 510 (1948)

For more information on trustee duties in case law see:

Lancaster County Bank v. Marshal, 264 N.W. 470 (Neb. 1936); and

Beals v. Coughwell, 299 N.W. 638 (1941); and

Jones v. Shrigley, 33 N.W. 2d 510; and

Active v. Passive Wills, 681(2)

Nevada

No land trust statute, however sections 73 and 74 of the Nevada Probate Code do support revocable inter-vivos trusts in general. Nevada Revised Statutes, Section 163 states that a trust may be created for any lawful purpose and that a trustee may be relieved of many of his duties by the grantor or beneficiary.

New Hampshire

No land trust statute. The 'statute of uses' does not apply to trusts in which the trustee has duties that require discretion.

Bellows v. Page, 188 A. 2 (1936)

New Jersey

No land trust statute, but New Jersey Statutes Annotated §~46:3 through 46:9 requires only that the trustee have some power to mortgage, sell, or lease the property, even if only at the beneficiary's direction.

Martling v. Martling, 39 A. 203 (1898); and

Skovberg v. Smith, 3 N.J. Super. 424, 72 A.2d 911 (1950); and

Speth v. Speth, 8 N.J. Super. 587, 74 A.2d 344 (1950)

New Mexico

No specific land trust statute, but cases have implied support for land trusts.

Wollard v. Sulier, 232 P.2d 991

Where realty is given to trustee with a direction to sell and distribute proceeds, the trust subject-matter is treated as personal property. New Mexico requires the registration of all living trusts, however do not confuse the common law land trust with the real estate investment trust authorized by Section 47-2-1 of the New Mexico Code.

New York

There is no specific land trust statute, but section 7-1.4 of the New York Estate Powers and Trusts Law states that a trust may be created for 'any lawful purpose'. This alone may be legislative authority for land trusts in New York.

G. Bogert, The Law of Trusts & Trustees §250 at 102 (2d ed 1964); and

H. 45 Notre Dame Lawyer 427. 461 (1970)

New York courts, however, strictly apply the 'statute of uses' on trusts. The trustee would need not only the duties of collecting rents and profits, but also the duty to exercise discretion in the exercise of his duties.

Land Trusts in New York, 37 St. John's Law Review 123 (1962); and

Cutler v. Winberry, 160 N.Y.S. 712 (1916)

North Carolina

No land trust statute, but some direction is given under North Carolina General Statutes Secion 41-7.

7 Wachovia Bank and Trust Co. v. Taylor, 255 N.C. 122, 120 S.E.2d 588 (1961)

Any duties of the trustee is sufficient to create a valid trust

Finch v. Honeycut, 975 S.E.2d 478 (1957)

For more information on trustee duties in case law see:

Fisher v. Fisher, 218 N.C. 42, 9 S.E.2d 493 (1940)); and

Security Natl Bank v. Starnberger, 207 N.C. 811, 178 S.E. 595 (1935)

North Dakota

Specifically authorized under North Dakota Century Codes, Section 59-03-02. No special duties required of the trustee other than holding legal and equitable title. North Dakota requires the registration of all living trusts.

Ohio

Specifically authorized under Ohio Revised Code Sections 5301.03, 1335.01 and 1335.04. No special duties required of the trustee other than holding legal and equitable title.

Ternansky v. Rabatin, 141 N.E.2d 189 (Ohio App. 1957)

For more information on trustee duties in case law see:

Knecht v. George, 69 N.E.2d 228 (Ohio App. 1943)

Oklahoma

No land trust statute, but Oklahoma Statutes Annotated 60-132, Section 175.4 validates all trusts where the trustee has 'some power of actual disposition'. Furthermore, §175.6a declares a trust to be a 'legal entity' which can hold title to real estate in its own name.

Oregon

No land trust statute. Oregon law strictly applies the 'statute of uses' requiring the trustee to exercise discretion and have the power to control, protect, manage and dispose of trust property. For more information on trustee duties in case law see:

Lee v. Malone, 10 Or. App. 30 527 P.2d 414 (1974); and

Closset v. Burtchaell, 112 Or. 685, 230 P. 554 (1924); and

Lent v. Title and Trust Co. of Portland, 137 Or. 511 3 P. 2d 755 (1931)

Pennsylvania

No land trust statute. Trustee must have the express or implied duties of collecting profits, paying taxes, assessments, repairs and other expenses.

For more information on trustee duties in case law see:

Sheasley Trust, 77 A.2d 448 (Pa 1951)

Duty to pay "net" income to beneficiaries implies discretion.

Sheridan v. Coughlin, 352 Pa. 226, 42 A.2d 618 (Pa. 1945); and

Eaves v. Snyder, 84 A.2d 195 (Pa. 1951); and

In Re Deckers Est., 46 A.2d 218 (Pa. 1946)

Transfers of property into a land trust are not exempt from real property transfer tax.

Rhode Island

No land trust statute. The law only requires that the trustee have the duty to convey title at the discretion of the beneficiary.

Read v. Power, 12 R.I. 16 (1878); and

Koehne v. Beattie, 36 R.I. 316 (1914)

South Carolina

No land trust statute. South Carolina Codes Annotated 62-7-107 (formerly under 21-27-70). The law only requires that the trustee have the duty to convey title at the discretion of the beneficiary.

Ramage v. Ramage, 283 S.C. 239, 322 S.E. 2nd 22 (Ct. App. 1984)

South Dakota

No land trust statute, but South Dakota Codified Laws Annotated § 43-10-1 through 43-10-4 validates trusts so long as the trustee has 'some active duties of management and discretion'. Case law has expressly recognized the land trust as a valid device.

Bank of Cody v. Fanning, 353 N.W.2d 352 (1984)

Power of trustee to convey under express trust agreement vests all title in trustee and judgment against beneficiary will not attach to realty under South Dakota Codified Laws Annotated 43-10-16 and 43-10-7 through 11.

Tennessee

Tennessee does not recognize land trusts.

Kelly v. Schwartz, 740 5. W.2d 719 (1987)

This decision does not make land trust illegal, just uncertain.

Linder v. Officer, 175 Tenn. 402, 135 S.W.2d 445 (1940)

Texas

No land trust statute. Vernon's Texas Statutes and Codes Annotated § 112.032 requires some active duties of management to validate a trust. See:

A Device for Land Development: The Illinois Land Trust, 10 Houston Law Review 692 (1973)

Texas Property Code Annotated 112.032

Vernon's Texas Statutes and Codes Annotated, Sections 101.001, 112.001, 112.004, 112.032, 112.033, 113.056, 114.081, 114.082, 114.0821

Utah

No land trust statute and no clear law on the duties required of a trustee to satisfy the 'statute of uses'. Chapter 75 of the Utah Probate Code does support the use of revocable inter-vivos trusts in general.

Schenck v. Wicks, 23 Utah 576, 65 P.732 (1901)

Vermont

No land trust statute. The 'statute of uses' is not in effect in Vermont, so any duties of the trustee will suffice.

Noyes v. Noyes, 9 A.2d 123 (1938) and Blair v. Blair, 111 Vt. 53; 10 A.2d 188 (1940)

Virginia

Specifically authorized under Virginia Codes Annotated, Section 55-17.1. No special duties required of the trustee other than holding legal and equitable title.

Burns v. Equitable Associates, 220 Va. 1020, 265 S.E.2d 737 (1980)

Washington

No land trust statute. The 'statute of uses' requires some active duties such as the payment of taxes and distribution of funds to beneficiaries.

Townsend v. Ranier National Bank, 751 P.2d 1214 (1988)

Washington does not recognize the 'doctrine of equitable conversion'.

Estate of Phillips, 874 P.2d 154

Thus, it is not clear whether the court will respect the grantor's intention of creating a personal property interest in the trust.

Welch v. Northern Bank & Trust, 170 P. 1029 (Wash. 1918); and

Teizel v. Valley, 1 Wash. App. 863, 466 P. 2d 169 (1970)

West Virginia

No land trust statute. West Virginia Codes §36-1-17 only requires some duty of care, management or disposition.

Rogerson v. Wheeling Dollar Savings & Trust Co., 222 S.E. 2d 816 (1976)

Wisconsin

No land trust statute. Land trusts are expressly recognized by case law under Wisconsin Statutes Annotated, Section 701.03.

Kinzer v. Bidwell, 201 N.W.2d 9 (1972)

Only duty required of trustee is to pay property taxes.

McMahon v. Standard Bank & Trust, 550 N.W.2d 727 (1996)

Wyoming

No land trust statute. Statute Sections. 2-3-301 to 2-3-304 and 4-8-101 to 4-8-109 require some duty of the trustee other than taking title and possession of the property. In addition to the 'statute of uses' issue, you must comply with state law regarding the filing of public documents.

Protecting Your Principle Residence

AssetProtectionServices.com

Introduction

There are 3 primary ways in which to protect the equity in your principle residence *without* risking the loss of your Capital Gains Exclusion:

    1. Encumbrance
    2. "Single-Member" Limited Liability Company (Nevada or Wyoming)
    3. Homestead Exemption

Capital Gains Exclusion

Thanks to The Taxpayer Relief Act of 1997, there exists a capital gains exclusion for a single person of $250,000 and $500,000 for a married couple. This exclusion translates in up to $75,000 in tax savings, so be aware of the tax consequences when choosing the type of trust or entity to protect your home. A 'principle residence' is considered a house, apartment, condominium, stock-cooperative or mobile home fixed to land. You can make use of the capital gains exclusion (every two years) as many times as you wish during your lifetime, as long as the applicable qualifications are met. In order to qualify for the capital gains exclusion:

1. Ownership must be held directly in your name or in the name of a qualifying trust or certain single-owner entities;

2. You must have resided in the property for a cumulative of 2 out of the 5 years prior to selling.

You may only have one principle residence at a time. And although you may spend time away from your home on say a two-month vacation, taking an eleven-month sabbatical would disqualify you from having 'resided' in the home during that year. If you are married, you must meet the following standards to qualify for the $500,000 capital gains exclusion, including:

    • filing a joint tax return;
    • having either spouse meet the 'ownership test';
    • having both you and your spouse meet the 'use test'; and
    • during the 2-year period ending on the date of the sale, neither you or your spouse excluded gain from the sale of another home.

If either spouse fails to satisfy all these requirements, the exclusion is figured separately for each spouse as if they were not married. If your spouse should die and you subsequently sell your home, you will still qualify for the $500,000 exclusion if the sale occurs within two years after the date of death and the other requirements discussed above were met immediately before the date of death.

When you transfer the property into a non-qualifying trust (such as a land trust utilizing an entity to hold the beneficial interests of the trust) or a non-qualifying 'single-owner' entity (such as a corporation), or a 'multi-member' entity (such as a limited partnership or a limited liability company filing a 1065 or 1120), **you** no longer hold ownership and after 3 years time may be at risk of losing your capital gains exclusion.

Although many (grantor) land trusts are afforded the capital gains exclusion under Internal Revenue Code (IRC) Sections 1.121 and 645(b)(1), as well as Treasury Regulation 301.7701-3 and Treasury Decision 9030, not all land trusts are drafted alike. Some land trusts may be considered a non-qualifying trust and prevent an individual from taking advantage of the capital gains exclusion.

Title 26 - Department of the Treasury Code of Regulations
Chapter 1 - Internal Revenue Service
SubChapter A - Income Tax
Part 1 - Income Taxes
Section 1.121 - Index

Exclusion of gain from sale or exchange of a principal residence.--

(3) *Ownership.--*

   (i) **Trusts**.*-- If a residence is owned by a trust, for the period that a taxpayer is treated under section 671 through 679 (relating to the treatment of grantors and others as substantial owners) as the owner of the trust or the portion of the trust that includes the residence, the taxpayer will be treated as owning the residence for purposes of satisfying the 2-year ownership requirement of section 121, and the sale or exchange by the trust will be treated as if made by the taxpayer. (See §672 below)*

   (ii) **Certain Single Owner Entities**.*-- If a residence is owned by an eligible entity (within the meaning of §301.7701-(3)a of this chapter) that has a single owner and is disregarded for federal tax purposes as an entity separate from its owner under §301.7701-(3)a of this chapter, the owner will be treated as owning the residence for purposes of satisfying the 2-year ownership requirement of section 121, and the sale or exchange by the entity will be treated as if made by the owner.*
   Title 26 --> Chapter 1 --> SubChapter J --> Part 1 --> SubPart E --> §672

   (f) *Subpart not to result in foreign ownership*

(2) Exceptions

   (A) *Certain revocable and irrevocable trusts Paragraph (1) shall not apply to any portion of a trust if --*
   the power to revest absolutely in the grantor title to the trust property to which such portions is attributable is exercised **solely by the grantor without the approval or consent of any other person or with the consent of a related or subordinate party who is subservient to the grantor**. *(Emphasis Added)*

Transfer Tax Exemption

The laws in most states exempt the transfer of property from transfer tax (Florida and Pennsylvania are two exceptions to this rule) because no tax can be charged if only the way you hold title to property has been undertaken. This process works because your 'beneficial' ownership interest remains exactly the same before and after the transfer and effectively only the name on the title has changed - but not the ownership.

As an example, here is how the State of California handles transfer taxes when a person transfers their property to an entity owned by them:

California Revenue and Taxation Code
Part 6.7 Documentary Transfer Tax Act
Chapter 3. Exemptions Section 11925

(d) ***No levy shall be imposed*** *pursuant to this part by reason of any transfer between an individual or individuals and a legal entity or between legal entities that results solely in a change in the method of holding title to the realty and in which proportional ownership interests in the realty, whether represented by stock, membership interest, partnership interest, co-tenancy interest, or otherwise, directly or indirectly, remain the same immediately after the transfer. (Emphasis Added)*

Notwithstanding the above statement, California has enacted a very onerous 3.33% tax on all property transfers consummated by individuals and/or foreign entities unless they are paying income taxes in California.

1.) Encumbrances

Encumbrances are bank loans which "encumber" a home with debt. If your home has no equity in it, then there is nothing available for a judgement creditor to seize. Mortgages may be used as a proactive means of asset protection, provided the loans were 'activated' or used at least one year prior to any knowledge of a summons and complaint (lawsuit). A traditional second mortgage has immense case law to substantiate defending against creditors. The bank is recognized as having the prior lien and is considered by the courts to be 'first in time, first in line'. Disadvantages to this strategy include the homeowner accruing interest and making payments on the full amount of money borrowed from the lender.

A Home Equity Line Of Credit (HELOC) is a collateralized loan, or line of credit, which allows a homeowner to draw upon the equity in their home as needed. In the event that the homeowner dishonors the note by failing to repay, the lender may foreclose on the property just as they would with a traditional mortgage. Lending institutions will normally only loan up to 80% of the available equity in a principle residence.

The advantage to a HELOC is that the homeowner need only accrue interest and make payment on the amount of money borrowed at any one given point in time. Disadvantages include a potential creditor trying to freeze the remaining funds or available credit after a lawsuit has been initiated. After which time, even if the homeowner successfully withdraws more money (equity) from the home, it is a matter of judicial determination if such a withdrawal is considered a fraudulent conveyance with intent to defraud a judgment creditor. Moreover, upon learning of the lawsuit, the lender may simply freeze the account out of self interest.

2.) 'Single-Member' Limited Liability Company

Nevada and Wyoming, in-particular, requires a court to rule on the charging order based on state statute and not judicial interpretation. Nevada and Wyoming 'single-member' limited liability companies are granted the same charging order protection as a 'multi-member' LLC under Nevada and Wyoming state statute.

According to the regulations of the Internal Revenue Service (IRS) Federal Registry on Single-Owner Entities 2002, a 'single-member' LLC is disregarded by the IRS for tax purposes and will **not** cause a homeowner to lose their capital gains tax exclusion.

Department of the Treasury
Internal Revenue Service
Federal Register
Volume 67, Number 247
Tuesday, December 24, 2002
Rules and Regulations
Explanation and Summary of Comments
Section 3. Ownership by Trusts

"The final regulations adopt these suggestions and provide that, if a residence is held by a (living) trust, a taxpayer is treated as the owner and the seller of the residence during the period that the taxpayer is treated as the owner of the trust or the portion of the trust that includes the residence under §671 and §679. The regulations provide similar treatment for certain single-owner entities."

Residents of foreign states such as California may take advantage of Nevada law by transferring their primary residence into a Nevada single-member LLC without the California Corporations Code, Section 17001 Limited Liability Companies considering the LLC to be conducting business within its borders.

In most states the ownership of real estate does not constitute the transaction of business. Thus a Nevada Corporation or LLC formed for the sole purpose of owning real estate is not required to 'foreign file' or register as a foreign entity (Corporation or LLC) in the state where the real estate is located. However, check with the laws of your resident state because at the time of this writing the only known exceptions to this rule are Florida, New York and Texas.

Deducting Home Mortgage Interest

If you are not interested in taking advantage of the capital gains exclusion (if you wished for your home to pass on to your children for example) and prefer to transfer your principle residence into an entity, such as a (Family) Limited Partnership, then one of the first questions raised is *"will I lose the income tax deduction for my home mortgage interest"?*

Section 163 of the Internal Revenue Code permits a deduction for a qualified residence interest. A 'qualified residence' is defined as the 'principal residence' of the taxpayer. The primary requirements described are:

1. the house is the principal residence of the taxpayer;
2. interest is paid by the taxpayer; and
3. the taxpayer has a beneficial interest in any entity that holds legal title to the property.

Based upon the language of the statute, the deduction for mortgage interest would, therefore, not seem to be adversely affected by a transfer into an entity (Corp, LLC or LP).

3.) Homestead Exemption

A State does not want a family to be destitute and without the necessities of food, clothing and shelter. States are entitled to grant protection to a family for their principle residence (or home) as a 'stead' and hence the term 'homestead'. There are no state homestead exemptions in Maryland, New Jersey and Pennsylvania, whereas Florida, Iowa, Kansas, Oklahoma and Texas have an unlimited homestead allowance. In addition to personal and corporate state income taxes, it may be wise to consider the state homestead allowances when determining where to reside.

The following list of Homestead Exemptions may not be current, but need not be current for its intended purpose. This illustration is designed to show the disparity between the homestead exemptions among the respective states. As with any tax advise, please seek competent counsel in your home jurisdiction.

Alabama [Section 6-10-2]
The homestead exemption limit in Alabama is $5,000 for real property. The property may not exceed 160 acres. A couple may double these amounts.

Alaska [Section 09.38.010]
The Homestead exemption limit in Alaska is $67,500.

Arizona [Statute 33-1101]
The homestead exemption in Arizona is $150,000. The sale proceeds are exempt for 18 months after the sale.

Arkansas [State Statute 16-66-210 and Federal Statute 16-66-218]
The Arkansas homestead exemption is classified into two types of homesteads: rural and urban. A debtor may only choose one type.

State Homestead Exemption
The homestead outside any city, town, or village, owned and occupied as a residence, shall consist of no more than one hundred sixty (160) acres of land, with the improvements thereon, to be selected by the owner. The homestead shall not exceed in value the sum of twenty-five hundred dollars ($2,500), but, in no event shall the homestead be reduced to less than eighty (80) acres, without regard to value.

Federal Homestead Exemption
Real or personal property if it is being used as a residence, is exempt. The homestead exemption limit for singles is $800 and $1,250 for couples.

California [Statute 704-730]
The homestead exemption limit is $50,000 in California for a single person, $75,000 for a couple, $150,000 if 65 or older, or physically or mentally disabled, $150,000 if 55 or older, and are single and earn under $15,000, or are married and earn under $20,000.

Colorado [Statutes 38-41-201 and 38-41-201.6]
The Colorado homestead exemption is $45,000, if the residence is occupied.

Connecticut [Section 52-352b(t)]
The homestead exemption limit is $75,000.

Delaware [Section 10-4914]
Delaware does limit the total amount in exemptions one can claim. A single person may exempt no more than $5,000 total in all exemptions and husband & wife may exempt no more than $10,000 total.

District of Columbia [Title 11, Chapter 5, Sub-Chapter II, Section 522]
The debtor's aggregate interest in real property used as the residence of the debtor, or property that the debtor or a dependent of the debtor in a cooperative that owns property that the debtor or a dependent of the debtor uses as a residence, or in a burial plot for the debtor or dependent of the debtor, is exempt. Debtors may choose from the state list of exemptions, or the federal list of exemptions. The federal list does allow for a homestead exemption.

Florida [Sections 222.01 and 222.02]
The Florida homestead exemption is mandated by state Constitution. The dollar value exemption is unlimited. The exemption is limited to a half acre tract within a city and one hundred and sixty contiguous acres, elsewhere. Property held in tenancy by the entirety may be exempt against debts owed by one spouse. The US Court of Appeals recently held that the exemption will apply even if the owner acquired the property or enlarged it, with the intent to defraud creditors.

Georgia [Section 44-13-100(A)(1)]
Real property is exempt up to $10,000. A couple may double this amount.

Hawaii [Section 246-26]
The Hawaii homestead exemption is $12,000. Those who are the head of household or individuals 60 years of age or over but not 70 years of age or over get 2.0 multiple or $24,000 exemption, and individuals who are 70 years of age or over get a 2.5 multiple of the $12,000 exemption or $30,000. The property must not exceed one acre. The sale proceeds of the homestead may be exempt for up to one year after the sale.

Idaho [Statutes 55-1001, 55-1002, 55-1003]
The homestead exemption limit in Idaho is $50,000 for real property.

Illinois [Statute 735-5, Section 12-901]
Illinois prohibits residents from using the federal bankruptcy exemptions, unless directed by Illinois law. The homestead exemption in Illinois is limited to $7,500. Additionally, the sale proceeds are exempt for one year from the sale of the property . A couple may double the homestead exemption.

Indiana [Statute 34-55-10]
The homestead exemption limit in Indiana is $7,500. The homestead plus any personal property may not exceed $10,000.

Iowa [Sections 499A.18, 561.16, 561.2]
The homestead exemption limit in Iowa is unlimited. The property may not exceed a 1/2 acre in a city or town, or 40 acres elsewhere.

Kansas [Section 59-401]
The homestead exemption limit in Kansas is unlimited.

Kentucky [Section 427.060]
The homestead exemption limit is $5,000.

Louisiana [Section 20.1]
The homestead exemption limit in Louisiana is $25,000 for real property. The property may not exceed 200 acres. A couple may not double these amounts. The homestead exemption may be claimed by the spouse or child of the deceased debtor.

Maine [Title 14, Section 4422]
The homestead exemption limit in Maine is $35,000. If the debtor is 60 or over or mentally or physically disabled, then the exemption limit is $70,000.

Maryland [Section 16-111]
There is no homestead exemption. However, property that is held in tenancy by the entirety may be exempt from the debts owed by one spouse.

Massachusetts [Chapter 188: Section 1 and Section 1A]
The Massachusetts homestead exemption is $500,000. Those disabled or over 62 qualify for a $500,000 exemption. Couples may not double the amount.

Michigan [Section 600.6023]
The Homestead exemption amount in Michigan is $3,500. The property may not exceed one lot in a town or city and 40 acres elsewhere.

Minnesota [Sections 510.01 thru 510.09]
The Homestead exemption amount in Minnesota is $200,000. If the homestead is used primarily for agricultural purposes, then the exemption limit is $500,000. The property can't exceed a half acre area within a city or town, or 160 acres everywhere else. It is important to note that certain exemptions can be adjusted for inflation during even-numbered years.

Mississippi [Sections 85-3-1, 85-3-21, 85-3-23, 85-3-27, 85-3-31]
The homestead exemption limit for those not widowed or over the age of 60 is $75,000. The property cannot exceed 160 acres. The proceeds of the homestead sale are exempt. A homestead declaration may be filed.

Missouri [Sections 513.430 and 513.475]
The homestead exemption in Missouri is $15,000. The homestead exemption for a mobile home is $1,000. Couples may not double these amounts. Property that is held in tenancy by the entirety may be exempt from the debts owed by one spouse.

Montana [Sections 70-32-104, 70-32-201, 70-32-210, 70-32-105]
The homestead exemption limit in Montana is $100,000. Farmland property must not exceed 320 acres. Property outside the city must not exceed 1 acre, and property within the city must not exceed 1/4 acre.

Nebraska [Sections 40-101, 40-111, 40-113, 40-105]
The homestead exemption limit in Nebraska is $12,500. The property may not exceed two lots in a city or town, or 160 acres elsewhere.

Nevada [Statutes 115.005 thru 115.090]
The homestead exemption limit is $550,000 in Nevada. Debtors must record the homestead declaration prior to filing for bankruptcy.

New Hampshire [Section 480.1]
The homestead exemption limit in New Hampshire is $100,000.

New Jersey [None]
While there is no statutory homestead exemption, a homestead exemption may be claimed under the federal bankruptcy exemptions.

New Mexico [Section 42-10-09]
Married, widowed, and caregiver debtors may claim a homestead exemption up to $30,000. Couples may double the amount.

New York
The New York homestead exemption is limited up to $10,000 for a single person. A couple may double the homestead exemption limit.

North Carolina [Section 1C-1601]
The North Carolina homestead exemption is $10,000. Up to $3,500 of the unused portion of the homestead may be applied to any property. Property held in tenancy by the entirety is exempt from the debts owed by one spouse.

North Dakota [Sections 28-22-02(10), 47-18-01]
The homestead exemption limit in North Dakota is $80,000.

Ohio [Section 2329.66(a)(1)(b)]
The homestead exemption amount in Ohio is $5,000. Property held in tenancy by the entirety is exempt from the debts of one spouse.

Oklahoma [Sections 31-1 and 31-2]
The homestead exemption limit in Oklahoma is unlimited.

Oregon [Sections 23.240 thru 23.250]
The homestead exemption amount in Oregon is $25,000. The limit for couples is $33,000. If you do not own the land a mobile home is located on, then the exemption limit for the home is $23,000, or $30,000 for couples. The property can't exceed a one block area within a city or town, or 160 acres everywhere else. Sale proceeds are exempt for one year from the sale date, if the debtor intends to purchase another home.

Pennsylvania [None]
There is no homestead exemption. However, property that is held in tenancy by the entirety may be exempt from the debts owed by one spouse.

Rhode Island [Section 9-26-4.1]
The Rhode Island homestead exemption is $200,000 in land and buildings for an owner or owners of a home.

South Carolina [Section 15-41-30(1)]
The homestead exemption limit is $5,000. Couples may double the amount.

South Dakota [Section 43-45-3]
The homestead in South Dakota is $30,000. For persons age 70 and above the homestead was previously unlimited, but the unlimited exemption was ruled unconstitutional. A new statute, effective July 1, 2005, sets the cap for seniors at $170,000.

Tennessee [Sections 26-2-301 thru 26-2-303]
The Tennessee homestead exemption is $5,000 for a single person and $7,500 for a couple. The homestead exemption applies to property held in a life estate. The homestead exemption applies to property held in a 2-15 year lease. The homestead exemption applies to the spouse and children of the deceased. Property held in tenancy by the entirety is exempt from the debts owed by one spouse.

Texas [Article 16, Section 51]
The Texas homestead exemption is mandated by state Constitution. The homestead exemption value is unlimited. The exemption is limited to ten acres in a city or town.

Utah [Section 78-23-3]
The homestead exemption limit on real property in Utah is $20,000. A couple may double that amount. A homestead declaration must be filed before the homestead is sold.

Vermont [Section 1.5401(7)]
Visit this website: http://www.state.vt.us/tax/pdf.word.excel/legal/regs/15401.pdf

---

Washington [Section 6.13.030 thru 6.13.040]

The Homestead exemption amount in Washington is $40,000. There is no exemption limit if the debtor is seeking to discharge a debt, which was accrued for failure to pay Washington state income taxes on retirement benefits, while a resident of Washington. A homestead declaration must be filed before the home sells, if the property is unimproved or unoccupied.

West Virginia [Section 38-10-4(a)]

The homestead exemption is $25,000.

Wisconsin [Section 815.20]

The Homestead exemption amount in Wisconsin is $40,000. A couple may not double the amount. Sale proceeds are exempt for up to two years after the sale date.

Wyoming [Sections 1-20-101 thru 1-20-104]

The homestead exemption limit in Wyoming is $10,000 for real property and $6,000 for a trailer. A couple may double these amounts. A deceased debtors spouse or child may claim the homestead exemption. Property held in tenancy by the entirety may be exempt from the debts owed by one of the spouses.

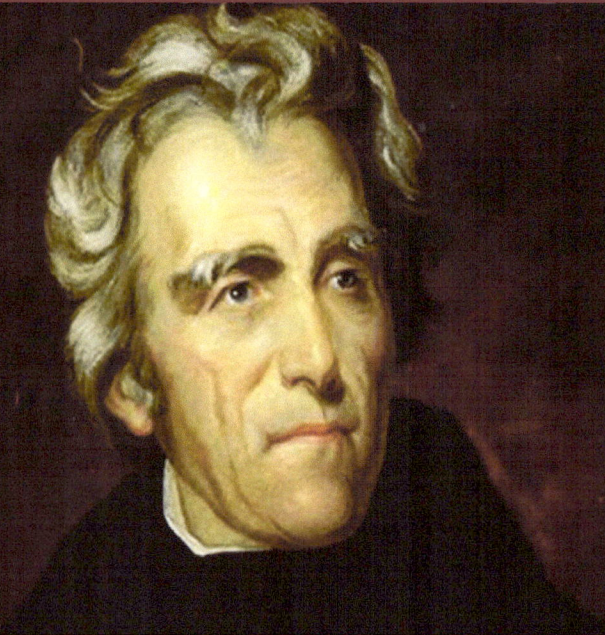

Equity Recovery Program

AssetProtectionServices.com

Introduction

The Equity Recovery Program works for you and not the private central bankers! Just as Andrew Jackson (7th President to the United States of America) fought tirelessly to keep the nation's issuance of currency and credit reserved to the States, our Equity Recovery Program keeps your hard-earned money in your pockets. Holding real property in your individual name provides no asset protection whatsoever and, upon selling the property, causes you to pay the maximum amount in capital gains tax, state tax and self-employment tax. As most real estate business deductions are not applicable for an individual filing a 1040 tax return, your silent partners (the Internal Revenue Service and State Taxing Agencies) will love being in business with you as they take a combined 30% to 40% of your hard-earned money from the sale of your property in taxes. Sadly this is the reality for over 50% of all escrows in the United States, but it doesn't have to be that way for you! By employing a Section 351-Transfer when selling your property, you can legitimately eliminate all federal capital gains tax, state tax and self-employment tax. Our nationally recognized Equity Recovery Program can increase your net earnings from the sale of your properties by 15% to 20% or more!

General Overview

The Equity Recovery Program is unique in that each program participant obtains a Nevada "C" Corporation specifically structured for real estate into which residential or commercial property is transferred under the Internal Revenue Code Section 351. Then, when the property is sold, the corporation sells the property and not the program participant.

By selling a property titled in the name of this corporation, the program participant eliminates state and self-employment taxes immediately [See IRS Publication 334]. The corporation pays no capital gains tax because it is **in** the real estate business and the income derived from the sale is considered 'ordinary income' to the corporation [See IRS Publication 544]. Additionally, federal taxes can be written down to almost nothing because of the many 'write-offs' available to a "C" Corporation, but not available to an individual, Limited Liability Company (LLC filing a 1065), Limited Partnership (LP) or even an "S" Corporation.
[See IRS Publication 535]

Corporate Tax Overview

Should the Nevada "C" Corporation not have enough 'write-offs' to eliminate its taxable income all together, the corporation would be required to pay taxes on the **net** amount remaining at the end of its fiscal year, if any. At the end of the (tax) year, should the corporation not 'spend' all its income on **allowable business expenses,** and provided the remaining net taxable amount did not exceed $50,000, the Nevada "C" Corporation taxable income (at the federal level) would be 15%. The great State of Nevada has no state corporate income tax, as well as no state individual income tax.

Title 26

The Internal Revenue Code is actually Title 26 of the United States Code. It was first put into a 'codified form' in 1939. Contrary to common perception, the 'code' actually shows people how to reduce their tax liability and not how to pay the most in taxes. The problem with the code is that no one section is taken alone as many code sections modify, or are otherwise affected by, other sections of code. Another problem is that Title 26 was written in 'legalese' and not plain English, so only the trained and/or informed can readily understand it.

The IRS

The Internal Revenue Service (IRS) is the agency for the government that has the responsibility to enforce Title 26 and to collect taxes from taxpayers. The IRS creates its own rules, commonly referred to as 'regulations' and licenses Certified Public Accountants (CPA) and Enrolled Agents to prepare the tax returns of taxpayers. Such professionals are not responsible to assist people in structuring their personal and business estates for tax reduction and are therefore generally not well-trained in the subject matter. Their primary job is to assist the IRS in collecting the maximum amount in taxes from the taxpayer and, unfortunately, are increasingly being pressured by the IRS *not* to assist clients in reducing their tax liability.

Title 26 and IRS Regulation Conflicts

It is important to note that people are required to follow Title 26 but not the IRS rules and regulations *when* the IRS rules are in conflict with Title 26 legislation.

Tax Court

The IRS has its own court system known as the 'Tax Court'. This court is operated by the IRS and its so-called 'judges' are IRS employees. It shouldn't require an advanced degree to figure out that this court is heavily biased in favor of the IRS.

Court of Appeals

If you take a case to Tax Court and loose, you can move your case into a 'real' court such as the Court of Appeals. Interestingly, these courts routinely overturn the IRS/Tax Court rulings. The reason for this is, as stated, that Title 26 laws must be followed and not the IRS Rules or Regulations *when* the two are in conflict.

IRC Title 26, Subtitle A, Chapter 1, Subchapter C, Part III, Section 351

The Internal Revenue Code, Section 351 was instituted in 1921 and can be found under Title 26, Subtitle A, Chapter 1, Subchapter C, Part III, Section 351. It wasn't widely used until Congress provided relief from its previously burdensome provisions in the Miscellaneous Trade and Technical Corrections Act of 1999, which for the first time allowed 351 transfers to include properties with liabilities such as a mortgage. Before that date, 351 transfers could only be undertaken with unencumbered (or fully-paid) properties.

IRC 351 Transfers

The government will assist people interested in venturing into business for themselves by allowing them to utilize previously owned assets to fund their new business venture. The IRC refers to this as a 'capital contribution'. The IRC further states categorically that in order for a transfer of real estate to a corporation to be tax-free, there must be a verifiable business reason for the transfer. Source of funding, necessary to undertake business, is in large part based upon the entity's 'business purpose' such as the acquisition and selling of real estate.

The Equity Recovery Program is a process whereby a "C" Corporation is specially drafted for the property owner to exchange the 'basis' of the property for the 'stock' of the corporation. Once transferred, the stock becomes valued at the same basis that the property was valued prior to the transfer. When the corporation sells the property, the code considers the income as **ordinary income** of the corporation and **not** as a capital gain of the corporation. Thus, the Equity Recovery Program (which utilizes a 351 Transfer) eliminates federal capital gains taxes when the property is sold. And, by having formed a "C" Corporation, there is no self-employment tax and no state tax in a state corporate income tax free jurisdiction like Nevada.

Comparing 351 Transfers and 1031 Exchanges

In the summer of 1990, the IRS drafted procedures for turning a 'sale and purchase' type transaction into an 'exchange' that came to be known as the 1031 Exchange. These new rules allowed owners of certain types of 'like kind' of real or personal property to exchange such property for another 'like kind' of property without immediately paying any Capital Gains Tax that otherwise would be payable if the property were 'sold' instead of 'exchanged'.

1031 exchanges are very well known because they are promoted by many companies who assist people through the process, which is quite cumbersome. If a 1031 Exchange is not handled correctly it can become a tax nightmare for the unwary. For example, participants in a 1031 exchange may not receive money from the exchange without it being taxed, and when the person stops trading / exchanging properties all the accumulated compounding capital gains taxes are due and payable at that time.

Conversely, very few companies promote the little known Internal Revenue Code Section 351 Transfer process. It requires no third-party to handle the process, has few restrictions and, unlike the 1031 exchange, has very few down sides. The 351 transfer process allows homeowners and real estate investors to eliminate self-employment tax, as well as state and federal tax liabilities entirely on the sale of real estate, vacant land, business and/or commercial property.

Additionally, after a property has been transferred into a "C" Corporation through a 351 Transfer, and monies are received from the sale, such funds are not required to be reinvested into real estate (as with a 1031 exchange). And, unlike 1031 exchanges, the transferring party (owner) will have until the end of the corporate fiscal year (without penalty) in which to 'spend' or otherwise 'reinvest' the proceeds from the sale.

Disadvantages of a 1031 Exchange

In a 1031 Exchange, the tax basis of a replacement property is essentially the purchase price of the replacement property, minus the gain which was deferred on the sale of the previously owned property in the exchange. Thus, the replacement property includes a deferred gain that will be taxed in the future when the taxpayer cashes out of his or her investment. So, you can use a 1031 exchange to defer your taxes, but it will likely push you into higher (if not the highest) tax brackets at the 'end of the exchanges' when the proverbial musical chairs stop and you are mandated to pay-up on your taxes. *Or* use the Equity Recovery Program and a 351 Transfer to *eliminate* capital gains tax, state tax and self-employment tax from the start.

Disqualified 1031 Exchange Properties

Land under development for resale
Construction or fix/flips for resale
Property purchased for resale

Asset Protection Benefits

1031 exchanges do **not** provide any asset protection from predatory attorneys whereas 351 Transfers conducted through our Equity Recovery Program can provide asset protection by way of the charging protection afforded to Nevada "C" Corporations containing between 2 and 99 shareholders.

Contribution of Services

Shareholders contributing services will always be taxed on the value of the services as compensation, and the shares are generally not counted in applying the 80% test. However shares received in return for services will be counted in the 80% control test if the shareholder also contributes property that is worth more than 10% of the total consideration transferred. In such a case, the taxpayer will be taxed on the stock received for services as compensation, though the remainder of the transaction will most likely be tax-free.

For example, if a shareholder contributes $20,000 in services, and $60,000 in property to a corporation that is being formed, the shares received by the contributor (in consideration for the $60,000 property) will be included in the 80% test but the shareholder shall be taxed on the $20,000 for services as compensation income.

351 Transfer Requirements

As a separate entity with its own legal personality, Corporations must follow certain business formalities when being formed including, but not limited to, articles of incorporation, bylaws, and electing directors. As for tax consequences on formation, it is important to distinguish **realized** gain and loss (aka 'accounting' gain or loss without reference to any special tax rules) from **recognized** gain or loss (aka actual 'reported' gain or loss for tax purposes).

IRS Code Section 351 states that no gain or loss is recognized by either the contributing shareholder or the recipient Corporation if three conditions are satisfied. Assuming that the transfers having a bona fide 'business purpose' in real estate, the said conditions are:

1.) There is a transfer of property (and not services)
2.) Solely in exchange for corporate stock, and
3.) After the exchange, the contributing shareholder(s) is (are) in control of the corporation (i.e. own at least 80% of the voting and outstanding stock).

Contributions by several shareholders may be aggregated in determining if the 80% test is satisfied, provided that all contributions were part of a single integrated transaction to form the business. Note that contributions of cash or property in return for long-term debt (e.g., bonds) do not qualify for a Section 351 transfer treatment.

If all Section 351 conditions are met, the transaction is treated as though 'nothing happened' in that no gain or loss is recognized. The basis of the shareholder's stock equals the basis of the property contributed, and the basis of the property to the corporation equals the contributing shareholder's basis. Holding periods also apply with all properties. Gain is generally recognized only if the 'boot' is received or mortgages in excess of the basis are assumed by the corporation.

Gain or Loss With Boot

The term 'boot' refers to any non-stock property received by the shareholder from the issuing corporation. The boot may be cash, debt (such as bonds), or other property. If boot is received by the shareholder, loss is never recognized; however, gain is recognized to the lesser extent of boot received or realized (accounting) gain.

Gain or Loss With Liabilities Assumed

Occasionally a corporation may assume outstanding liabilities of the shareholder on contributed property. Normally, this assumption of shareholder liability would be considered 'boot received' by the shareholder (the same as though the shareholder received cash and paid off the liability). However, to remove a potential tax barrier to incorporation, Section 351 states that liabilities assumed by the corporation are not treated as boot received for purposes of determining gain on the contributing transfer. Such liabilities are treated as boot received for purposes of determining *the basis of the shares to the shareholder*. If the liabilities assumed exceed the tax basis of the property, such excess must be recognized as taxable gain, as this prevents a negative basis in the stock received.

Corporate Capital Contributions

The Equity Recovery Program, indeed the IRS 351 Transfer, relies heavily on the principals relating to corporate capital contributions. Contributions of capital to a corporation are called 'paid-in capital'. A corporation does not recognize gain or loss when it issues stock in exchange for cash or property. [See IRC §1032] Generally, when property is transferred to a corporation in exchange for stock, the transaction is treated as if the property were sold to the corporation at fair market value.

Non-Recognition of Gain or Loss

Under Section 351, shareholder(s) control the corporation if, immediately after the transfer, they own at least 80% of the combined voting power of all outstanding voting stock and 80% of the shares of all classes of corporation stock.

"No gain or loss shall be recognized if property is transferred to a corporation by one or more persons solely in exchange for stock in such corporation and immediately after the exchange such person or persons are in control of the corporation."   – IRS Regulation §1.351-1(a)(1)

Non-recognition of gain under §351 only applies to amounts paid *"solely in exchange for stock"*. If the shareholder receives cash or other property in addition to corporation stock, gain is recognized up to the amount of cash or fair market value of the other property received. According to Reg. §1.351-1(a)(1), the phrase *"immediately after the exchange"* does not necessarily require simultaneous exchanges as long as the transfers are made pursuant to a predetermined agreement.

Property Subject to Liabilities

In a Section 351 Transfer, if a corporate shareholder contributes property subject to liabilities the shareholder's basis in the corporate stock received is reduced by the amount of liability relief. 'Relief' of liabilities is generally not considered in determining gain on the transaction. However, if liabilities exceed the shareholder's adjusted basis in the property, gain is recognized on the excess and the shareholder's basis in the corporation stock is zero. [See IRC §357(c)]

Short-Term Capital Gains Tax

Properties held for 365 days or less are considered 'short-term' sales (also known as 'flips') and are taxed at the same rate as your personal income tax bracket / level (on a 1040 tax return), which could be as high as 39.6%. This scenario is true if the property is owned in your individual name or that of a pass-through entity such as an "S" Corp, an LLC (filing a 1065), an LP or Sole Proprietorship. Taxes paid at the 1040 tax rate on gain ranges anywhere from 10% to 39.6% for calendar year 2013. This could be a real killer should your taxable gain, plus any other 1040 income, push you into the higher tax brackets.

Long-Term Capital Gains Tax

The following tax levels are known as 'long-term' capital gains (known as 'holds') and apply to property that you held for more than 365 days (more than one year). Long-term capital gains tax rates depend on which ordinary income tax bracket you fall under.

0%	if in the 10% or 15% tax brackets
15%	if in the 25%, 28%, 33%, or 35% tax brackets
20%	if in the 39.6% tax bracket

In both 'short-term' and 'long-term' capital gains tax scenarios, there are no allowable deductions that you may 'take' in order to reduce your personal capital gains tax liability other than capital improvements and selling expenses such as commissions, closing costs and inspections. Please note that short and long term capital gains taxes do not apply to any "C" Corporation or LLC filing an 1120 tax return. The gains from such a sale are considered 'ordinary business income' if the said entity is in the real estate business.

Double Taxation

Tax planners often spread fear concerning the potential for double taxation with "C" Corporations. Double taxation comes into play where after-tax earnings of a "C" Corporation are distributed to shareholders as dividends. This is rarely a problem in small corporations with earnings under 5 million and/or non-publicly traded corporations because there are so many legitimate ways to pull money out of the "C" Corporation in a manner that is deductible, and thus only taxed once.

Ordinary Income

Ordinary income is the income generated during the 'ordinary course' of a company's business activities. For example, a new car dealership purchases cars to sell. The Internal Revenue Code considers these cars 'inventory'. When a car is sold, the income derived from the sale is commingled with the income derived from servicing the cars and the parts the dealership sells for the cars. This income is never considered capital gains. This is a very important concept to understand as its application is equivalent to that of a business whose 'business purpose' is the purchasing and selling of real estate.

Should the corporation not have enough write-offs to eliminate its taxable income all together, the corporation would be required to pay taxes on the net amount remaining at the end of the tax year, if any. In other words, should the corporation not 'spend' all its income on allowable business expenses by the end of its fiscal calendar year, the remaining net taxable income would be taxed at the corporate level. It is important to remember that "C" Corporations invariably pay less in taxes than do individuals filing a 1040, LLC's filing a 1065 or "S" Corporations filing an 1120-S on incomes up to $250,000.

Owning Property in Other States

Nevada Corporations can hold title directly to property in most every state without being considered 'conducting business' in the state where the property is located. The three exceptions to that rule are Florida, New York and Texas wherein the entity must be formed or foreign filed prior to owning property. Having this knowledge is very advantageous when holding property in any of the other 47 States. For example, take a property in Arizona, which is titled directly into say a Nevada "C" Corporation, when the property is sold any state taxes that might be due and payable on the income from the sale will be due and payable in Nevada and not Arizona. Knowing this fact alone can save you (tens of) thousands of dollars.

Phantom Income

In an "S" Corporation or Limited Liability Company (filing a 1065), the shareholders / members are required to pay income tax on their share of the entity's income regardless as to whether or not they took any money out of the entity's account or left it there. This is known as 'Phantom Income' and is **not** applicable to "C" Corporations.

Writing-Off Real Estate Losses

An individual (or pass-through entity, "S" Corp, an LLC (filing a 1065), an LP or Sole Proprietorship) engaged in the business of buying and selling real estate may only 'write-off' 25% of any losses incurred under IRS passive loss rules. However, 100% of any such losses may be 'written-off' by a "C" Corporation engaged in the business of buying and selling real estate.

Down Markets

In a collapsing or 'down' real estate market, property sellers need all the help they can get in order to retain as much of their hard earned equity (profit) as they can. Unfortunately, declining markets generally worsen sales while the housing market attempts to stabilize. It is interesting to note that real estate **is** selling in almost every market, but the properties which are selling are those 'priced right' in a specific area. In a down market, having your property 'priced to sell' will likely make the difference between selling and not selling. If you, as the seller, continue to try to sell your property using outmoded methods of selling a property titled in your name (or undertaking a 1031 exchange), you will face the maximum in taxability and needlessly lose far too much of your hard-earned equity / profits.

Calculating Your Cost Basis and Capital Gain

The formula for calculating the gain or loss involves subtracting your cost basis from your selling price. The formula is as follows:

Purchase Price
      Purchase costs (Including Title and Escrow Fees, Realtor Commissions, etc)
  + Capital Improvements (See 'Real Estate Forms')
  + Selling Costs (Including Title and Escrow Fees, Realtor Commissions, etc)
  – Accumulated Depreciation
  = **Cost Basis**

Profit or Loss
      Selling price
  – Cost Basis
  = **Gain or Loss**

If the resulting number is positive, you made a profit when you sold your home. If the resulting number is negative, you incurred a loss.

Capital Assets
IRS Publication 544

Generally, you will have a capital gain or loss if you sell or exchange a capital asset. You also may have a capital gain if your section 1231 transactions result in a net gain. Section 1231 transactions are sales and exchanges of property held longer than 1 year and either used in a trade or business or held for the production of rents or royalties. Almost everything you own and use for personal purposes or investment is a capital asset, including the following.

- **Stocks and Bonds**
- **A Home** owned and occupied by you and your family
- **Household Furnishings**
- **A Car** used for pleasure or commuting
- **Personal-Use Property** Property held for personal use is a capital asset. Gain from a sale or exchange of that property is a capital gain. Loss from the sale or exchange of that property is *not deductible*. You can deduct a loss relating to personal-use property only if the loss was the result of a casualty or theft.
- **Investment Property** Investment property (such as stocks and bonds) is a capital asset, and a gain or loss from its sale or exchange is a capital gain or loss. This treatment does not apply to property used to produce rental income.

Personal gain from a sale or exchange of a capital asset is a capital gain and is taxed as such.

What are Non-Capital Assets?

A non-capital asset is property that is not a capital asset. The following kinds of property are not capital assets.

- **Property** (including real estate) held mainly for sale to customers or property that will physically become part of merchandise for sale. This includes stock in trade, inventory and other property you hold mainly for sale in your trade or business.
- **Accounts or Notes Receivable** acquired in the ordinary course of a trade or business for services rendered or from the sale of any properties.
- **Depreciable Property** used in your trade or business or as rental property (including section 197 intangibles), even if the property is fully depreciated or amortized.
- **Real Property** (including real estate) used in your trade or business or as rental property, even if the property is fully depreciated.
- **Property held mainly for sale** Stock in trade, inventory, and other property you hold mainly for sale in your trade or business.
  (See IRS Publication 538 for the tax considerations relating to inventories).
- **Business Assets** Real property and depreciable property used in your trade or business or as rental property.

Peracchi v. Commissioner

In 1997, the U.S. 9th Circuit Court of Appeals heard the case of *Peracchi v. Commissioner*. Herein is what the court had to say regarding capital contributions:

"The Internal Revenue Code (IRC) tries to make organizing a corporation pain-free from a tax point of view. In 1997, the United States 9th Circuit Court of Appeals heard the case of Peracchi vs Commissioner wherein the court ruled on capital contributions. A capital contribution is, in tax lingo, a 'non-recognition' event. A shareholder can generally contribute capital without recognizing gain on the exchange as it is merely a change in the form of ownership, like moving a billfold from one pocket to another [See IRC §351]. So long as the shareholders contributing the property remain in control of the corporation after the exchange, Section 351 applies.

It doesn't matter if the capital contribution occurs at the creation of the corporation or if the company is already up and running. Corporations may be funded with any kind of asset, such as equipment, real estate, intellectual property, contracts, leaseholds, securities or letters of credit. The tax consequences can get a little complicated because a shareholder's basis in the property contributed often differs from its fair market value. The general rule is that an asset's basis is equal to its 'cost'. [See IRC §1012] Continuity of investment is the cornerstone of non-recognition under section 351.

When a shareholder like Peracchi contributes property to a corporation in a non-recognition transaction, a cost basis does not preserve the unrecognized gain. Rather than take a basis equal to the fair market value of the property exchanged, the shareholder must substitute the basis of that property for what would otherwise be the cost basis of the stock. This preserves the gain for recognition at a later day. The gain is built into the shareholder's new basis in the stock, and he will recognize income if he disposes of the stock.

Continuity of investment is the cornerstone of non-recognition under section 351. Non-recognition assumes that a capital contribution amounts to nothing more than a nominal change in the form of ownership; in substance the shareholder's investment in the property continues."

The court when on to say . . .

"The Internal Revenue Code seems to recognize that economic exposure of the shareholder is the ultimate measuring rod of a shareholder's investment [Cf. I.R.C. S 465 (at-risk rules for partnership investments)]. Peracchi therefore is entitled to a step-up in basis to the extent he will be subjected to economic loss if the underlying investment turns unprofitable [Cf. HGA Cinema Trust v. Commissioner, 950 F.2d 1357, 1363 (7th Cir. 1991)]."

Lessinger v. Commissioner

In *Lessinger v. Commissioner, 872 F2d 519, 89-1 USTC Para. 9254, (1989)*, the 2nd Circuit held that *"Where the transferor undertakes genuine personal liability to the transferee, adjusted basis in IRC §357(c) refers to the transferee basis in the obligation, which is its face amount."* The court reasoned that the corporation must have a basis in the note equal to its principal amount since a later receipt of the principal does not result in income recognition.

Most taxpayers would much prefer to pay tax (if any) on contributed property years later when they sell their stock, rather than when they contribute the property. Continuity of investment is the cornerstone of non-recognition under section 351 transfers. Non-recognition assumes that a capital contribution amounts to nothing more than a nominal change in the form of ownership; in substance the shareholder's investment in the property continues.

Corporation Capital Contributions

Generally, when property is transferred to a corporation in exchange for stock, the transaction is treated as if the property were sold to the corporation at FMV.

- A corporation does not recognize gain or loss when it issues stock in exchange for cash or property. [IRC §1032]
- A shareholder does not recognize gain or loss upon contribution of cash in exchange for corporation stock. A shareholder may recognize gain or loss upon exchange of property for corporation stock.
- When services are performed in exchange for corporation stock, the FMV of the service is taxable compensation. The amount included in income is the shareholder's basis in the corporation stock received.

The basis of property contributed to a corporation by a non-shareholder is zero.

Properties Subject to a Mortgage

A central issue relating to the transfer of real estate, are properties subject to a mortgage. To understand this issue of relating transfers subject to liabilities, take a look at USC Title 26.

USC Title 26
Section 357(a) and 357(b)
Assumption of Liabilities

(a) (1)   *The taxpayer receives property which would be permitted to be received under section 351 or 361 without the recognition of gain if it were the sole consideration, and;*

(2)   As part of the consideration, another party to the exchange assumes a liability of the taxpayer, and then such assumption shall not be treated as money or other property, and shall not prevent the exchange from being within the provisions of section 351 or 361, as the case may be.

(b) (1)   In general: For purposes of this section, section 358(d), section 362(d), section 368(a)(1)(C), and section 368(a)(2)(B), except as provided in regulations:

   (A)   A recourse liability (or portion thereof) shall be treated as having been assumed if, as determined on the basis of all facts and circumstances, the transferee has agreed to, and is expected to, satisfy such liability (or portion), whether or not the transferor has been relieved of such liability; and

   (B)   Except to the extent provided in paragraph (2), a non-recourse liability shall be treated as having been assumed by the transferee of any asset subject to such liability.

(2)   Exception for non-recourse liability.

   The amount of the non-recourse liability treated as described in paragraph (1)(B) shall be reduced by the lesser of:

   (A)   The amount of such liability which an owner of other assets not transferred to the transferee and also subject to such liability has agreed with the transferee to, and is expected to, satisfy; or

   (B)   The fair market value of such other assets (determined without regard to section 7701(g)).

If the transfer of the real estate is without the transfer of liability, where the corporation is not liable for the mortgage on the real estate, then the transfer is a non-recourse transfer and acceptable under the IRC.

If a transfer were undertaken wherein the corporation assumes the full liability for the mortgage and any other debt on the property, the extent of the assumption of that debt would be taxable to the person transferring the property. Again, this is called 'boot' in the IRC. Boot amounts to cashing out of the liability for the transferring party (in many cases referred to as the 'shareholders' in the code), which is fully taxable.

That is why we **only transfer the current and future equity and income derived** from the property and the transferring party remains solely liable for all the debt associated with the property. The only allowable part of the income derived from the sale of the property that could be reimbursed to the transferring party would be for documented expenses personally paid for from the personal funds of the transferring party. Those expenses are very narrowly focused on items that are acceptable deductions at the time of sale of the property or would be classified as normal and ordinary for a corporation in the real estate business.

IRC §351 Legislation

"No gain or loss shall be recognized if property is transferred to a corporation by one or more persons solely in exchange for stock in such corporation and immediately after the exchange such person or persons are in control…of the corporation."

Non-recognition treatment does not apply to transfers of property to an investment company. Additionally, Cash Is considered property for purposes of Section 351. Shareholder(s) control the corporation if, immediately after the transfer, they own at least:
(1) 80% of the combined voting power of all outstanding voting stock, and;
(2) 80% of the shares of all other classes of corporation stock, this is not a maybe it is a must.

Non-recognition of gain under §351 only apply to amounts paid "solely in exchange for stock". If the shareholder receives cash or other property in addition to corporation stock, gain will be recognized up to the amount of cash or FMV of other property received. Additionally, Securities are considered property for purposes of IRC §351. According to Reg. §1.351-1(a)(1), the phrase "immediately after the exchange" does not necessarily require simultaneous exchanges, as long as the transfers are made pursuant to a predetermined agreement.

Under a Section 351 exchange, if a corporation shareholder contributes property subject to liabilities, the shareholder's basis in the corporation stock received is reduced by the amount of liability relief. Relief of liabilities is generally not considered in determining gain on the transaction. However, if liabilities exceed the shareholder's adjusted basis in the property, gain is recognized on the excess, and the shareholder's basis in the corporation stock is zero. [See IRC §357(c)] Technical know-how such as trade secrets or processes may be considered property for purposes of Section 351, even though related services are provided. The importance of the services to the principal business purpose is the main factor in making the determination.

When a Section 351 transfer occurs, the corporation and the controlling shareholders must attach a statement to their tax returns describing the details of the transaction. Non-qualified preferred stock is seen as 'boot'. Preferred stock is non-qualified if:
- *the stockholder has the right to require the issuer or a related person to redeem or purchase the corporation stock;*
- *the issuer or a related person is required to redeem or purchase the corporation stock;*
- *on the issue date it is more likely than not that the right to redemption will be exercised; or Dividend rate varies with reference to interest rates, commodity prices, or other similar indices.*

Exceptions apply if the stock must be held for 20 years or more before redemption, or in cases of death, disability or mental incompetence of the owner. Applies to transfers made after 6/8/97.

IRS Publication 542

A. Sec. 351 Transfers – Basic Requirements

1. *Sec. 351 General Rule - As a separate business entity, corporations must follow certain business formalities when forming; these include articles of incorporation, bylaws, and electing directors. As for tax consequences on formation, it is important to distinguish realized gain or loss (the "accounting" gain or loss, without reference to any special tax rules) from the recognized gain or loss (the gain or loss actually reported for tax purposes).*

2. *Code Sec. 351 states that no gain or loss is recognized by either the contributing shareholder or the recipient corporation if three conditions are satisfied. These conditions are (assuming that the transfers having a bona fide business purpose):*

   - *There is a transfer of property (and not services),*
   - *Solely in exchange for corporate stock, and*
   - *After the exchange the contributing shareholder(s) is (are) in control of the corporation (e.g., own at least 80% of the voting and 80% of the outstanding stock).*

3. *Contributions by several shareholders may be aggregated in determining if the 80% test is satisfied, provided that all contributions were part of a single integrated transaction to form the business.*

4. *Note that contributions of cash or property in return for long-term debt (e.g., bonds) do not qualify for Sec. 351 treatment. Also, in some cases, certain preferred stock that has characteristics similar to long-term debt may be treated as not qualifying for Sec. 351 non-recognition. These characteristics include:*

   - *A right to have the stock bought or redeemed by the issuer (or related party)*
   - *The issuer or related party is required to buy or redeem the stock*
   - *The issuer or related party has a right to buy or redeem the stock, and it is likely that such right will be exercised, or*
   - *The dividend rate on the stock varies with reference to interest rates, commodity prices, or other such indices*

5. *As explained below, if all Sec. 351 conditions are met, the transaction is treated as though* **"nothing happened,"** *in that no gain or loss is recognized, the basis of the shareholder's stock equals the basis of the property contributed, and the basis of the property to the corporation equals the contributing shareholder's basis. Holding periods*

   also tack with all properties. (Note—Gain is generally recognized only if boot is received or mortgages in excess of basis are assumed by the corporation.)

B. Sec. 351 Transfers – Gain or Loss on Contribution of Services:

1. Shareholders contributing services will always be taxed on the value of the services as compensation, and the shares are generally not counted in applying the 80% test.

2. However, shares received in return for services will be counted in the 80% control test if the shareholder also contributes property that is worth more than 10% of the total consideration transferred . In such a case, the taxpayer will be taxed on the stock received for services as compensation, though the remainder of the transaction will most likely be tax-free under the general rules explained below.

   Example - A shareholder contributes $20,000 services and $60,000 property to a corporation that is being formed. In this case, the shares received by the contributor will be included in the 80% test, although the shareholder is still taxed on the $20,000 for services as compensation income.

C. Sec. 351 Transfers – Gain or Loss Without Boot Received:

1. If all of the Sec. 351 conditions are met, no gain is recognized by either the contributing shareholder or the corporation, and the basis of the shares to the shareholder equals the basis of the property transferred to the corporation (and the corporation has the same basis in the property).

2. In essence, the transaction is treated as if nothing has changed. If the 80% control test is not met, the exchange will be fully taxable (i.e., compare the fair market value of the stock received with the tax (adjusted) basis of the property contributed to the corporation. (See Examples 1 and 2 of comprehensive Figure 1 below.)

D. Sec. 351 Transfers – Gain or Loss With Boot Received:

1. The term "boot" refers to any non-stock property received by the shareholder from the issuing corporation. The boot may be cash, debt (such as bonds), or other properties. The 1997 Act also treats certain preferred stock that has "debt-like" characteristics as boot.

2. If boot is received by the shareholder, loss is never recognized; however, gain is recognized to the extent of the lesser of the boot received or the realized (accounting) gain. In effect, the boot received represents an upper bound on the

   taxpayer's wherewithal to pay tax; the taxable gain may not exceed this amount. See Example 3 of comprehensive Figure 1 below.

A. Sec. 351 Transfers – Basis of Stock Received by Contributors

1. The shareholder's basis in the shares is determined as follows:

	Adjusted **B**asis of property transferred to the corporation	**AB** $ xxx.xx
Plus	Gain recognized (for tax purposes) on the transfer	+ $ xxx.xx
Less	Boot recognized (including liabilities assumed by Corporation)	− $ xxx.xx
Equals	Adjusted Basis of Shares received	$ xxx.xx

2. Note that the shareholder does pay a price in basis for all liabilities assumed by the corporation, even though they may not exceed basis and not cause gain.

3. Note the parallels in the basis formula to the basis formulas used for like-kind exchanges that were discussed in Part 1 and also earlier in this part.

B. Sec. 351 Transfers – Basis of Property Received by Corporation

1. The corporation's basis in the property received is determined as follows:

	Adjusted **B**asis of property transferred to the Shareholder	**AB** $ xxx.xx
Plus	Gain recognized (for tax purposes) by the Shareholder	+ $ xxx.xx
Equals	Adjusted Basis of Shares received	$ xxx.xx

2. Figure 1 presents a variety of transactions involving Sec. 351 transfers. Gain computations and basis computations are included. Review these examples carefully.

3. In Figure 1, note particularly the effects of liabilities on recognized gain and on basis.

4. As mentioned earlier, liabilities assumed are NOT considered boot for determining gain (unless the liabilities exceed basis).

5. However, the liabilities assumed ARE considered boot for purposes of determining the adjusted basis of the stock to the shareholder.

Treasury Regulations
Subchapter A, Sec. 1.351-1

Sec. 1.351-1 Transfer to corporation controlled by transferor

(a) *(1) Section 351(a) provides, in general, for the non-recognition of gain or loss upon the transfer by one or more persons of property to a corporation solely in exchange for stock or securities in such corporation, if immediately after the exchange, such person or persons are in control of the corporation to which the property was transferred. As used in section 351, the phrase "one or more persons" includes individuals, trusts, estates, partnerships, associations, companies, or corporations (see section 7701(a)(1)). To be in control of the transferee corporation, such person or persons must own immediately after the transfer stock possessing at least 80 percent of the total combined voting power of all classes of stock entitled to vote and at least 80 percent of the total number of shares of all other classes of stock of such corporation (see section 368(c)). In determining control under this section, the fact that any corporate transferor distributes part or all of the stock which it receives in the exchange to its shareholders shall not be taken into account. The phrase "immediately after the exchange" does not necessarily require simultaneous exchanges by two or more persons, but comprehends a situation where the rights of the parties have been previously defined and the execution of the agreement proceeds with an expedition consistent with orderly procedure. For purposes of this section—*

(i) *Stock or securities issued for services rendered or to be rendered to or for the benefit of the issuing corporation will not be treated as having been issued in return for property, and*

(ii) *Stock or securities issued for property which is of relatively small value in comparison to the value of the stock and securities already owned (or to be received for services) by the person who transferred such property, shall not be treated as having been issued in return for property if the primary purpose of the transfer is to qualify under this section the exchanges of property by other persons transferring property.*

For the purpose of section 351, stock rights or stock warrants are not included in the term "stock or securities."

IRS Eases Reporting Burden on
Corporations and Shareholders
October 18, 2012IR-2006-83, May 26, 2006

WASHINGTON — The Internal Revenue Service today announced new regulatory revisions that will reduce the reporting burden on corporations and shareholders while also making it easier for them to file their tax returns electronically....

The regulations for Section 351 imposed reporting requirements on anyone who owned a share of a company involved in a Section 351 transfer and on the company itself. Those reporting requirements involved 18 information items from shareholders and 20 information items from corporations.

The revised regulations will limit the Section 351 reporting requirement to only those stockholders who own either 5 percent or more of a public company or 1 percent or more of a privately held company – drastically reducing the number of stockholders who must file a report. Also, the revised regulations will reduce the reportable information to four items:

> *1.) The name and employer identification of the company;*
> *2.) The date of the asset transfer;*
> *3.) The fair market value and basis of the assets transferred; and*
> *4.) The date of any IRS private letter ruling.*

Savings with No Depreciation
(Example Taken from a Real Client in Washington D.C. on April 12th, 2007)

Original Purchase Price	$ 115,000	
(+) Capital improvements	+ $ 80,000	
(–) Depreciation	– $ 0	
	$ 195,000	**Adjusted Basis**

Selling Price	$ 495,000	
(–) Cost of Sale	– $ 45,000	
(–) Adjusted Basis	– $ 195,000	
	$ 255,000	**Capital Gains**

Before

Federal Recapture Depreciation	(25% of $0)	$ 0	
(+) Federal Capital Gains Tax Rate	(15% Tax Bracket)	+ $ 38,250	
(+) Federal Self Employment Tax	(15.3% of $97,500)	+ $ 0	
(+) Washington D.C. Tax Rate	(9%)	+ $ 22,950	
		$ 61,200	**Taxes Due**

Capital Gains	$ 255,000	
(–) Taxes Due	– $ 61,200	
(–) Equity Recovery Program	– $ 0	
	$ 193,800	**Net Income**

After

Federal Recapture Depreciation	(25% of $0)	$ 0	
(+) Federal Capital Gains Tax Rate	(15% Tax Bracket)	+ $ 0	
(+) Federal Self Employment Tax	(15.3% of $97,500)	+ $ 0	
(+) Washington D.C. Tax Rate	(9%)	+ $ 0	
		$ 0	**Taxes Due**

Capital Gains	$ 255,000	
(–) Taxes Due	– $ 0	
(–) Equity Recovery Program	– $ 6,000	
	$ 249,000	**Net Income**

$ 55,200 Total Money Saved!

Savings with Depreciation and Self-Employment Tax
(Example Taken from a Real Client in California on September 2nd, 2007)

Original Purchase Price		$ 46,980	
(+) Capital improvements		+ $ 1,000	
(–) Depreciation		– $ 25,000	
		$ 22,980	**Adjusted Basis**

Selling Price		$ 400,000	
(–) Cost of Sale		– $ 16,000	
(–) Adjusted Basis		– $ 22,980	
		$ 361,020	**Capital Gains**

Before

Federal Recapture Depreciation	(25% of $25,000)	$ 6,250	
(+) Federal Capital Gains Tax Rate	(15% Tax Bracket)	+ $ 54,153	
(+) Federal Self Employment Tax	(15.3% of $97,500)	+ $ 22,823	
(+) State Tax Rate	(10.3%)	+ $ 37,185	
		$ 120,411	**Taxes Due**

Capital Gains		$ 361,020	
(–) Taxes Due		– $ 120,411	
(–) Equity Recovery Program		– $ 0	
		$ 240,609	**Net Income**

After

Federal Recapture Depreciation	(25% of $25,000)	$ 6,250	
(+) Federal Capital Gains Tax Rate	(15% Tax Bracket)	+ $ 0	
(+) Federal Self Employment Tax	(15.3% of $97,500)	+ $ 0	
(+) California Withholding Tax	(3.3% of $400,000)	+ $ 13,200	
(+) California State Tax Rate	(10.3%)	+ $ 0	
		$ 19,450	**Taxes Due**

Capital Gains		$ 361,020	
(–) Taxes Due		– $ 19,450	
(–) Equity Recovery Program		– $ 6,000	
		$ 335,570	**Net Income**

$ 94,961 Total Money Saved!

Real Estate Transfer Taxes

Real Estate Transfer Taxes

Real estate transfer taxes are taxes imposed by states, counties and municipalities on the transfer of the title of real property within the jurisdiction. Real estate transfer taxes can also be used for specific purposes, such as affordable housing and open space development. The following table lists real estate transfer taxes for 37 states and the District of Columbia.

State	Tax Description	Transfer Fee Rate
Alabama	Deeds are $0.50 / $500 Mortgages are $0.15 / $100 **Conveyance is by warranty deed**	0.1% 0.15%
Alaska	None **Conveyance is by warranty deed**	None
Arizona	$2 Fee per deed or contract **Conveyance is by warranty deed**	Flat Fee
Arkansas	$3.30 / $1,000 **Conveyance is by warranty deed**	0.33%
California	Local option transfer tax $.55/$500 for counties. The city tax rate is half of the county rate and the city tax is allowed as a credit against the county tax. **Conveyance is by grant deed**	0.11%
Colorado	Transfer tax is $0.01 / $100 **Conveyance is by warranty deed**	0.01%
Connecticut	State residential transfer tax has two tiers of either 0.75% or 1.25%, based on value. Nonresidential is 1.25% Municipal transfer tax is from 0.11% to 0.36% **Conveyance is by warranty deed**	0.75% up to $800k 1.25% over $800k Plus Municipal Tax
Delaware	2% tax on value of property unless there is also a local transfer tax; then the maximum rate is 1.5% **Conveyance is by warranty deed**	1.5% to 2.0% 1.0% for Construction Projects over $10k

State	Tax Description	Transfer Fee Rate
District of Columbia	Transfer tax is 1.1%	1.1%
	Mortgage recordation tax is 1.5% of 1.1% for values up to $250k.	1.1% to 1.5%
	There are varying rates for different types of property $5 surcharge per document.	
	Conveyance is by bargain-and-sale deed	
Florida	Conveyance of realty is $0.70 / $100 ($0.60 in Miami-Dade County plus a $0.45 surtax on documents transferring anything other than a single-family residence)	0.7%
	Mortgage tax is $0.35 / $100	0.35%
	Conveyance is by warranty deed	
Georgia	$0.10 / $100	0.1%
	Conveyance is by warranty deed	
Hawaii	Transfer tax is $0.10 to $1 / $100, based on property value.	0.1% to 1.0%
	$0.15 to $1.25 / $100 without homeowner exemption, based on value.	0.15% to 1.25%
	Conveyance is by warranty deed	
Idaho	None	None
	Conveyance is by warranty deed	
Illinois	State is $0.50 / $500	0.1%
	County is $0.25 / $500	0.05%
	Chicago is $5.25 / $500	1.05%
	Conveyance is by warranty deed	
Indiana	None	None
	Conveyance is by warranty deed	
Iowa	Transfer tax is $0.80 / $500	0.16%
	Conveyance is by warranty deed	
Kansas	Mortgage fee is $0.26 / $100	0.26%
	Conveyance is by warranty deed	

State	Tax Description	Transfer Fee Rate
Kentucky	Transfer tax is $0.50 / $500 **Conveyance is by bargain-and-sale deed**	0.1%
Louisiana	None **Conveyance is by warranty deed**	None
Maine	Transfer tax is $2.20 / $500 **Conveyance is by warranty deed**	0.44%
Maryland	Transfer tax is $0.5% (or 0.25% for 1st-time buyers) County transfer tax varies by county Recordation tax varies by county **Conveyance is by grant deed**	0.5%
Massachusetts	Transfer tax is $4.56 / $1,000 ($2 / $500 plus 14% surtax) Barnstable Country transfer tax $3.42 / $1,000 ($1.50 / $500 plus 14% surtax) Plus $10 to $20 document fee **Conveyance is by warranty deed**	0.456% 0.342%
Michigan	State is $3.75 / $500 County is $0.55 / $500 to $0.75 / $500 depending on (+/-) 2 million population **Conveyance is by warranty deed**	0.75% 0.11% to 0.15%
Minnesota	Deed tax of $1.65 / $500 Mortgage registry tax $0.23 / $100 **Conveyance is by warranty deed**	0.33% 0.23%
Mississippi	None **Conveyance is by warranty deed**	None
Missouri	None **Conveyance is by warranty deed**	None
Montana	None **Conveyance is by warranty deed**	None

State	Tax Description	Transfer Fee Rate
Nebraska	Transfer tax is $2.25 / $1,000 **Conveyance is by warranty deed**	0.225%
Nevada	$0.65 / $500 up to 700,000 county population $1.25 / $500 over 700,000 county population County tax regardless of size $1.30 / $500 Counties may impose an additional $0.10 / $500 **Conveyance is by bargain-and-sale deed**	0.13% 0.25% 0.26%
New Hampshire	Transfer tax is $0.75 / $100 Paid by buyer and by seller $20 minimum tax on transfers of $4,000 or less **Conveyance is by warranty deed**	1.5%
New Jersey	Transfer tax varies, based on price and tax status (i.e. seniors or disabilities, etc) Homes over $1 million add $5 / $500 surtax Commercial sales over $1 million have a 1% fee County is up to 0.1% additional tax **Conveyance is by bargain-and-sale deed**	0.4% to 1.21% Based on Value 1.0% 1.0% 0.1%
New Mexico	None **Conveyance is by warranty deed**	None
New York	Realty transfer state is $2 / $500 up to $1 million 1% additional over $1 million (Some counties may levy more) Mortgage recording tax $1 / $100 Mortgage New York City $1 to $1.75 / $100 Realty transfer New York City 1% to 2.625% based on (+/-) $550,000 home value (There may be additional local taxes) **Conveyance is by bargain-and-sale deed**	0.4% or 1.4% over $1 million 1.0% 1% to 1.75% 1% to 2.625% Rates Vary
North Carolina	Transfer tax is $1 / $500 Local option is to increase by up to 0.4% **Conveyance is by warranty deed**	0.2% 0.4%

State	Tax Description	Transfer Fee Rate
North Dakota	None **Conveyance is by warranty deed**	None
Ohio	Transfer tax is $0.10 / $100 Mortgage registration tax $0.02 to $0.10 / $100 **Conveyance is by warranty deed**	0.4% 0.02% to 0.1%
Oregon	None **Conveyance is by bargain-and-sale deed**	None
Pennsylvania	Documentary stamp tax is 1% County rates vary **Conveyance is by warranty deed**	1%
Rhode Island	Realty conveyance tax is $2 / $500 **Conveyance is by warranty deed**	0.4%
South Carolina	Deed recording fee is $1.85 / $500 State $1.30 County $0.55 **Conveyance is by warranty deed**	0.37%
South Dakota	$0.50 / $500 **Conveyance is by warranty deed**	0.1%
Tennessee	Transfer tax $0.37 / $100 Mortgage tax $0.115 / $100 **Conveyance is by warranty deed**	0.37% 0.12%
Texas	None **Conveyance is by warranty deed**	None
Utah	None **Conveyance is by warranty deed**	None

State	Tax Description	Transfer Fee Rate
Vermont	Property tax is 1.25% Unless property is owner-occupied, in which case, tax is 0.5% on the first $100,000 of value and 1.25% over $100,000 in value. Qualified farms 0.5% Plus capital gains tax on land sales, based on length of ownership. **Conveyance is by warranty deed**	1.25%
Virginia	Transfer tax is $0.50 / $500 Mortgage tax is $0.25 / $100 up to $10 million value; more thereafter Local option for 1/3 more of state recordation tax $20 fee on every deed collected Northern Virginia Transportation Authority and the Hampton Roads Transportation Authority are authorized to impose a local realty grantor's fee of $0.40 per $100 **Conveyance is by bargain-and-sale deed**	0.1% 0.25%
Washington	Real property sale excise tax 1.28% of sales price plus local option tax, currently ranging from 0.25% to 0.75% **Conveyance is by warranty deed**	1.28% 1.53% to 2.03%
West Virginia	Transfer tax is $1.65 / $500 State $1.10 County $0.55 (Local option for $0.55 more) $20 Flat fee on all transfers **Conveyance is by warranty deed**	1.28% $20
Wisconsin	Transfer tax is $0.30 / $100 **Conveyance is by warranty deed**	0.3%
Wyoming	None **Conveyance is by warranty deed**	None

Sources: National Conference of State Legislatures (NCSL) Fiscal Affairs Program
and The Commerce Clearing House State Tax Guide

Escrow Procedures

Escrow Procedures

Alabama

Attorneys and title companies handle closings. Conveyance is by warranty deed. Mortgages are the customary security instruments. Foreclosures are non-judicial. Foreclosure notices are published once a week for three weeks on a county-by-county basis. The foreclosure process takes a minimum of 21 days from the date of first publication. After the sale, there is a one-year redemption period. Alabamans use ALTA policies to insure titles. Buyers and sellers negotiate who is going to pay the closing costs and usually split them equally. Property taxes are due and payable annually on October 1st.

Alaska

Title companies, lenders, and private escrow companies all handle real estate escrows. Conveyance is by warranty deed. Deeds of trust with private power of sale are the customary security instruments. Foreclosures take 90-120 days. Alaskans use ALTA owner's and lender's policies with standard endorsements. There are no documentary or transfer taxes. Buyer and seller usually split the closing costs. Property tax payment dates vary throughout the state.

Arizona

Title companies and title agents both handle closings. Conveyance is by warranty deed. Whereas deeds of trust are the security instruments most often used, mortgages and "agreements for sale" are used approximately 20% of the time. Foreclosure depends upon the security instrument. For deeds of trust, the foreclosure process takes about 91 days. Arizonans use ALTA owner's and lender's policies, standard or extended, with standard endorsements. The seller customarily pays for the owner's policy, and the buyer pays for the lender's policy. They split escrow costs otherwise. There are no documentary, transfer, or mortgage taxes. The first property tax installment is due October 1st and delinquent November 1st; the second half is due March 1st and delinquent May 1st. Arizona is a community-property state.

Arkansas

Title agents handle escrows, and attorneys conduct closings. Conveyance is by warranty deed. Mortgages are the customary security instruments. Foreclosure requires judicial proceedings, but there are no minimum time limits for completion. Arkansans use ALTA policies and endorsements and receive a 40% discount for reissuance of prior policies. Buyers and sellers pay their own escrow costs. The buyer pays for the lender's policy; the seller pays for the owner's. The buyer and seller split the state documentary tax. Property taxes come due three times a year as follows: the third Monday in April, the third Monday in July, and the tenth day of October.

California

Not only do escrow procedures differ between Northern and Southern California, they also vary somewhat from county to county. Title companies handle closings through escrow in Northern California, whereas escrow companies and lenders handle them in Southern California.

Conveyance is by grant deed. Deeds of trust with private power of sale are the security instruments used throughout the state. Foreclosure requires a three-month waiting period after the recording of the notice of default. After the waiting period, the notice of sale is published each week for three consecutive weeks.

The borrower may reinstate the loan at any time prior to five business days before the foreclosure sale. All in all, the procedure takes about four months. Californians have both ALTA and CLTA policies available. In Southern California, sellers pay the title insurance premium and the transfer tax. Buyer and seller split the escrow costs. In the Northern California counties of Amador, Merced, Plumas, San Joaquin, and Siskiyou, buyers and sellers share title insurance and escrow costs equally. In Butte County, sellers pay 75%; buyers pay 25%. In Alameda, Calaveras, Colusa, Contra Costa, Lake, Marin, Mendocino, San Francisco, San Mateo, Solano, and Sonoma counties, buyers pay for the title insurance policy, whereas sellers pay in the other Northern California counties. Each California county has its own transfer tax; some cities have additional charges. Property taxes may be paid annually on or before December 10th, or semiannually by December 10th and April 10th. Annual taxes are set at no more than 1 percent of the property's base value or purchase price. Each year following this, a two percent increase is permissible. (Proposition 13). A property transfer between husband and wife will not result in a new tax assessment of one percent of the fair market value.

The homeowner's exemption allows an owner to be exempt of the first $7,000 of the property's full cash value. This exemption is allowed only for primary residences. Homeowner must obtain a form from the county tax assessor, and submit it by February 15 of the current tax year to be eligible for the exemption. Californians over the age of 55 also have the option of moving primary residences and taking their prior "old" tax base with them to the new property. This exception may be used only once in a lifetime. Referred to as the" Senior Citizen's Replacement Dwelling Benefit", Proposition 60 was a constitutional amendment approved by the voters in 1986. It is codified in Section 69.5 of the *Revenue & Taxation Code*, and allows the transfer of an existing Proposition 13 base year value from a former residence to a replacement residence, if certain conditions are met. California is a community-property state.

Colorado

Title companies, brokers, and attorneys all may handle closings. Conveyance is by warranty deed. Deeds of trust are the customary security instruments. Public trustees must sell foreclosure properties within 45-60 days after the filing of a notice of election and demand for sale, but they will grant extensions up to six months following the date of the originally scheduled sale. Subdivided properties may be redeemed within 75 days after sale; agricultural properties may be redeemed within 6 months after sale. The first junior lien holder has 10 additional days to redeem, and the second and other junior lien-holders have an additional 5 days each. The public trustee is normally the trustee shown on the deed of trust, a practice unique to Colorado. Foreclosures may be handled judicially. Coloradans have these title insurance policy options: ALTA owner's, lender's, leasehold, and construction loan; endorsements are used, too. Although they are negotiable, closing costs are generally split between buyer and seller, and seller normally pays for title insurance. Sellers pay the title insurance premium and the documentary transfer tax. Property taxes may be paid annually at the end of April or semiannually at the ends of February and July.

Connecticut

Attorneys normally conduct closings. Most often conveyance is by warranty deed, but quitclaim deeds do appear. Mortgages are the security instruments. Judicial foreclosures are the rule, either by a suit in equity for strict foreclosure or by a court decree of sale. Court decreed sales preclude redemption, but strict foreclosures allow redemption for 3-6 months, depending upon court discretion. Lender and owner title insurance policies are available with various endorsements. Buyers customarily pay for examination and title insurance, while sellers pay documentary and conveyance taxes. Property tax payment dates vary by town.

Delaware

Attorneys handle closings. Although quitclaim and general warranty deeds are sometimes used, most conveyances are by special warranty deeds. Mortgages are the security instruments. Foreclosures are judicial and require 90-120 days to complete. ALTA policies and endorsements are prevalent. Buyers pay closing costs and the owner's title insurance premiums. Buyers and sellers share the state transfer tax. Property taxes are on an annual basis and vary by county.

District of Columbia

Attorneys, title insurance companies, or their agents may conduct closings. Conveyances are by bargain-and-sale deeds. Though mortgages are available, the deed of trust, containing private power of sale, is the security instrument of choice. Foreclosures require at least six weeks and start with a 30-day notice of sale sent by certified mail. ALTA policies and endorsements insure title. Buyers generally pay closing costs, title insurance premiums, and recording taxes. Sellers pay the transfer tax. Property taxes fall due annually or if they're less than $100,000, semiannually, on September 15th and March 31st.

Florida

Title companies and attorneys handle closings. Conveyance is by warranty deed. Mortgages are the customary security instruments. Foreclosures are judicial and take about 3 months. They involve service by the sheriff, a judgment of foreclosure and sale, advertising, public sale, and finally issuance of a certificate of sale and certificate of title. ALTA policies are commonplace. Buyers pay the escrow and closing costs, while county custom determines who pays for the title insurance. Sellers pay the documentary tax. Property taxes are payable annually, but the due and delinquent dates are months apart, November 1st and April 1st. Under Florida law, a widow or widower has the right to live in their deceased spouse's house for the remainder of his or her life, even if the home is willed to someone else.   A Homestead Exemption exists for an owner's residence in Florida. Florida's exemption is unique because it lacks any monetary cap on the homestead protection, while other states which offer a homestead exemption usually place a limit on the valuation which can be protected.

Georgia

Attorneys generally take care of closings. Conveyance is by warranty deed. Security deeds are the security instruments. Foreclosures are non-judicial and take little more than a month because there's a power of attorney right in the security deed. Foreclosure advertising must appear for 4 consecutive weeks prior to the first Tuesday of the month; that's when foreclosure sales take place. Georgians use ALTA title insurance policies, including owners and lenders, and they use binders and endorsements. Buyers pay title insurance premiums and also closing costs usually. Sellers pay transfer taxes. Property tax payment dates vary across the state.

Hawaii

By law, only attorneys may prepare property transfer documents, but there are title and escrow companies available to handle escrows and escrow instructions. Conveyance of fee-simple property is by warranty deed; conveyance of leasehold property, which is common throughout the state, is by assignment of lease. Condominiums are everywhere in Hawaii and may be fee simple or leasehold. Sales of some properties, whether fee simple or leasehold, are by agreement of sale. Mortgages are the security instruments. Hawaiians use judicial foreclosures rather than powers of sale for both mortgages and agreements of sale. These foreclosures take 6-12 months and sometimes more, depending upon court schedules. Title companies issue ALTA owner's and lender's policies and make numerous endorsements available. Buyers and sellers split escrow fees. Sellers pay the title search costs and the conveyance tax. Buyers pay title insurance premiums for the owner's and lender's policies. Property taxes come due twice a year, on February 20th and again on August 20th.

Idaho

Closings are handled through escrow. Conveyance is by warranty deed or corporate deed, though often there are contracts of sale involved. Either mortgages or deeds of trust may be the security instruments. Deeds of trust which include power of sale provisions are restricted to properties in incorporated areas and properties elsewhere which don't exceed 20 acres. After the notice of default has been recorded, deed-of-trust foreclosures take at least 120 days, and there's no redemption period. Judicial foreclosures for mortgages take about a year, depending upon court availability, and there's a 6-12 month redemption period after that, depending on the type of property involved. Idahoans use ALTA policies and various endorsements. Buyers and sellers split escrow costs in general and negotiate who's going to pay the title insurance premiums. There are no documentary taxes, mortgage taxes, or transfer taxes, but there are property taxes, and they're due annually in November and delinquent on December 20th or semiannually on December 20th and June 20th. Idaho is a community-property state.

Illinois

Title companies, lenders, and attorneys may conduct closings, but only attorneys may prepare documents. Lenders generally hire attorneys and have them prepare all the paperwork. Conveyance is by warranty deed. Recorded deeds must include a declaration of the sales price. Mortgages are the customary security instruments. Judicial foreclosure is mandatory and takes at least a year from the filing of the default notice to the expiration of the redemption period. Illinoisans use ALTA policies. Buyers usually pay the closing costs and the lender's title insurance premiums; sellers pay the owner's title insurance premiums and the state and county transfer taxes. Property tax payment dates vary. Larger counties typically schedule them for March 1st and September 1st, and smaller counties schedule them for June 1st and September 1st.

Indiana

Title companies, lenders, real estate agents, and attorneys handle closings. Conveyance is by warranty deed. Mortgages are the customary security instruments. Judicial foreclosures are required; execution of judgments varies from 3 months after filing of the complaint in cases involving mortgages drawn up since July 1, 1975, to 6 months for those drawn up between January 1, 1958, and July 1, 1975, to 12 months for those drawn up before that. Immediately following the execution sale, the highest bidder receives a sheriff's deed. Hoosiers use ALTA policies and certain endorsements. Buyers usually pay closing costs and the lender's title insurance costs, while sellers pay for the owner's policy. There are no documentary, mortgage, or transfer taxes. Property taxes fall due on May 10th and November 10th.

Iowa

Attorneys and real estate agents may conduct closings. Conveyance is usually by warranty deed. Mortgages and deeds of trust are both authorized security instruments, but lenders prefer mortgages because deeds of trust do not circumvent judicial foreclosure proceedings. Such proceedings take at least 4 -6 months. Since Iowa is the only state which does not authorize private title insurance, Iowans who want it must go through a state administered title company or fund. Buyers and sellers share the closing costs; sellers pay the documentary taxes. Property taxes are due July 1st based upon the previous January's assessment.

Kansas

Title companies, lenders, real estate agents, attorneys, and independent escrow firms all conduct closings. Anyone who conducts a title search must be a licensed abstracter, a designation one receives after passing strict tests and meeting various requirements. Because many land titles stem from Indian origins, deeds involving Indians as parties to a transaction go before the Indian Commission for approval. Conveyance is by warranty deed. Mortgages are the customary security instruments. Judicial foreclosures, the only ones allowed, take about 6 months from filing to sale. Redemption periods vary, the longest being 12 months. Kansan's use ALTA policies and endorsements. Buyers and sellers divide closing costs. Buyers pay the lender's policy costs and the state mortgage taxes; sellers pay for the owner's policy. Property taxes come due November 1st, but they needn't be paid in a lump sum until December 31st. They may be paid in two installments, the first on December 20th and the second on June 20th.

Kentucky

Attorneys conduct closings. Conveyance is by grant deed or by bargain-and-sale deed. Deeds must show the name of the preparer, the amount of the total transaction, and the recording reference by which the grantor obtained title. Mortgages are the principal security instruments because deeds of trust offer no power-of-sale advantages. Enforcement of any security instrument requires a decree in equity, a judicial foreclosure proceeding. Kentuckians use ALTA policies and endorsements. Sellers pay closing costs; buyers pay recording fees. Responsibility for payment of title insurance premiums varies according to locale. Property taxes are payable on an annual basis; due dates vary from county to county.

Louisiana

Either attorneys or corporate title agents may conduct closings, but a notary must authenticate the documentation. Conveyance is by warranty deed or by act of sale. Mortgages are the security instruments generally used in commercial transactions, while vendor's liens and seller's privileges are used in other purchase money situations. Foreclosures are swift (60 days) and sure (no right of redemption). Successful foreclosure sale bidders receive adjudication from the sheriff. Louisianan's use ALTA owner's and lender's policies and endorsements. Buyers generally pay the title insurance and closing costs. There are no mortgage or transfer taxes. Property tax payment dates vary from parish to parish (parishes are like counties). Louisiana is a community-property state.

Maine

Attorneys conduct closings. Conveyance is by warranty or quitclaim deed. Mortgages are the security instruments. Foreclosures may be initiated by any of the following: an act of law for possession; entering into possession and holding the premises by written consent of the mortgagor; entering peaceably, openly, and unopposed in the presence of two witnesses and taking possession; giving public notice in a newspaper for three successive weeks and recording copies of the notice in the Registry of Deeds, and then recording the mortgage within 30 days of the last publication; or by a bill in equity (special cases). In every case, the creditor must record a notice of foreclosure within 30 days. Judicial foreclosure proceedings are also available. Redemption periods vary from 90-365 days depending on the method of foreclosure. Mainers use ALTA owner's and lender's policies and endorsements. Buyers pay closing costs and title insurance fees; buyers and sellers share the documentary transfer taxes. Property taxes are due annually on April 1st.

Maryland

Attorneys conduct closings, and there has to be a local attorney involved. Conveyance is by grant deed, and the deed must state the consideration involved. Although mortgages are common in some areas, deeds of trust are more prevalent as security instruments. Security instruments may include a private power of sale, so it naturally is the foreclosure method of choice. Marylanders use ALTA policies and endorsements. Buyers pay closing costs, title insurance premiums, and transfer taxes. Property taxes are due annually on July 1st. Police officers in Prince George's County who are first-time home buyers get a break on their transfer taxes at closing under a law that took effect July 1, 2006. Officers pay one-percent of the purchase price rather than 14%, the regular rate. County school teachers were made eligible for the same tax break in an earlier law without the first-time buyer limitation. Teachers must commit to living in the house for at least three years and maintain their teaching position with the county during that time.

Massachusetts

Attorneys handle closings. Conveyance is by warranty deed in the western part of the state and by quitclaim deed in the eastern part. Mortgages with private power of sale are the customary security instruments. Creditors forced to foreclose generally take advantage of the private power of sale, but they may foreclose through peaceable entry (entering unopposed in the presence of two witnesses and taking possession for 3 years) or through the rarely used judicial writ of entry. Frequently, cautious creditors will foreclose through both power of sale and peaceable entry. People in Massachusetts use ALTA owner's and lender's title insurance policies and endorsements. Buyers pay closing costs and title insurance fees, except in Worcester, where sellers pay. Sellers pay the documentary taxes. Property taxes are payable in two installments, November 1st and May 1st.

Michigan

Title companies, lenders, real estate agents, and attorneys may conduct closings. Conveyance is by warranty deed which must give the full consideration involved or be accompanied by an affidavit which does. Many transactions involve land contracts. Mortgages are the security instruments. Private foreclosure is permitted; it requires advertising for 4 consecutive weeks and a sale at least 28 days following the date of first publication. The redemption period ranges from 1 to 12 months. Michiganders use ALTA policies and endorsements. Buyers generally pay closing costs and the lender's title insurance premium, and sellers pay the state transfer tax and the owner's title insurance premium. Those property taxes which pay for city and school expenses fall due July 1st; others (county taxes, township taxes, and some school taxes) fall due on the first of December. In many tax jurisdictions, taxpayers may opt to pay their taxes in two equal installments without penalty.

Minnesota

Title companies, lenders, real estate agents, and attorneys may conduct closings. Conveyance is by warranty deed. Although deeds of trust are authorized, mortgages are the customary security instruments. The redemption period following a foreclosure is 6 months in most cases; it is 12 months if the property is larger than 10 acres or the amount claimed to be due is less than 2/3 of the original debt. This is a strong abstract state. Typically a buyer will accept an abstract and an attorney's opinion as evidence of title, even though the lender may require title insurance. People in the Minneapolis-St. Paul area use the Torrens system. Minnesotans use ALTA policies. Buyers pay the lender's and owner's title insurance premiums and the mortgage tax. Sellers usually pay the closing fees and the transfer taxes. Property taxes are due on May 15th and October 15th.

Mississippi

Attorneys conduct real estate closings. Conveyance is by warranty deed. Deeds of trust are the customary security instruments. Foreclosure involves a non-judicial process which takes 21-45 days. Mississippians use ALTA policies and endorsements. Buyers and sellers negotiate the payment of title insurance premiums and closing costs. There are no documentary, mortgage, or transfer taxes. Property taxes are payable on an annual basis and become delinquent February 1st.

Missouri

Title companies, lenders, real estate agents, and attorneys may conduct closings. In the St. Louis area, title company closings predominate. In the Kansas City area, an escrow company or a title company generally conducts the closing. Conveyance is by warranty deed.

Deeds of trust are the customary security instruments and allow private power of sale. The trustee must be named in the deed of trust and must be a Missouri resident. Foreclosure involves publication of a sale notice for 21 days, during which time the debtor may redeem the property or file a notice of redemption. The foreclosure sale buyer receives a trustee's deed. Missourians use ALTA policies and endorsements. Buyers and sellers generally split the closing costs. Sellers in western Missouri usually pay for the title insurance polices, while elsewhere the buyers pay. There are no documentary, mortgage, or transfer taxes. Property taxes are payable annually and become delinquent January 1st for the previous year.

Montana

Real estate closings are handled through escrow. Conveyance is by warranty deed, corporate deed, or grant deed. Mortgages, deeds of trust, and unrecorded contracts of sale are the security instruments. Mortgages require judicial foreclosure, and there's a 6-12-month redemption period following sale. Foreclosure on deeds of trust involves filing a notice of default and then holding a trustee sale 120 days later. Montanans use ALTA policies and endorsements. Buyers and sellers split the escrow and closing costs; sellers usually pay for the title insurance policies. There are no documentary, mortgage, or transfer taxes. Montanans may pay their property taxes annually by November 30th or semi-annually by November 30th and May 31st.

Nebraska

Title companies, lenders, real estate agents, and attorneys all conduct closings. Conveyance is by warranty deed. Mortgages and deeds of trust are the security instruments. Mortgage foreclosures require judicial proceedings and take about 6 months from the date of the first notice when they're uncontested. Deeds of trust do not require judicial proceedings and take about 90 days. Nebraskan's use ALTA policies and endorsements. Buyers and sellers split escrow and closing costs; sellers pay the state's documentary taxes. Property taxes fall due April 1st and August 1st.

Nevada

Escrow similar to California's is used for closings. Conveyance is by grant deed, bargain-and-sale deed, or quitclaim deed. Deeds of trust are the customary security instruments. Foreclosure involves recording a notice of default and mailing a copy within 10 days. Following the mailing there is a 35-day reinstatement period. After that, the beneficiary may accept partial payment or payment in full for a 3-month period. Then come advertising the property for sale for 3 consecutive weeks and finally the sale itself. All of this takes about 4 1/2 months. Nevadans use both ALTA and CLTA policies and endorsements. Buyers and sellers share escrow costs. Buyers pay the lender's title insurance premiums; sellers pay the owner's and the state's transfer tax. Property taxes are payable in one, two, or four payments, the first one being due July 1st. Nevada is a community-property state.

New Hampshire

Attorneys conduct real estate closings. Conveyance is by warranty or quitclaim deed. Mortgages are the customary security instruments. Lenders may foreclosure through judicial action or through whatever power of sale was written into the mortgage originally. Entry, either by legal action or by taking possession peaceably in the presence of two witnesses, is possible under certain legally stated conditions. There is a one-year right-of-redemption period. The people of New Hampshire use ALTA owner's and lender's policies. Buyers pay all closing costs and title fees except for the documentary tax; that's shared with the sellers. Property tax payment dates vary across the state.

New Jersey

Attorneys handle closings in northern New Jersey, and title agents customarily handle them elsewhere. Conveyance is by bargain-and-sale deed with covenants against grantors' acts (equivalent to a special warranty deed). Mortgages are the most common security instruments though deeds of trust are authorized. Foreclosures require judicial action which takes 6-9 months if they're uncontested. New Jerseyites use ALTA owner's and lender's policies. Both buyer and seller pay the escrow and closing costs. The buyer pays the title insurance fees, and the seller pays the transfer tax. Property taxes are payable quarterly on the first of April, July, October, and January.

New Mexico

Real estate closings are conducted through escrows. Conveyance is by warranty or quitclaim deed. Deeds of trust and mortgages are the security instruments. Foreclosures require judicial proceedings, and there's a 9-month redemption period after judgment. New Mexicans use ALTA owner's policies, lender's policies, and construction and leasehold policies; they also use endorsements. Buyers and sellers share escrow costs equally; sellers pay the title insurance premiums. There are no documentary, mortgage, or transfer taxes. Property taxes are payable November 5th and April 5th. New Mexico is a community-property state.

New York

All parties to a transaction appear with their attorneys for closing. Conveyance is by bargain-and-sale deed. Mortgages are the security instruments in this lien-theory state. Foreclosures require judicial action and take several months if uncontested or longer if contested. New Yorkers use policies of the New York Board of Title Underwriters almost exclusively, though some use the New York State 1946 ALTA Loan Policy. Buyers generally pay most closing costs, including all title insurance fees and mortgage taxes. Sellers pay the state and city transfer taxes. Property tax payment dates vary across the state.

North Carolina

Attorneys or lenders may handle closings, and corporate agents issue title insurance. Conveyance is by warranty deed. Deeds of trust with private power of sale are the customary security instruments. Foreclosures are non-judicial, with a 10-day redemption period following the sale. The entire process takes between 45 and 60 days. North Carolinians use ALTA policies, but these require an attorney's opinion before they're issued. Buyers and sellers negotiate the closing costs, except that buyers pay the recording costs, and sellers pay the document preparation and transfer tax costs. Property taxes fall due annually on the last day of the year.

North Dakota

Lenders, together with attorneys, conduct closings. Conveyance is by warranty deed. Mortgages are the security instruments. Foreclosures require about 6 months, including the redemption period. North Dakotans base their title insurance on abstracts and attorneys' opinions. Buyers usually pay for the closing, the attorney's opinion, and the title insurance; sellers pay for the abstract. There are no documentary or transfer taxes. Property taxes are due March 15th and October 15th.

Ohio

Title companies and lenders handle closings. Conveyance is by warranty deed. Dower rights require that all documents involving a married person must be executed by both spouses. Mortgages are the security instruments. Judicial foreclosures, the only kind allowed, require about 6-12 months. People in Ohio use ALTA policies; they get a commitment at closing and a policy following the recording of documents. Buyers and sellers negotiate who's going to pay closing costs and title insurance premiums, but sellers pay the transfer taxes. Property tax payment dates vary throughout the state.

Oklahoma

Title companies, lenders, real estate agents, and attorneys may conduct closings. Conveyance is by warranty deed. Mortgages are the usual security instruments. Foreclosures may be by judicial action or by power of sale if properly allowed for in the security instrument. Oklahomans use ALTA policies and endorsements. Buyers and sellers share the closing costs, except that the buyer pays the lender's policy premium, the seller pays the documentary transfer tax, and the lender pays the mortgage tax. Property taxes may be paid annually on or before the last day of the year or semi-annually by December 31st and March 31st.

Oregon

Closings are handled through escrow. Conveyance is by warranty or bargain-and-sale deed, but land sales contracts are common. Mortgage deeds and deeds of trust are the security instruments. Oregon attorneys usually act as trustees in non-judicial trust-deed foreclosures. Such foreclosures take 5 months from the date of the sale notice; defaults may be cured as late as 5 days prior to sale. Judicial foreclosures on either mortgages or trust deeds allow for a one-year redemption period following sale. Oregonians use ALTA and Oregon Land Title Association policies. Buyers and sellers split escrow costs and transfer taxes; the buyer pays for the lender's title insurance policy, and the seller pays for the owner's policy. Property taxes are payable the 15th of November, February, and May; if paid in full by November 15th, owners receive a 3% reduction.

Pennsylvania

Title companies, real estate agents, and approved attorneys may handle closings. Conveyance is by special or general warranty deed. Mortgages are the security instruments. Foreclosures take 1-6 months from filing through judgment plus another 2 months or more from judgment through sale. State law restricts aliens in owning real property with respect to acreage and income and includes special restrictions affecting farmland. Pennsylvanians use ALTA owners, lenders, and leasehold policies. Buyers pay closing costs and title insurance fees; buyers and sellers split the transfer taxes. Property tax payment dates differ across the state.

Rhode Island

Attorneys usually conduct closings, but banks and title companies may also conduct them. Conveyance is by warranty or quitclaim deed. Mortgages are the usual security instruments. Foreclosures follow the power-of-sale provisions contained in mortgage agreements and take about 45 days. Power-of-sale foreclosures offer no redemption provisions, whereas any other foreclosure method carries a 3-year right of redemption. Rhode Islanders use ALTA policies and endorsements. Buyers pay title insurance premiums and closing costs; sellers pay documentary taxes. Property taxes are payable annually, semi-annually, or quarterly with the first payment due in July.

South Carolina

Attorneys customarily handle closings. Conveyance is by warranty deed. Mortgages are most often the security instruments. Foreclosures are judicial and take 3-5 months depending on court schedules. Foreclosure sales take place on the first Monday of every month following publication of notice once a week for 3 consecutive weeks. South Carolinians use owner's and lender's ALTA policies and endorsements. Buyers pay closing costs, title insurance premiums, and state mortgage taxes; sellers pay the transfer taxes. Property tax payment dates vary across the state from September 15 to December 31.

South Dakota

Title companies, lenders, real estate agents, and attorneys may handle closings. Conveyance is by warranty deed. Mortgages are the usual security instruments. Foreclosures may occur through judicial proceedings or through the power-of-sale provisions contained in certain mortgage agreements. Sheriff's sales follow publication of notice by 30 days. The redemption period allowed after sale of parcels smaller than 40 acres and encumbered by mortgages containing power of sale is 180 days; in all other cases, it's a year. There's a unique statute which stipulates that all land must be platted in lots or described by sectional references rather than by metes and bounds unless it involves property described in documents recorded prior to 1945. There's another unique statute called the Affidavit of Possession Statute. Certain exceptions aside, it provides that any person having an unbroken chain of title for 22 years thereafter has a marketable title free of any defects occurring prior to that 22-year period. South Dakotans use ALTA policies and endorsements. Sellers pay the transfer taxes and split the other closing costs, fees, and premiums with the buyers. Property taxes come due May 1st and November 1st.

Tennessee

A title company attorney, a party to the contract, a lender's representative, or an outside attorney may conduct a closing. Conveyance is by warranty or quitclaim deed. Deeds of trust are the customary security instruments. Foreclosures, which are handled according to trustee sale provisions, are swift, that is, 22 days from the first publication of the notice until the public sale, and there is normally no right of redemption after that. Tennesseans use ALTA policies and endorsements. The payment of title insurance premiums, closing costs, mortgage taxes, and transfer taxes varies according to local practice. Property taxes are payable annually on the first Monday in October.

Texas

Title companies normally handle closings. Conveyance is by warranty deed. Deeds of trust are the most common security instruments. Following the posting of foreclosure sales at the local courthouse for at least 21 days, the sales themselves take place at the courthouse on the first Tuesday of the month. Texans use only Texas standard policy forms of title insurance. Buyers and sellers negotiate closing costs. There aren't any documentary, transfer, or mortgage taxes. Property taxes notices are send around October 1st, but are not due until the end of the year. Texas is a community-property state.

Utah

Lenders handle about 60% of the escrows and title companies handle the rest. Conveyance is by warranty deed. Mortgages and deeds of trust with private power of sale are the security instruments. Mortgage foreclosures require judicial proceedings which take about a year; deed-of-trust foreclosures take advantage of private power-of-sale provisions and take about 4 months. Utahans use ALTA owner's and lender's policies and endorsements. Buyers and sellers split escrow fees, and sellers pay the title insurance premiums. There is no documentary, transfer, or mortgage tax. Property taxes are payable November 30th.

Vermont

Attorneys take care of closings. Conveyance is by warranty or quitclaim deed. Mortgages are the customary security instruments, but large commercial transactions often employ deeds of trust. Mortgage foreclosures require judicial proceedings for „strict foreclosure‰; after sale, there is a redemption period of one year for mortgages dated prior to April 1, 1968, and 6 months for all others. Vermonters use ALTA owners and lenders policies and endorsements. Buyers pay recording fees, title insurance premiums, and transfer taxes. Property tax payment dates vary across the state.

Virginia

Attorneys and title companies conduct real estate closings. Conveyance is by bargain-and-sale deed. Deeds of trust are the customary security instruments. Foreclosure takes about 2 months. Virginians use ALTA policies and endorsements. Buyers pay the title insurance premiums and the various taxes. Property tax payment dates vary.

Washington

Title companies, independent escrow companies, lenders, and attorneys may handle escrows. An attorney must prepare real estate documents, but there is a limited practice rule which lets licensed non-attorneys prepare most of the commonly used real estate documents. Conveyance is by warranty deed. Both deeds of trust with private power of sale and mortgages are used as security instruments. Mortgages require judicial foreclosure. Deeds of trust require that a notice of default be sent first and 30 days later, a notice of sale. The notice of sale must be recorded, posted, and mailed at least 90 days before the sale, and the sale cannot take place any earlier than 190 days after the actual default. Sellers generally pay the title insurance premiums and the revenue tax; buyers and sellers split everything else. Property taxes are payable April 30th and October 31st. Washington is a community-property state.

West Virginia

Attorneys conduct escrow closings, although lenders and real estate agents do them occasionally. Conveyance is by warranty deed, bargain-and-sale deed, or grant deed. Deeds of trust are the customary security instruments. Foreclosures are great for lenders; when uncontested, they take only a month. West Virginians use ALTA policies and endorsements. Buyers pay the title insurance premiums and sellers pay the documentary taxes; they divide the other closing costs. Property taxes may be paid in a lump sum after July 6th or in two installments on September 1st and March 1st.

Wisconsin

Lenders and title companies conduct what are called "table closings" throughout the state, except in the Milwaukee area, where attorneys conduct the closings. Conveyance is by warranty deed, but installment land contracts are used extensively, too. Mortgages are the customary security instruments. Within limits, the actual mortgage wording determines foreclosure requirements; redemption varies from 2 months for abandoned property to a full year in some cases. Lenders generally waive their right to a deficiency judgment in order to reduce the redemption period to 6 months. Wisconsinites use ALTA policies and endorsements. Buyers generally pay closing costs and the lender's policy fees; sellers pay the owner's policy fees and the transfer taxes. In transactions involving homesteads, conveyances may be void if not joined into by the spouse. Property taxes may be paid in full on February 28th, or they may be paid half on January 31st and half on July 31st. Wisconsin is a quasi-community-property state.

Wyoming

Real estate agents generally conduct closings. Conveyance is by warranty deed. Mortgages are the usual security instruments. Foreclosures may follow judicial or power-of-sale proceedings. Residential foreclosures take around 120 days; agricultural foreclosures, around 13 months. Wyomingites use ALTA owner's and lender's policies and endorsements. Buyer and seller negotiate who's going to pay the various closing costs and title insurance fees. There are no documentary, mortgage, or transfer taxes. Property taxes may be paid annually December 31st or semi-annually September 1st and March 1st.

Deeds for Transferring Real Property

Introduction

A deed is a written instrument used to convey title to property. Deeds differ usually by the type of guarantee or "warranty" that they give. For our discussion, there are basically three different types of deeds you should be familiar with. These deeds are:

Grant Deed

("Special Warranty Deed") This type of deed only warrants that the grantor has acquired title and did nothing to impair it while he held title. Public officials, such as a Sheriff after a foreclosure sale, use a special warranty deed. California and Maryland use a slightly modified version of a Special Warranty Deed, which is called a grant deed.

Quitclaim Deed

A Quitclaim Deed contains no promises or warranties about title. The grantor simply gives up whatever claim he may or may not have. A quitclaim deed is commonly used to transfer an interest between spouses or to clear up a title defect. If the seller has good title, a quitclaim deed will transfer the property the same as a warranty deed. However, the grantor makes no guarantee that title is good.

Warranty Deed

A Warranty Deed is the most complete guarantee of title. The warranty deed promises that the grantor (seller) has full and complete title and forever warrants against any claims against said title. If anyone makes a claim to the property, no matter how old the claim is the grantor of a warranty deed must fix the problem.

Elements of a Deed

There are certain elements a deed must contain to be considered a legal and valid transfer. Make sure if you execute a deed or pay someone else for a deed to real estate, the following elements are present:

Have it in Writing

A deed must be in writing to be enforceable. It does not necessarily need to be typed, but it may not be accepted for public recording at the county if it is not legible.

Parties to the Transaction

The deed must state the names of the giver of the deed (the "grantor") and the receiver of the deed (the "grantee"). The grantor's name must be spelled exactly as it appears on the deed that gave him/her/it title, even if that spelling is incorrect. In community property states (CA, LA, TX, WI, ID, AZ, NV, NM, WA), you also need a separate quitclaim deed from the grantor's spouse, even if his/her name is not on title.

Consideration

The deed must state that the grantor received consideration even though no actual money changed hands. You can insert the purchase price or simply the words: *"the grantee has received ten dollars in hand and other good and valuable consideration, the sufficiency of which is hereby acknowledged."*

Legal Description

The legal description of the property must be exactly as it appears from the previous deed. It will usually read something like, *"Lot 25, block 21, Harris Subdivision, County of Barrington, State of Illinois."* This designation comes from a plat map that was previously filed in the county records. If the description is more complicated than a simple lot and block or government survey description, simply photocopy the description from the previous deed and paste it in the appropriate place on the new deed.

Conveyance

This language spells out what type of deed is given. It usually reads something like *"the grantor hereby grants, conveys and warrants"* (warranty deed) or *"the grantor hereby remises, releases and quit-claims"* (quitclaim deed).

Grantor Signature

The grantor must sign his/her name exactly as it appears on the previous deed. If the grantor is not available for signature an authorized agent or "attorney-in-fact" can sign on his/her behalf. This process is accomplished by a power of attorney that authorizes an agent to act for the grantor in signing the deed. The power of attorney should include a legal description of the property and should be recorded with the deed that is signed by the agent. The agent does not sign the grantor's name, but rather signs his/her own name "as attorney-in-fact" for the grantor.

Acknowledgment

The deed should be acknowledged before a notary public. An acknowledgment is a declaration that the person signing is whom he/she claims he/she is and that he/she is signing the deed voluntarily. The notary signs the deed affirming that the grantor appeared before him/her and that he/she knows the person or was provided with sufficient proof of identity. Although acknowledgment is not required to make a deed valid, it is usually required for recording. Although the notary acknowledgment provided by the California Secretary of State is generally accepted in all 50 states, notary requirements may differ from state to state so make certain your deed complies with your state laws.

Form of Deed

The form of deed you use (***quitclaim, warranty or grant deed***) will depend on the circumstances surrounding the transfer. If you are transferring title from your own name to an entity that you "own", then the warranty of title is a moot issue, so a quitclaim deed will suffice.

Deed Recording   Recording is the process of bringing a legal document to your county office (usually called a *County Clerk* or *Registrar of Deeds)* and handing over the document. The county official will give you back the original after it is copied and indexed in their records. The county charges a filing fee for recording deeds, usually about $5 to $10 per page. In addition, the county, city or state may charge a documentary transfer tax, although this fee is usually waived for transfers into an entity that is wholly owned by you. You may also have to file some informational forms with the county clerk or treasurer's office. Ask your local title company or attorney if such forms are required or call your county government offices.

Bargain-and-Sale Deed

District of Columbia	Kentucky	Nevada	New Jersey
New York	Oregon	Virginia	

Grant Deed

California	Maryland

Warranty Deed States

Alabama	Alaska	Arizona	Arkansas
Colorado	Connecticut	Delaware	Florida
Georgia	Hawaii	Idaho	Illinois
Indiana	Iowa	Kansas	Louisiana
Maine	Massachusetts	Michigan	Minnesota
Mississippi	Missouri	Montana	Nebraska
New Hampshire	New Mexico	North Carolina	North Dakota
Ohio	Oklahoma	Pennsylvania	Rhode Island
South Dakota	Tennessee	Texas	Vermont
Washington	West Virginia	Wisconsin	Wyoming

Checklist for Transferring Property

States differ in their requirements as to which of the following forms they require to be recorded at the county recorder in order for you to acquire a tax-free title transfer. When you create and file these documents with the county recorder and/or your lender, there is no guarantee that they will not be included in the 'public records', which can be viewed by any interested party including an attorney doing an asset search on you. It would behoove you to ask the county recorder's office what they will need before you try to transfer your property.

Forms

Once completed, these documents should be placed into your Records Book!

Resolution For Authorized Signatory
This document proves that you are the authorized signatory for your entity.

Resolution For Purchase Of Real Property
This document proves that your entity has approved the purchase of the property.

Resolution To Sell Real Property
This document proves that your entity has approved the sale of the property.

Real Estate Purchase Service Agreement
A lender may want a copy of this agreement (and possibly the Declaration of Beneficial Interest) in order to accept the transfer of title from you to your entity without activating the "due on sale clause" (aka 'loan acceleration') found in most mortgages.

Declaration of Beneficial Interest
This document is your notarized statement that you own your entity. Only provide a copy of this document when absolutely required to do so.

Additional Documents
Should you need additional documents such as a 'Promissory Note' or 'Assignment' they can be found in our publication entitled 'Operations Manual' available through My Biz Publishing at AssetProtectionServices.com.

When you are ready to record the transfer of the property to your controlled entity, take the above completed documents to the Recorders Office in the county where the property is located. File the State transfer forms and provide any additional forms required. Then create the insurance letter and lender letter contained herein and, when the transfer is completed, mail the respective letters to your insurance company and lender. Your lender may ask for supporting documentation to prove that you are still the owner of the property.

If you have not already done so, open a bank account for your entity (not applicable for land trusts, as land trusts are not entities). From this account start paying the bills relating to the property. This would also include paying the mortgage payments, insurance and/or property taxes. Remember too that all the expenses that you incurred in structuring your entities and paying for transferring the property should be reimbursed to you upon you providing receipts to your controlled entity. You can find more information regarding reimbursement in the Real Estate Purchase Service Agreement that can be found in our publication entitled 'Operations Manual' available through My Biz Publishing at AssetProtectionServices.com.

State Specific Documents

Many states have specific documentation requirements for filing the transfer of property to a controlled entity beyond simply filing a deed. However most all states allow a transfer of real property to be tax-free when you transfer it to a controlled entity. We are unable to include such state specific documentation in this publication as it differs from one state to the next. Should you desire assistance transferring property to your controlled entity in any state, please undertake the following and then contact our offices:

Step 1 Contact a title company or the county recorder's office in the state where the property is located and request a copy of the state approved title-transferring documents. In most states this would be a Grant Deed, Warrantee Deed and/or a Quit Claim Deed.

Step 2 While talking to the county recorder's office in the state where the property is located, request a copy of the state's transfer tax exemptions list. Explain to them that this transfer is from you as an individual to an entity that is wholly-owned by you. In other words you are only changing the name on the title. You will still own the property because you own the entity that is to be named as the owner on the new title.

Step 3 While talking to the county recorder's office in the state where the property is located, ask them to tell you the appropriate code section in their state statutes where the property transfer tax exemptions can be found. In addition, request a copy of all the forms (or at least the form numbers) that are required to claim the exemption.

When all of the aforementioned information is received, we will be able to assist you.

This Document Was Prepared by:

_____
_____
_____

After Recording Please Return to:

_____
_____
_____
_____

This Space Reserved for Recording Purposes

GRANT DEED

Assessor's Parcel Number (APN): _____

The full value of the interest in the property conveyed is _____
dollars ($ _____).

The full value, less the value of any liens and/or encumbrances remaining at the time of sale is
_____ dollars ($ _____).

WITNESSETH, this transfer is one in which the proportional interest remains the same. The property is situate and being in the County of _____, State of _____, described as follows (enter legal description): also known as street and number
_____ with Tax Parcel ID#_____.

For a valuable consideration, receipt of which is hereby acknowledged, the current title holder
_____ **HEREBY GRANTS** _____ a
(Name of State) (Type of Entity) the following real property located at _____, the which legal description for which is found on the attached document entitled "EXHIBIT A".

(Attach the legal description from your current deed on a separate page)

IN WITNESS WHEREOF, I/We have hereunto set my hand/our hands on this the _____ day of _____, 20___.

_____
Printed Name

_____
Signature

_____
Printed Name

_____
Signature

GRANT DEED

NOTARY ACKNOWLEDGEMENT

STATE OF _____)

) SS.

COUNTY OF _____)

On _____ before me, _____

(insert name and title of the officer)

personally appeared _____, who proved to me on the basis of satisfactory evidence to be the person(s) whose name(s) is are subscribed to the within instrument and acknowledged to me that he/she/they executed the same in his/her/their authorized capacity(ies), and that by his/her/their signature(s) on the instrument the person(s), or the entity upon behalf of which the person(s) acted, executed the instrument.

I certify under PENALTY OF PERJURY under the laws of the State of _____ that the foregoing paragraph is true and correct.

WITNESS my hand and official seal.

_____

Notary Public Signature

- -

INSTRUCTIONS FOR COMPLETING THE GRANT DEED

The Assessor's Parcel Number (APN) can be found on another deed, tax coupon or deed of trust, etc. You can call the county assessor's office for this information too.

The Legal Description of a property being granted can be found on a tax coupon or another deed.

This Document Was Prepared by:

_____

_____

_____

After Recording Please Return to:

_____

_____

_____

This Space Reserved for Recording Purposes

GRANT, BARGAIN AND SALE DEED

Assessor's Parcel Number (APN): _____

Return Preparation Utility (RPU): _____

THIS INDENTURE WITNESS that _____ and _____ (Hereinafter called Grantors) in consideration of _____ dollars ($ _____), the receipt of which is hereby acknowledged, do hereby GRANT, BARGAIN, SALE and CONVEY to:_____ and _____ (Hereinafter called Grantees) all that real property situated in the City of _____ County of _____ State of _____ bounded and described as follows (enter legal description): also known as street and number _____ with Tax Parcel ID#_____. Together with all and singular hereditament and appurtenances thereunto belonging or in any way appertaining to.

IN WITNESS WHEREOF, I/We have hereunto set my hand/our hands on this the _____ day of _____, 20___.

_____

Signature of Grantor

_____

Signature of Grantor

GRANT, BARGAIN AND SALE DEED

NOTARY ACKNOWLEDGEMENT

STATE OF _____)

) SS.

COUNTY OF _____)

On _____ before me, _____

(insert name and title of the officer)

personally appeared _____, who proved to me on the basis of satisfactory evidence to be the person(s) whose name(s) is are subscribed to the within instrument and acknowledged to me that he/she/they executed the same in his/her/their authorized capacity(ies), and that by his/her/their signature(s) on the instrument the person(s), or the entity upon behalf of which the person(s) acted, executed the instrument.

I certify under PENALTY OF PERJURY under the laws of the State of _____ that the foregoing paragraph is true and correct.

WITNESS my hand and official seal.

_____

Notary Public Signature

INSTRUCTIONS FOR COMPLETING THE
GRANT, BARGAIN, AND SALE DEED

The Assessor's Parcel Number (APN) can be found on another deed, tax coupon or deed of trust, etc. You can call the county assessor's office for this information too.

The Return Preparation Utility (RPU) is the transfer tax exemption number (determined by declaration of value form. Certain transfers are exempt from a transfer tax per Nevada revised statutes (NRS 375.090). This is not property taxes.

The Legal Description of a property being granted can be found on a tax coupon or another deed.

QUITCLAIM DEED

THIS QUITCLAIM DEED, Executed on this the _____ day of _____, 20___, by and between _____ (hereinafter 'First Party) whose address is _____ to _____ (hereinafter 'Second Party) whose address is _____.

WITNESSETH, that the said First Party, for good consideration and for the sum of $_____ Dollars ($_____) paid by the said Second Party, the receipt whereof is hereby acknowledged, does hereby remise, release and quitclaim unto the said second party forever, all the right, title, interest and claim which the said First Party has in and to the following described property, parcel of land, and improvements and appurtenances thereto in the County of _____, State of_____, to wit:

IN WITNESS WHEREOF, The said First Party has signed and sealed these presents the day and year first above written.   Signed, sealed and delivered:

_____   _____
First Party   Second Party

NOTARY ACKNOWLEDGEMENT

STATE OF _____   )
) SS.
COUNTY OF _____   )

On _____ before me, _____
                                                            (insert name and title of the officer)

personally appeared _____, who proved to me on the basis of satisfactory evidence to be the person(s) whose name(s) is are subscribed to the within instrument and acknowledged to me that he/she/they executed the same in his/her/their authorized capacity(ies), and that by his/her/their signature(s) on the instrument the person(s), or the entity upon behalf of which the person(s) acted, executed the instrument.

I certify under PENALTY OF PERJURY under the laws of the State of _____ that the foregoing paragraph is true and correct.

                                                            WITNESS my hand and official seal.

                                        _____
                                        Notary Public Signature

This Document Was Prepared by:

_____
_____
_____

After Recording Please Return to:

_____
_____
_____
_____

This Space Reserved for Recording Purposes

WARRANTY DEED

THIS DEED, made on this the _____ day of _____, 20___ by and between _____ the grantor, and _____ the grantee, whose address is _____.

WITNESSETH, that the grantor, for and in consideration of the sum of _____ Dollars ($_____), the receipt and sufficiency of which is hereby acknowledged and received, and for other good and valuable consideration, has granted, bargained sold and conveyed, and by these presents does grant, bargain sell, convey and confirm unto the grantee, their heirs and assigns forever, all the real property, together with improvements, if any, situate and being in the County of _____, State of _____, described as follows (enter legal description): also known as street and number _____ with Tax Parcel ID#_____.

TOGETHER with all and singular hereditaments and appurtenances thereunto belonging, or in anywise appertaining and the reversion and reversions, remainder and remainders, rents, issues, and profits thereof, and all the estate, right, title, interest, claim and demand whatsoever of the said grantor, either in law or equity, of, in and to the above bargained premises, with the hereditaments and appurtenances.

TO HAVE AND TO HOLD the said premises above bargained and described, with the appurtenances, unto the said grantee, their heirs and assigns forever. And the said grantor, for himself, his heirs, and personal representatives, does covenant, grant bargain and agree to and with the grantee, their heirs and assigns, that at the time of the ensealing and delivery of these presents, is well seized of the premises above conveyed, has good, sure, perfect, absolute indefeasible estate if inheritance, in law, in fee simple, and has good right, full power and lawful authority to grant, bargain, sell and convey the same in manner and form aforesaid, and that the same are free and clear from all former and other grants, bargains, sales, liens, taxes, assessments, encumbrances and restrictions of any kind or nature whatsoever, except

_____.

The grantor shall and will **WARRANT AND FOREVER DEFEND** the above bargained premises in the quiet and peaceable possession of the grantee, his heirs, and assigns, against all and every person or persons lawfully claiming the whole or any part thereof. The singular shall include the plural, the plural shall include the singular, and the use of any gender shall be applicable to all genders.

IN WITNESS WHEREOF, the grantor has executed this deed on the date set forth above.

_____   _____
Grantor   Grantor

NOTARY ACKNOWLEDGEMENT

STATE OF _____)
) SS.
COUNTY OF _____)

On _____ before me, _____
                                                                  (insert name and title of the officer)

personally appeared _____, who proved to me on the basis of satisfactory evidence to be the person(s) whose name(s) is are subscribed to the within instrument and acknowledged to me that he/she/they executed the same in his/her/their authorized capacity(ies), and that by his/her/their signature(s) on the instrument the person(s), or the entity upon behalf of which the person(s) acted, executed the instrument.

I certify under PENALTY OF PERJURY under the laws of the State of _____ that the foregoing paragraph is true and correct.

WITNESS my hand and official seal.

_____
Notary Public Signature

Real Estate Forms

'AS-IS' ADDENDUM TO CONTRACT
(Short Form)

In reference to a contract and agreement dated on the _____ day of _____, 20___ by and between _____ as Buyer(s) and _____ as Seller(s), it is further agreed as follows:

The property that is being transferred is located at:

_____

_____

And is being done so in an "As-Is" / "Where-Is" condition. There are no warranties, guarantees or any obligations being given by the Seller(s) to repair any defects. Further Seller(s) state(s) that he/she/they have never lived in the property and can only rely on the previous Owner's disclosures which have been given to the Buyer(s), if available.

Buyer accepts this property in the condition in which it exists as of the date shown above and fully agrees with the statements made above by affixing his/her/their signature(s) below.

This addendum, upon signing by all parties involved in the transaction, is herewith made an integral part of the original contract and agreement.

Date: _____/____/20___

_____   _____
Buyer - Printed Name   Signature

Date: _____/____/20___

_____   _____
Buyer - Printed Name   Signature

ADDENDUM FOR THE
ASSIGNMENT OF A LAND CONTRACT
FOR SELLER / OPTIONOR

This Addendum is for the assignment of an agreement dated on the _____ day of _____, 20___ between _____ (Hereby "Assignor") and _____ (Hereby "Assignee") which has been exercised as an assignment of the Land Contract agreement between Assignor and _____ (Hereby "Seller") for the property located at:

_____

_____

Seller fully acknowledges and accepts this assignment and further agrees to in no way hold Assignor responsible for any obligations, payments or conditions for any reason written or verbal whatsoever.

Seller also agrees that Assignor is acting as a principle in this acquisition and is not a licensed realtor, real estate broker, mortgage broker or attorney and no claims stating otherwise have been made.

Seller hereby accepts that the assignment fee paid to assignor by assignee shall be credited in full towards the purchase price as down payment as specified in the Land Contract Agreements.

Assignee hereby acknowledges Seller's acceptance to this assignment and its terms herein.

_____   Date:_____
Seller

_____   Date:_____
Assignor

_____   Date:_____
Assignee

ADDENDUM TO CONTRACT OF SALE

Company Name Here
Company Address Here
Company City, State & Zip Here
Phone Here
Fax Here

Disclosure, Hold Harmless and "As Is" / "Where Is" Addendum

The property that is being purchased is located at:

_____

_____

On this the _____ day of _____, 20___, The undersigned Buyer acknowledges that he/she/it is purchasing the above named property in its **"EXISTING CONDITION", WITHOUT REPRESENTATION OR WARRANTIES OF ANY KIND OR NATURE**.

Buyer further acknowledges on behalf of buyer and buyer's successors, heirs and assignees, that buyer has been given a reasonable opportunity to inspect and investigate the property and all improvements thereon, either independently or through agents of buyer's choosing at buyer's expense and that in purchasing the property, Buyer is not relying on Seller or Seller's Agent, as to the condition of the property and/or any improvements thereon, including but not necessarily limited to,

All existing window coverings, floor coverings, electrical, plumbing, heating, sewage, septic, roof, foundation, soils and geology, lot size or suitability of the property and/or its improvements for any particular purposes, or that the improvements are structurally sound and/or in compliance with any city, county, state and/or federal codes or ordinances.

Additionally, Buyer acknowledges that the Seller makes no promises, guarantees, representations or warranties, either expressed or implied, as to the present or future market value of the subject property, encroachments, easements or profitability nor the presence or absence of any hazardous or toxic substances or contamination including but not limited to:

Radon, lead, electromagnetic radiation, mold, mildew, microscopic organisms, lead paint, fuel oil, allergens or asbestos, whether known or unknown and whether or not such defects or conditions were discoverable through inspection.

Buyer and Seller both waive the right to Seller's disclosure form, if applicable.

Seller does not warrant existing structure as to its habitability or suitability for occupancy. Buyer (s) assumes responsibility to check the appropriate planning authority for intended use and holds Seller and broker harmless as to the suitability for Buyer (s) intended use.

Buyer(s) further states that they are relying solely upon their own inspections of the subject property and not upon any representation made to them by any person whomsoever, and is purchasing the subject property in the condition in which it now currently listed, without any obligation on the part of the Seller to make any changes, alterations, repairs or future obligations of any nature whatsoever.

Any report (s) that is required by the Buyer's Lender is to be the sole responsibility of the Buyer. Buyer shall neither make nor cause to be made: (i) invasive or destructive investigations; or (ii) inspections by any governmental building or zoning inspector or government employee, unless required by Law. Buyer is not allowed to perform order or otherwise cause any repair (s) and/or work to be done on the property prior to closing.

When visiting or inspecting the property, Buyer's and Buyer's Representative (s) enter the premises at their own risk, and Seller shall not be liable for any injuries, or damage suffered or incurred, to any Buyer's or Buyer's Representative (s) person or personal property, as a result of such entry.

The undersigned, Buyer, acting personally and for his/her/their representatives, affiliates and or organization if any each hereby agrees to defend, indemnify, and hold harmless Sellers, and any affiliate and all employees, officers and directors from and against any and all claims, demands, suits, actions, damages, judgments, cost, charges and expenses including, without limitation, court cost and attorneys fees, of any nature whatsoever that any such, Buyer and or their affiliate, representative or organization may suffer, sustain or incur resulting from, arising out of or in any way connected with any action taken by, or inaction on the part of, any Buyer or their affiliate, representative or organization in connection with this transaction.

Information given to the Buyer may not have been verified by the Seller and is not guaranteed to be accurate. Therefore, Buyer should not rely on such information in deciding to purchase property. It is the Buyers responsibility to conduct his/her/its own inspections to verify any information, including square footage, provided to him. ***Should the Buyer rely on advice or representations made by Seller in deciding to purchase said property, Buyer is doing so at his/her/its own risk.***

It is the policy of the Seller to make no promises, guarantees, representations or warranties, either expressed or implied. If any expressed or implied promises, guarantees, representations or warranties were made, they should be disregarded.

If the property was built before 1978, the Buyer acknowledges receipt of a lead based paint brochure and disclosure available on the Internet and must sign and attach the lead based paint disclosure as part of this contract and addendum.

Seller recommends that Purchaser obtain a survey and plat of the property.

BUYER

_____	_____
[Authorized Signatory]	[Print Name]
_____	_____
[Authorized Signatory]	[Print Name]

ADDENDUM TO PURCHASE AGREEMENT
EXHIBIT A

Addendum to Purchase Agreement pertaining to the purchase and sale of the property at:

_____

_____

A.)   All parties expressly understand that this property is being sold "as is". As a stipulation of this agreement, seller will under no circumstances be held liable or responsible to repair or replace any item(s) located on the inside, outside, or near the subject property.

B.)   All parties expressly understand that this real estate sales contract is contingent upon final inspection of the subject property by buyer and/or buyer's agent.

1.)   The inspection shall be done within 10 business days of final acceptance of this Purchase Agreement. If Buyer or anyone representing Buyer discovers any unacceptable defects relating to the property and/or its structures, Buyer must notify Seller or Seller's agent in writing, describing such defects within 5 business days after the inspection.

2.)   If Buyer fails to have the inspection performed, or does not notify Seller within time specified above, this contingency shall be deemed removed and the Purchase Agreement shall be in full force and effect.

SELLER

Dated _____/_____/20____

_____   _____
[Signature of authorized Signatory]   [Print Name]

BUYER

Dated _____/_____/20____

_____   _____
[Signature of authorized Signatory]   [Print Name]

ADDENDUM TO PURCHASE AGREEMENT
EXHIBIT B

Addendum to Purchase Agreement pertaining to the purchase and sale of the property located at:

_____

_____

Regarding the attached Purchase Agreement pertaining to the agreement(s) between all parties involved: Any/all typewritten or handwritten provisions contained within this addendum shall control all printed provisions of any part of the attached contract. Also, all handwritten items must be initialed by all parties involved.

The following items are hereby added to the Agreement:

_____

_____

_____

_____

_____

SELLER

Dated _____/_____/20____

_____   _____
[Signature of authorized Signatory]   [Print Name]

_____   _____
[Signature of authorized Signatory]   [Print Name]

BUYER

Dated _____/_____/20____

_____   _____
[Signature of authorized Signatory]   [Print Name]

_____   _____
[Signature of authorized Signatory]   [Print Name]

AGREEMENT AND ADDENDUM FOR SALE OF REAL ESTATE

Concerning Sale of Property, to wit:

To: _____

Date _____ 20___

I have been made aware that the loan on the property I am purchasing contains a due on sale clause, which means the lender may call the loan due upon transfer of the property to me.

I agree if this should happen it would be my responsibility to either assume the loan or pay it off. If I am unable to do either or make other arrangements with the lender I may lose the house to foreclosure.

I understand that if I do not make timely payments that the property I am purchasing could go into default. If this should happen, I can cure the defaulted payments and all amounts will first be applied to my default, and then will be applied to the purchase price of the property, less any late charges or fees. I also understand, that I am purchasing the property "AS-IS". I am responsible for any and all repairs. If any single repair exceeds $_____, I will inform the seller in writing who shall be given the opportunity to arrange for the repair. Seller would be responsible for any amount over $_____. Buyer(s) must pay up to this amount directly to the repair person/supplier at the time of purchase or repair. As the future purchases of the property, Buyer(s) further waive any right they may have under repair provisions under applicable _____ law regarding the landlord being responsible for all repairs.

If this should happen I will hold the seller harmless for any loss, which may occur.

_____   _____   _____
Signature   Printed Name   Date

_____   _____   _____
Signature   Printed Name   Date

APPLICATION FOR RENTAL-LEASE
(Must be completed by each adult applicant intending to reside in the property)

All Potential Applicants Are Evaluated Without Regard To Race, Color, Religion, Gender, National Origin, Age, Marital Or Veteran Status. The Presence Of A Non-Job Related Handicap Or Any Other Legally Protected Status.

Credit Application for Address:

_____

_____

How did you learn about the property? _____

Applicant Information

Name _____

Address _____

_____

Phone: Day (_____) _____ - _____   Evening (_____) _____ - _____

Email: _____

Social Security Number: _____ / ____ / _____   DOB: _____ / _____ / _____

Drivers License #: _____   State of Issuance: _____

Vehicle #1   [ ] Personal   [ ] Work
License Plate #: _____ Year _____ Make _____ Model _____
Do you own the vehicle outright?   [ ] Yes   [ ] No
If no, what are your monthly payments? $_____

Vehicle #2   [ ] Personal   [ ] Work
License Plate #: _____ Year _____ Make _____ Model _____
Do you own the vehicle outright?   [ ] Yes   [ ] No
If no, what are your monthly payments? $_____

On what date would you be available to move in?   _____ / _____ / 20___
Desired Rental \ Lease Amount $_____

Are you a U.S. citizen or authorized to work in the U.S.?   [ ] Yes   [ ] No

Have you ever been convicted of a felony?   [ ] Yes   [ ] No
If yes, please explain:_____
Have you ever been evicted from a property?   [ ] Yes   [ ] No
If yes, please explain:_____
Have you ever filed for bankruptcy?   [ ] Yes   [ ] No
If yes, when? _____
If approved, are you willing to submit to a drug-screening test?   [ ] Yes   [ ] No
If approved, are you willing to submit to a criminal & background check?   [ ] Yes   [ ] No

Previous Addresses for Last 5 Years
(Complete Address)

1. Address:_____
   City:_____ State:_____ Zip:_____
   How Long At This Address?   _____ Years _____ Months
   What was your Rent-Lease Payment: $ _____
   Why did You Move: _____
   Landlord's Name:_____
   Landlord's Phone #: (_____) _____ - _____ Ext. #_____
   E-Mail: _____
   May We Contact the Landlord: [ ] Yes   [ ] No

2. Address:_____
   City:_____ State:_____ Zip:_____
   How Long At This Address?   _____ Years _____ Months
   What was your Rent-Lease Payment: $ _____
   Why did You Move: _____
   Landlord's Name:_____
   Landlord's Phone #: (_____) _____ - _____ Ext. #_____
   E-Mail: _____
   May We Contact the Landlord: [ ] Yes   [ ] No

3. Address:_____
   City:_____ State:_____ Zip:_____
   How Long At This Address?   _____ Years _____ Months
   What was your Rent-Lease Payment: $ _____
   Why did You Move: _____
   Landlord's Name:_____
   Landlord's Phone #: (_____) _____ - _____ Ext. #_____
   E-Mail: _____
   May We Contact the Landlord: [ ] Yes   [ ] No

Employment
(Most Recent First)

Employer _____

Address _____ City _____

State _____ Zip _____ Phone (_____)_____

Job Title _____ Supervisor _____

Start Date _____/_____/_____ Ending Date _____/_____/_____

Starting Salary $ _____ Ending Salary $ _____

Special Skills or Responsibilities:_____

Reason for Leaving:_____

Manager's Name:_____

Manager's Phone #: (_____) _____ - _____ Ext. #_____

E-Mail: _____

May We Contact the Manager: [ ] Yes   [ ] No

Employer _____

Address _____ City _____

State _____ Zip _____ Phone (_____)_____

Job Title _____ Supervisor _____

Start Date _____/_____/_____ Ending Date _____/_____/_____

Starting Salary $ _____ Ending Salary $ _____

Special Skills or Responsibilities:_____

Reason for Leaving:_____

Manager's Name:_____

Manager's Phone #: (_____) _____ - _____ Ext. #_____

E-Mail: _____

May We Contact the Manager: [ ] Yes   [ ] No

Employer _____

Address _____ City _____

State _____ Zip _____ Phone (_____)_____

Job Title _____ Supervisor _____

Start Date _____/_____/_____ Ending Date _____/_____/_____

Starting Salary $ _____ Ending Salary $ _____

Special Skills or Responsibilities:_____

Reason for Leaving:_____

Manager's Name:_____

Manager's Phone #: (_____) _____ - _____ Ext. #_____

E-Mail: _____

May We Contact the Manager: [ ] Yes   [ ] No

Debts and Income

Do you pay alimony or child support?   [ ] Yes   [ ] No $_____

Do you receive ANY other monthly income?   [ ] Yes   [ ] No $_____

Are you interested in purchasing a home?   [ ] Yes   [ ] No $_____

Bank Reference

Bank Name _____   [ ] Checking   [ ] Savings

Bank Branch Address: _____

Bank Branch Contact Person: _____   Phone #: (_____) _____ - _____

Credit Information

Creditor Name _____   [ ] Credit Card   [ ] Loan

Account Number:_____   Type of Debt _____

Names of People Who Will Be Living At This Address

Name _____   Age _____   Relationship _____

Name _____   Age _____   Relationship _____

Name _____   Age _____   Relationship _____

Name _____   Age _____   Relationship _____

Do You Have Any Pets?

Name _____   Age _____   [ ] Dog   [ ] Cat

Name _____   Age _____   [ ] Dog   [ ] Cat

Personal References

1. Name: _____   Years Known: _____

    Phone: (_____) _____ - _____   E-Mail: _____

2. Name: _____   Years Known: _____

    Phone: (_____) _____ - _____   E-Mail: _____

Emergency Contact

1. Name: _____   Relationship: _____

    Phone: (_____) _____ - _____   E-Mail: _____

Acknowledgment and Authorization

I certify that answers given herein are true and complete to the best of my knowledge. I authorize investigation of all statements contained in this application for rental or lease as may be necessary in arriving at a tenant decision.

This application for rental or lease shall be considered active for a period-of-time not to exceed 45 days. Any applicant wishing to be considered for rental or lease beyond this time-period should inquire as to whether or not applications are being accepted at that time.

I hereby understand and acknowledge that, unless otherwise defined by applicable law, any tenant relationship with this company is of an "at will" nature, which means that the Tenant may terminate tenancy at any time with a 30 day written notice. The Landlord may terminate Tenant at any time with cause, or at any time without cause and a 30-day written notice.

Any security deposit and cleaning deposit will be considered for refund after final inspection and keys have been turned in. Any refund will be based upon duration of tenancy, condition of property and a full decision of the Landlord.

In the event of tenancy, I understand that false or misleading information given in my application or interview(s) may result in cancellation. I understand, also, that I am required to abide by all terms and conditions of the Landlord including any rules and regulations for the property.

_____
Signature of Applicant

_____
Applicant's Printed Full Name

_____
Today's Date

NON-REFUNDABLE CREDIT CHECKING FEE OF $_____
IS DUE AT THE TIME THE RENTAL APPLICATION IS FILED

I/We hereby authorize _____ or their assigns and/or any Credit Information Services company to obtain information concerning my banking, past credit, and/or tenant-landlord history now or at anytime in the future. I hereby authorize any sources including but not limited to banks, landlords, current or past creditors, governmental agencies, and/or other credit reporting agencies to release any information to the above named person/entity or their assigns and/or any Credit Information Services company concerning me. Further, I hereby release any of the above sources, their officers, agents, or employees from any liability or damages of whatsoever kind or nature by reason of their compliance with the above mentioned inquiry which may include the answering of specific questions and the giving of any information concerning my past records.

I HAVE READ THE ABOVE AND I AM IN COMPLETE AGREEMENT WITH IT.

_____
Signature of Applicant

_____
Applicant's Printed Full Name

_____
Today's Date

THIS SECTION FOR INTERVIEWER

Credit: [ ] Favorable   [ ] Unfavorable   [ ] Other:_____

Comments: _____

Deposit: $_____   Monthly Rent: $_____   Option: $_____

Term of Lease: _____ in Months   Option to Renew: [ ] Yes   [ ] No

Move in Date: _____/____/20___   Lease Expires: _____/____/20___

Total number of Occupants: _____ Adults _____ Children _____Pets

APPLICATION FEE RECEIPT

An application fee of $25.00 will be charged to each prospective tenant wanting to complete a rental application. This fee will cover the cost of processing and initiating a credit check. The amount is non-refundable, should the prospective tenant withdraw their application.

Should a rental agreement not be completed because of **undisclosed** credit or past landlord problems, the $25.00 application fee is non-refundable.

_____
(Authorized Signature)

_____
Applicant

_____
Applicant

I would like to disclose any potential credit problems that may be revealed through a normal credit check and provide a short explanation. I understand this disclosure is optional and I am providing information voluntarily to aid the application process.

_____
_____
_____
_____
_____
_____
_____
_____
_____
_____
_____
_____
_____
_____
_____

_____
Applicant

_____
Applicant

ASSIGNMENT AGREEMENT
Assignment of Cooperative Option

This Assignment agreement is for the property located at:

_____

_____

This agreement, made and entered into this _____ day of _____, 20___, by: _____ (hereinafter "Assignor") the original buyer/optionee under the agreement dated this _____ day of _____, 20___, (hereinafter "Agreement") hereby assigns all right, title and interest of said agreement to _____ (hereinafter "Assignee") for the sum and consideration of: $_____ ($_____)

Assignee agrees to perform all covenants, conditions, and obligations required by Assignor under the aforementioned Agreements and furthermore agree to indemnify, defend and hold Assignor harmless from any liabilities, restrictions or obligations under said Agreements. Assignee further agrees to hold Assignor harmless from any deficiencies or defects in the legality or enforceability of the terms of said Agreements.

Assignor _____ Date: _____

Assignee _____ Date: _____

ASSIGNMENT AGREEMENT
Land Contract Assignment

This Assignment agreement is for the property located at:

_____

_____

This agreement hereby enforces an assignment of the Land Contract agreements (hereinafter "Agreements") dated on the _____ day of _____, 20___ between _____ (hereinafter, "Assignor"), the original Buyer and _____ (hereinafter, "Seller"). Assignor hereby assigns all of their rights, title and interest to _____, (hereinafter, "Assignee"), for the sum and consideration of _____ ($_____).

Assignee agrees to perform all covenants, conditions, and obligations required by Assignor under the aforementioned Agreements and furthermore agree to indemnify, defend and hold Assignor harmless from any liabilities, restrictions or obligations under said Agreements. Assignee further agrees to hold Assignor harmless from any deficiencies or defects in the legality or enforceability of the terms of said Agreements.

Assignor _____ Date: _____

Assignee _____ Date: _____

ASSIGNMENT AGREEMENT
Lease Option Assignment

This assignment agreement is for the property located at:

_____

_____

This Agreement hereby enforces an assignment of the lease with option to purchase agreements (hereinafter "Agreements") dated on the _____ day of _____, 20___ between _____ (hereinafter, "Assignor"), the original Tenant / Buyer / Optionee and _____(hereinafter, "Seller / Optionor"). Assignor hereby assigns all of their rights, title and interest to _____, (hereinafter, "Assignee"), for the sum and consideration of $_____ ($_____).

Assignee agrees to perform all covenants, conditions, and obligations required by Assignor under the aforementioned Agreements and furthermore agree to indemnify, defend and hold Assignor harmless from any liabilities, restrictions or obligations under said Agreements. Assignee further agrees to hold Assignor harmless from any deficiencies or defects in the legality or enforceability of the terms of said Agreements.

Assignor _____ Date: _____

Assignee _____ Date: _____

ASSIGNMENT OF BENEFICIAL INTEREST IN TRUST

The undersigned ("Assignor"), for $_____ received in hand and other valuable consideration received, hereby assigns all rights, title and interest in the beneficial interest, including the power of direction and revocation, under a certain Trust Agreement created the _____ day of _____, 20___ by and between _____ _____, as Grantor(s)/Settlor(s) and _____, as Trustee(s) known as the _____Trust", which owns title to certain real property located at _____ in the County of _____ State of _____ to _____, ("Assignee") whose address is _____.

I/We hereby affirm and warrant that the beneficial interest assigned herein is 100% of the total beneficial interest in the aforesaid Trust, and that I/We have the full power and authority to assign and transfer said interest. I/We further agree to waive any right to revoke or amend said trust or in any way to direct, influence or control the actions of the trustee(s) which would create an ownership interest as defined in Section 671-678 of the Internal Revenue Code.   I/We intend this transfer to be a transfer of real estate for federal income tax purposes, and we agree to report the same to the Internal Revenue Service. I/We further understand that if the real property held in trust is encumbered by a security instrument containing a "due-on-sale" provision, that this assignment may violate said security instrument, giving the holder of said security instrument the right to call any underlying debt due and payable.

_____   _____
Assignor   Assignor

ASSIGNMENT OF BENEFICIAL INTEREST IN TRUST

NOTARY ACKNOWLEDGEMENT

STATE OF _____)

) SS.

COUNTY OF _____)

On _____ before me, _____

(insert name and title of the officer)

personally appeared _____, who proved to me on the basis of satisfactory evidence to be the person(s) whose name(s) is are subscribed to the within instrument and acknowledged to me that he/she/they executed the same in his/her/their authorized capacity(ies), and that by his/her/their signature(s) on the instrument the person(s), or the entity upon behalf of which the person(s) acted, executed the instrument.

I certify under PENALTY OF PERJURY under the laws of the State of _____ that the foregoing paragraph is true and correct.

WITNESS my hand and official seal.

_____

Notary Public Signature

TRUSTEE ACKNOWLEDGEMENT

I have received a copy of this assignment of beneficial interest and acknowledge the validity of said assignment subject to all of the terms and conditions of the trust agreement and addendum thereto.

_____

Trustee

ASSIGNMENT OF CONTRACT / INTEREST

I the undersigned _____ (Assignor) hereby assigns, transfers and/or sells his/her/its Contract/Interest, whether written or verbal in the property located at:

_____

_____

to _____ (Assignee). The assignment fee of $_____ ($_____) is to be paid from proceeds at closing. Assignor has negotiated a purchase price on the above referenced property of $ _____ which is an "as is" / "where is" price with no warranties or guarantees whatsoever. Adding the assignment fee of $ _____, the assignees total purchase price is $_____ plus any inspection fees, repairs, due diligence, and/or closing costs. In addition to the assignment fee, the assignee shall reimburse assignor the deposit amount of $_____ which has already been paid by assignor. This assignment is made with no warranties, guarantees, or claims to condition of property, size, title, or the present or future value of the property and it is the assignees responsibility to perform their own due diligence before closing. This assignment shall survive the closing.

The undersigned agrees that they have the full authority to execute this document personally and/or on behalf of any organization they represent or will represent. By signing, the signatories agree that they have read, understand and have the full power and authority to enter into this legal agreement. The undersigned acknowledges receipt of a copy of this document.

_____   _____   _____
Witness   Assignor   Date

_____   _____   _____
Witness   Assignee   Date

ASSIGNMENT OF
LEASE AGREEMENT AND OPTION TO PURCHASE

THIS ASSIGNMENT OF LEASE AGREEMENT AND OPTION TO PURCHASE is made by and between _____, whose address is _____ (hereinafter called "Assignor") and _____ whose address is _____ (hereinafter called "Assignee").

NOW, THEREFORE, for good and valuable consideration, the sufficiency of which is expressly acknowledged, Assignor and Assignee hereby agree as follows:

1.   ASSIGNMENT OF RIGHTS, INTEREST AND PRIVILEGES: Assignor hereby conveys, transfers and assigns unto Assignee, his/her/its successors and assigns, all the rights, interest and privileges, which the Assignor Possess in the Lease Agreement and Option to Purchase Agreement (*attached hereto and thereby made a part hereto and hereinafter referred to as the "Agreements"*) by and between _____ (as the "Landlord/Optionor"), and Assignor (as the Tenant/Optionee), for the Premises (Property), as defined in the subject Agreements for certain real property lying and situated in the County of _____, and having the street address of _____ City of _____ State of _____ Zip Code _____.

2.   CONSIDERATION: In consideration of this Assignment of the Lease Agreement and Option to Purchase Agreement, the Assignee shall pay Assignor the sum of _____ ($_____) Dollars and hereby shall acquire and assume all of Assignor's rights, interest and privileges as well as Assignor's obligations under the Agreements and further agrees to make all payments of rent relating to the Lease Agreement and to perform and abide by all of the obligations of Assignor in the Agreements attached hereto.

3.   REPRESENTATIONS: Assignor represents and warrants that the Agreements attached hereto including all addenda thereto, have not been modified or amended in any way, nor have they been assigned or encumbered by Assignor to any other party.

4.   ASSIGNEE SHALL PAY ALL LEASE PAYMENTS TO:

_____

Whose address is _____

5. **HOLD HARMLESS**: Assignee shall protect, save and keep Assignor harmless and indemnified against any and all liability, loss, cost, damages, or expenses arising out of any this Assignment.

IN TESTIMONY WHEREOF, the above named parties have executed this Assignment of the Lease Agreement and Option to Purchase Agreement for the above stated Property on this the _____ day of _____, 20___.

<table>
<tr><td align="center">**ASSIGNEE**</td><td align="center">**ASSIGNOR**</td></tr>
<tr><td></td><td></td></tr>
<tr><td>_____</td><td>_____</td></tr>
<tr><td>[Signature of authorized Signatory]</td><td>[Signature of authorized Signatory]</td></tr>
<tr><td></td><td></td></tr>
<tr><td>_____</td><td>_____</td></tr>
<tr><td>[Print Name]</td><td>[Print Name]</td></tr>
</table>

NOTIFICATION OF ASSIGNMENT OF LEASE AND OPTION TO PURCHASE

To: _____ (Hereby "Seller" - Landlord / Optionor).

Whose mailing address is: _____

city _____ state _____ Zip _____

contact Phone (_____) _____ E-mail:_____

This Assignment Notification Addendum dated on the _____ day of _____, 20___, to advise you that _____ (Hereby "Assignor") has exercised its option to assign its rights and obligations in the lease and option to purchase agreements for your property located at:

_____

_____

to _____ (Hereby "Assignee").

1.) Seller agrees that Assignor has been and is acting as a principle in this transaction and is not a licensed realtor, real estate broker, mortgage broker or attorney and no claims stating otherwise have been made.

2.) Said lease and option agreements were previously signed by you as the Seller (Landlord / Optionor) and by _____ as Assignor (Tenant / Optionee). They provide for the un-contested right of Assignor to assign its rights and obligations thereto to a 3rd party Assignee.

3.) Further, in the lease and option agreements you as the Seller (Landlord / Optionor) have agreed that Assignor shall have the un-contested right to receive an assignment fee which shall be paid directly to Assignor by the Assignee.

4.) And lastly, in the lease and option agreements you as the Seller (Landlord / Optionor) have agreed that said fee shall be credited towards the purchase price of the above named property as part of the non-refundable option consideration of Assignee.

ASSIGNOR (Tenant / Optionee)

_____   _____

[Signature of authorized Signatory]   [Print Name]

ACKNOWLEDGED BY ASSIGNEE

_____   _____

[Signature of authorized Signatory]   [Print Name]

ASSIGNMENT OF REAL ESTATE PURCHASE AND SALE AGREEMENT

THIS ASSIGNMENT is made this _____ day of _____, 20___ by
_____ (hereinafter referred to as "Assignor") to
_____ (hereinafter referred to as "Assignee").

WHEREAS, Assignor has entered into a certain Real Estate Purchase and Sale Agreement
with _____ as "Seller" and Assignor as "Buyer" which Agreement was executed
on the _____ day of _____, 20___ by said Assignor and said Seller for the purchase
and sale of certain real property being, lying and situate in _____ County, in the
state of _____ and more particularly described in said Agreement, copy of said
Agreement being attached hereto as Exhibit "A"; and,

WHEREAS, Assignor desires to assign, transfer, sell and convey to Assignee all of Assignor's
right, title and interest in, to and under said Real Estate Purchase and Sale Agreement; and,

WHEREAS, Assignee is desirous of receiving all of Assignor's right, title and interest in, to and
under said Real Estate Purchase and Sale Agreement;

NOW, **THEREFORE**, for and in consideration of the sum of _____ ($_____)
and other good and valuable considerations, the sufficiency of which is hereby acknowledged,
Assignor has assigned, transferred, sold and conveyed and by these presents does hereby
assign, transfer, sell and convey unto Assignee all of Assignor's right, title and interest in, to and
under said Real Estate Purchase and Sale Agreement.

Assignor agrees to receive and Assignee agrees to pay in full said assignment consideration on
or before the closing date of said Real Estate Purchase and Sale Agreement.

This Assignment shall be binding upon Assignor and shall inure to the benefit of Assignee and
its successors, heirs and assigns.

Assignee hereby assumes all of Assignor's duties and obligations under said Real Estate
Purchase and Sale Agreement. Assignee agrees to perform all covenants, conditions and
obligations required by Assignor under said Agreement and agrees to defend, indemnify and
hold Assignor harmless from any liability or obligation under said Agreement. Assignee further
agrees to hold Assignor harmless from any deficiency or defect in the legality or enforceability
of the terms of said agreement.

Assignee agrees and understands that Assignor is not acting as a real estate broker or agent in
this transaction and is not representing either party, but rather is acting as a principal in selling
his interest in the above-referenced agreement to Assignee.

Time is of the essence in this agreement.

Assignee is in possession of the original agreement.

_____   _____ / ____ / 20____
                      Assignor   Date

_____   _____ / ____ / 20____
                      Assignee   Date

BUYER FORM

Buyer Name: _____

Address: _____

City: _____ State: _____ Zip: _____

Home Phone   (_____) _____   Fax   (_____) _____

Mobile Phone   (_____) _____   Other   (_____) _____

Email: _____   Website: _____

Property Desired

Price Range: From $_____   to $ _____

Bedrooms ____   Baths: ____   Square Feet: _____

Location Desired:_____

Other Desires: _____

How Much Cash Do You Have For Down Payment: $ _____

What Types of Properties are You Interested in Purchasing?

_____ Single Family Homes
_____ Condos
_____ Foreclosures
_____ Pre-Foreclosures
_____ Other _____

What Constitutes a Good Deal for You?

_____ % of value (_____%)
_____ minimum profit ($_____)
_____ minimum cash flow ($_____)
_____ Other _____

How Quickly Can You Close?

_____ 0-3 weeks
_____ 4-5 weeks
_____ 6-10 weeks
_____ Other _____

Type of financing available to you?

_____ Pre-Qualified loan
_____ Private lender
_____ Your Own Cash
_____ Other _____

Comments and/or Questions

_____

_____

_____

_____

_____

_____

_____

Notes

CALIFORNIA NOTARY ACKNOWLEDGMENT

The Notary Acknowledgment provided by the California Secretary of State is considered to be a 'perfected' notary acknowledgement and widely accepted by all 50 states. Therefore, this is the notary acknowledgment we have elected to use on all our documentation, as taken directly from the California Secretary of State Website:

http://www.sos.ca.gov/business/notary/forms/notary_ack.pdf

ACKNOWLEDGMENT

State of California
County of _____)

On _____ before me, _____
(insert name and title of the officer)

personally appeared _____,
who proved to me on the basis of satisfactory evidence to be the person(s) whose name(s) is/are subscribed to the within instrument and acknowledged to me that he/she/they executed the same in his/her/their authorized capacity(ies), and that by his/her/their signature(s) on the instrument the person(s), or the entity upon behalf of which the person(s) acted, executed the instrument.

I certify under PENALTY OF PERJURY under the laws of the State of California that the foregoing paragraph is true and correct.

WITNESS my hand and official seal.

Signature _____ **(Seal)**

Capital Improvements
(Always keep receipts for your records)

The following list are examples of capital improvements from IRS Publication 523 which can increase the basis of your home and are considered tax deductible expenses against your taxable gains.

Improvement	Date	Cost
Air Conditioning	____/ ____/ 20___	$_____
Appliances	____/ ____/ 20___	$_____
Bedroom	____/ ____/ 20___	$_____
Bathroom	____/ ____/ 20___	$_____
Carpeting	____/ ____/ 20___	$_____
Deck *(Addition)*	____/ ____/ 20___	$_____
Driveway	____/ ____/ 20___	$_____
Duct Work	____/ ____/ 20___	$_____
Fencing	____/ ____/ 20___	$_____
Filtration System	____/ ____/ 20___	$_____
Flooring	____/ ____/ 20___	$_____
Furnace Duct Work	____/ ____/ 20___	$_____
Garage	____/ ____/ 20___	$_____
Heating System	____/ ____/ 20___	$_____
Hot-Water Heater	____/ ____/ 20___	$_____
Humidifier	____/ ____/ 20___	$_____
Insulation	____/ ____/ 20___	$_____
Kitchen	____/ ____/ 20___	$_____

Landscaping _____ _____ / _____ / 20___ $_____

Patio / Porch _____ _____ / _____ / 20___ $_____

Piping _____ _____ / _____ / 20___ $_____

Retaining Wall _____ _____ / _____ / 20___ $_____

Roofing _____ _____ / _____ / 20___ $_____

Security System _____ _____ / _____ / 20___ $_____

Septic System _____ _____ / _____ / 20___ $_____

Soft-Water System _____ _____ / _____ / 20___ $_____

Sprinkler System _____ _____ / _____ / 20___ $_____

Storm Doors _____ _____ / _____ / 20___ $_____

Storm Windows _____ _____ / _____ / 20___ $_____

Swimming Pool _____ _____ / _____ / 20___ $_____

Vacuum (Central) _____ _____ / _____ / 20___ $_____

Walkway _____ _____ / _____ / 20___ $_____

Wiring _____ _____ / _____ / 20___ $_____

_____ _____ _____ / _____ / 20___ $_____

_____ _____ _____ / _____ / 20___ $_____

_____ _____ _____ / _____ / 20___ $_____

_____ _____ _____ / _____ / 20___ $_____

_____ _____ _____ / _____ / 20___ $_____

DECLARATION OF BENEFICIAL INTEREST
FOR
(Replace This With The Name Of Your Corp)
A *(Name of State) (Type of Entity)*

I/We the undersigned as the actual holders of all the beneficial Interest (ownership) in the above named entity (in good standing), hereby declare and say that;

All of the actual beneficial interest in the stock, and assets as well as all rights, powers, privileges and/or control over the day-to-day operations of said entity are held by the undersigned individual(s) *only*; and, The undersigned states that they fully understand their legal rights and obligations in connection herewith and that having understood the rights and obligations detailed herein, has executed this instrument on the _____ day of _____, 20___.

Beneficial Interest Holder Signature: *(**Sign Your Name Here**)*
Printed Name: *(**Type In Your Name Here**)*

Beneficial Interest Holder Signature: *(**Second Person Signs Name Here** (if any)*
Printed Name: *(**Type In Second Person's Namer Here** (if any)*

NOTARY ACKNOWLEDGEMENT

STATE OF _____)

) SS.

COUNTY OF _____)

On _____ before me, _____

                                           (insert name and title of the officer)

personally appeared _____, who proved to me on the basis of satisfactory evidence to be the person(s) whose name(s) is are subscribed to the within instrument and acknowledged to me that he/she/they executed the same in his/her/their authorized capacity(ies), and that by his/her/their signature(s) on the instrument the person(s), or the entity upon behalf of which the person(s) acted, executed the instrument.

I certify under PENALTY OF PERJURY under the laws of the State of _____ that the foregoing paragraph is true and correct.

                                 WITNESS my hand and official seal.

                                 _____

                                 Notary Public Signature

DEPOSIT OF
NON-REFUNDABLE ASSIGNMENT FEE

Date: _____/_____/20____

I/We the undersigned hereby pay to Assignor a **NON REFUNDABLE** Deposit of
_____ ($_____) Dollars toward the assignment
of a lease/option on the home located at: _____ in the city
of _____ _____ in the state of _____ with
zip code of _____ Under the following terms:

Assignee Applicant: _____

Assignee Applicant: _____

LEASE INFORMATION

Approximate Lease Start Date   _____/_____/20____
Lease Term   _____ (____) months
Monthly Rent   ($_____)
Security Deposit   ($_____)

OPTION INFORMATION

Home Purchase Price   ($_____)
Allowable Monthly Rent Credits   ($_____)

IMPORTANT NOTE: If you are not completely committed to leasing this home please do
not put down a deposit. There will be no refund in the event that YOU or any co-applicants
decide to withdraw your/their application(s). Your deposit shall also be forfeited if you, or any
co-applicants, fail to execute a lease after our approval of your application.

ASSIGNEE APPLICANT _____   _____
                                              [Print Name]   [Signature]

ASSIGNEE CO-APPLICANT_____   _____
                                              [Print Name]   [Signature]

ASSIGNOR _____   _____
                            [Print Name]   [Signature]

ASSIGNOR _____   _____
                            [Print Name]   [Signature]

GOOD FAITH DEPOSIT RECEIPT

To lock-in the property for you while your references are being reviewed,
we require a "good faith" deposit.

_____ (Applicant) has made a deposit of _____ ($_____) on this the day _____ of _____ 201__ in good faith in order to hold the property located at _____ for the intended purpose of leasing and/or purchasing said property. I/we the undersigned contemplate taking physical possession of said property on or before the _____ day of _____ 20___.

Further, I/we the undersigned Applicant(s) understand that this deposit, and/or any future deposits tendered by me/us will not be refunded should I/we elect not to complete the transaction(s) contemplated herein by the above physical possession date.

In Addition, Applicant(s) also understand that if they are "*turned down*" for the property for any reason before the possession date stated above that this deposit shall be refunded in full within fourteen (10) business days.

_____
Applicant

_____
Printed Name

_____
Applicant

_____
Printed Name

DISCLOSURE OF INFORMATION ON LEAD-BASED PAINT AND/OR LEAD-BASED PAINT HAZARDS LEAD WARNING STATEMENT

Housing built before 1978 may contain lead-based paint. Lead from paint, paint chips, and dust can pose health hazards if not managed properly. Lead exposure is especially harmful to young children and pregnant women. Before renting pre-1978 housing, lessors **MUST** disclose the presence of known lead-based paint and/or lead-based paint hazards in the dwelling.

LESSOR'S DISCLOSURE

(a) Presence of lead-based paint and/or lead-based paint hazards (check (i) or (ii) below):

(i) _____ Known lead-based paint and/or lead-based paint hazards are present in the housing and reasonably known to be located:

_____

_____

(ii) _____ Lessor has no knowledge of lead-based paint and/or lead-based paint hazards in the housing.

(b) Records and reports available to the lessor (check (i) or (ii) below):

(i) _____ Lessor has provided the lessee with all available records and reports pertaining to lead-based paint and/or lead-based paint hazards in the housing.
Such document include:

_____

_____

(ii) _____ Lessor has no reports or records pertaining to lead-based paint and/or lead-based paint hazards in the housing.

LESSEE'S ACKNOWLEDGMENT (INITIAL)

(c) _____ Lessee has received copies of all information listed above.

DISCLOSURE OF INFORMATION ON LEAD-BASED PAINT AND/OR LEAD-BASED PAINT HAZARDS LEAD WARNING STATEMENT

CERTIFICATION OF ACCURACY

The following parties have reviewed the information above and certify, to the best of their knowledge, that the information they have provided is true and accurate.

IN WITNESS WHEREOF, Lessor and Lessee have executed this Disclosure on the _____ day of _____, 20___.

LESSEE

_____   _____
[Signature of authorized Signatory]   [Print Name]

LESSOR

_____   _____
[Signature of authorized Signatory]   [Print Name]

EQUITY PURCHASE AGREEMENT

THIS AGREEMENT is made this _____ day of _____, 20___ between the undersigned (Seller) and _____ and/or assignees ("Buyer") whose business address is _____.

Buyer [   ] does or [   ] does not hold an active real estate license issued by the State of _____.

In consideration of the covenants and agreements hereinafter contained, Seller agrees to sell and convey to Buyer and Buyer agrees to purchase from Seller, the following real property which is commonly described as:

(Attach legal description as Exhibit "A").

The following personal property is also included in this purchase:

_____
_____
_____

Said real and personal property is collectively known as the **"Property"**.

Consideration.   In consideration for said property, Buyer agrees to pay to Seller, as Sellers equity in the Property, the total sum of $_____ payable at the time, **1** Seller delivers to Buyer a properly prepared and executed Grant Deed to the Property (and a Bill of Sale for any personal property included in this sale) and, **2** Seller surrenders to Buyer possession of the Property that is vacant, clean and in good condition.

In No Event Shall Any Money Or Other Consideration Be Transferred To Seller By Buyer At Any Time Prior To Expiration Of Seller's Right To Cancel This Contract.

Seller represents that **the** following **are** all **the unpaid deeds of trusts,** liens and assessments ("Encumbrances").

1st LIEN $_____ payable $_____ per month @ _____% Interest (Taxes & Ins.)

2nd LIEN $_____ payable $_____ per month @ _____% Interest. All due

3rd LIEN $_____ payable $_____ per month @ _____% Interest. All due

Seller represents that said Encumbrances are delinquent in the following amounts:

_____.

All delinquent payments that are due as of the _____ day of _____, 20___ will be deducted from the NET amount due Seller. Also all taxes, judgments, bonds, assessments, association dues, prepayment penalties, and other liens are to be offset against the NET amount due Seller. Impounds, if any, are to be assigned without charge to the Buyer and any impound shortage will be deducted from the funds due Seller. The fire/casualty insurance policy will be assigned to Buyer without charge.

Buyer shall take title to the Property, subject to all said Encumbrances and amounts past due except _____.

Furthermore, Buyer shall take title subject to all easements, zoning restrictions, and covenants, conditions and restrictions of record.

Buyer's Rescission Right. Buyer shall have the right to rescind this Agreement and receive a refund of all consideration paid to Seller if, within (5) days after receiving a Grant Deed to the Property, Buyer notifies Seller in writing that the principal amounts of, and/or the amounts due or past due on one or more of the Encumbrances, are greater than as represented hereinabove, Said notice shall demand rescission and shall specify the Encumbrance(s) which are not in compliance with the representations made by Seller. Upon receipt of said notice Seller shall immediately cooperate with Buyer to execute all documents and do all things necessary to fully rescind the sale and return the full amount of money and/or other property transferred to Seller in connection with this sale, If Seller shall fail or refuse to cooperate Seller shall be liable for all loss or harm caused by said failure or refusal.

Buyer shall pay all the following, if any: escrow fees, title insurance fees, transfer taxes, recording fees and notary fees whereas Seller agrees to pay for any damages found by termite and roof inspections.

Possession. Possession of the Property shall be transferred to Buyer on the _____ day of _____, 20___. Any and all risk of loss of the Property or any part thereof shall be born by Seller until possession of the Property has passed to Buyer. Any possession, occupancy, or tenancy by the Seller at any time after the Deed has been delivered to Buyer shall be on the following terms. Rent to be paid by Seller to Buyer: $_____ per day _____, month _____, year _____, or _____.

Seller to vacate Property on or before _____. Seller agrees to pay for any damage done to the property that is caused by the seller or tenants after the date this contract is signed. Balance of funds due Seller are to be paid after the premises are vacated.

Seller is not entitled to receive any other consideration or thing of value for services from Buyer in connection or incident to the sale of the Property to Buyer except as stated hereinabove and except for the following:_____

_____

Appraisal. The Property MUST appraise for a minimum of $_____, any amount less than that will be DEDUCTED from Seller's net proceeds.

Attorney's Fees. In the event any legal or equitable action is brought to enforce the terms of this agreement including but not limited to specific performance or rescission of contract, the prevailing party in such action shall be entitled to collect reasonable attorney's fees, except witness fees and cost of suit determined by the court. Said legal or equitable action shall be filed and tried in the county of _____, State of _____.

Partial Invalidity. The provisions of this Agreement are agreed to severally by the undersigned, and the invalidity or partial invalidity of one or more provisions of this Agreement shall not deem the remaining provisions invalid or unenforceable.

Binding Upon Heirs, Assigns. This Agreement and all terms hereof, shall be binding on the heirs, devisees, executors, personal representative, conservators, successors, and assigns of the undersigned Buyer or Seller.

Warranty Of Title. Seller hereby warrants, jointly and severally, that each of the undersigned, as Seller, is the lawful owner of any ownership interest in the Property, and that collectively the Seller has the right and authority to convey said ownership to Buyer. This warranty, and all warranties, terms and conditions hereof, shall survive the delivery and recordation of any deed to Buyer, and the close of any escrow.

Condition Of Property. Seller warrants the Property is free of all defects in its structure and operating system. Such as foundations, roof, heating, air conditioning, plumbing, electrical, gas, sewer, pool, etc.. Except for the following:

_____

_____.

Seller agrees to pay for all damages and repairs found by termite and roof inspectors. Buyer takes the property subject to the above-disclosed defects. Seller hereby warrants that the property is free of other defects, as of the delivery date of both the title and possession of the Property to the Buyer.

Sales Commissions. Seller hereby represents that there is no licensed real estate salesperson or **Broker** representing Seller In any way in connection with this purchase and sale, and Seller agrees to hold Buyers harmless and defend Buyer from any claim to commission In connection with this purchase and sale.

Unconscionability. Seller hereby represents that all negotiations and dealings with Buyer have been and are at arm's length and that no duress or undue influence has been exerted by Buyer over Seller or Seller's family in connection with this purchase. Seller is aware that the Buyer may be purchasing property for immediate resale.

Seller's Acknowledgment. Seller is aware and understands that the present fair market value of the Property probably is higher than the purchase price set forth herein. Seller hereby expressly waives any and all claims to any potential or actual income, profits, or other sums in excess of the above-cited purchase price, which may be realized by Buyer or others as a result of any transaction involving the Property. Seller acknowledges that the purchase price stated herein is fair and equitable and is in the Seller's best interests, and that Seller's decision to sell was not made in reliance on any representations of Buyer, which are not expressly contained herein.

Seller _____   Date _____/_____/20____

Seller _____   Date _____/_____/20____

Buyer _____   Date _____/_____/20____

Buyer _____   Date _____/_____/20____

LEASE AGREEMENT

THIS LEASE AGREEMENT made by and between: _____, whose address is _____ (hereinafter called "Landlord") and _____, whose address is _____ (hereinafter called "Tenant"). The masculine singular pronoun shall be used throughout this Agreement, regardless of the sex or number of parties.

1. **LEASE PREMISES**: Landlord, in consideration of the rents to be paid and covenants to be performed by Tenant hereunder, hereby rents to Tenant for the Term and subject to the covenants and conditions hereinafter set forth, the following described premises lying and situated in the County of _____, in the State of _____, such real property having the street address of _____, together with all improvements thereon, all privileges, appurtenances, easements and all fixtures presently situated in said building, including appliances:

2. **TERM**: The term of this Agreement shall be twelve (12) months beginning on the _____ day of _____, 20___, and ending on the last day of _____, 20___. However, Landlord agrees that this Agreement may be extended at the option of the Tenant for two (2) additional terms of twelve (12) months each.

3. **RENT**: Tenant will pay Landlord each month during the term of this Agreement the sum of _____ ($_____) Dollars as rent for the premises, which payment shall be due on or before the first day of each month. If the payment is not received by the Landlord or their agent by 5:30 PM on the fourth day of the month a late charge of five percent five (5%) percent of the monthly payment shall also be due.

4. **SECURITY DEPOSIT**: Simultaneous with the execution of this Agreement, Tenant shall also deposit the sum of _____ ($_____) Dollars with Landlord as a security deposit. Said deposit shall serve as security for the faithful performance of this Agreement, including the repair and maintenance obligations set forth in Paragraph 7 herein, and all other obligations imposed on tenants by any applicable landlord-tenant legislation. Within thirty (30) days after the termination of this Agreement, the security deposit or that portion thereof to which Tenant is entitled shall be returned to Tenant.

5. **USE OF THE PREMISES**: Tenant covenants that he/she/it shall not commit or suffer any waste in the premises, use the premises or permit them to be used for drugs or any unlawful purpose or any dangerous, noxious or offensive activity or cause or maintain any nuisance in the premises, nor operate a business for which the property is not zoned. At the end of the term of this Agreement, Tenant will deliver up the premises in as good an order and condition as they were received, reasonable use and ordinary wear and tear thereof and damage by fire or other casualty, excepted.

6. **UTILITIES**: Tenant is responsible for paying for all water, sewage, fuel, electric current and trash removal which may be charged against said premises during the term of this Agreement. Tenant further agrees to notify the appropriate utilities that he/she/it is occupying the property on the beginning date of this Agreement.

7. **REPAIRS AND MAINTENANCE**: Tenant agrees to maintain the lawn, remove snow, repair and/or replace any and all facilities related to the premises, to provide ordinary and customary preventive maintenance, and to maintain the property in good to excellent condition throughout the term of this Agreement. The costs of such maintenance and repairs shall be allocated as follows:

> 7.1 The cost of repairs, maintenance and improvements, which are less than or equal to one hundred ($100.00) Dollars per repair shall be paid by Tenant.

> 7.2 The cost of repairs and maintenance in excess of one hundred ($100.00) Dollars shall be paid by Landlord, provided that Landlord has approved of each expenditure in writing prior to the commencement of any work on the premises, and provided that the work is performed by a licensed contractor.

> 7.3 Notwithstanding the above, the cost of all repairs required as a result of negligence by Tenant or his/her/its guests shall be paid in full by Tenant.

> 7.4 Tenant may only make improvements or modifications to the property upon written approval of the Landlord. Any unapproved improvements or modifications to the property must be removed at Tenant's expense within seven (7) days of written notice to Tenant by Landlord.

8. **RIGHT TO INSPECT**: Landlord shall have the right to inspect the premises at any time upon a twenty four (24) hour notice to Tenant, unless such entry is required for emergency repairs in the absence of the Tenant.

9. **LANDLORD'S REMEDIES ON DEFAULT**: If default shall at any time be made by the Tenant in the performance of any of the covenants and duties articulated herein or otherwise imposed on tenants by any applicable landlord tenant legislation, or if Tenant shall be declared bankrupt or make a general assignment for the benefit of creditors, or have a receiver appointed for him/her/it, then in each and every such event, Landlord may, at his/her/its election (at any time thereafter), without any demand or notice and without declaring the said term ended as he/she/it may see fit, to re-enter the premises and each and every part thereof either with or without process of law, and to expel and remove Tenant and every other person occupying the Property. Further, Tenant agrees that all expense reasonably incurred in recovering possession of the demised premises, including all costs of attorneys' fees in connection with such terminating and recovering possession of the demised premises shall be paid by Tenant.

10. **QUIET ENJOYMENT**: Landlord agrees that if Tenant pays the rent on time and keeps and performs the covenants of this Agreement, Tenant will peaceably and quietly hold the premises during the term hereof without any hindrance, ejection or molestation by Landlord or any person lawfully claiming authority under Landlord.

11. **LIABILITY**: Tenant agrees that Landlord and its employees and agents shall not be liable to Tenant for any damage to or loss of personal property located in the premises or for injuries to persons occurring in the premises.

12. **HOLD HARMLESS AGREEMENT**: Tenant shall protect, save and keep the Landlord harmless and indemnified against any and all liability, loss, cost, damages, or expenses arising out of any accident or other occurrence on the demised premises, causing death, injury or damage to any person or property due to any act or neglect of the Tenant, its agents, employees, assigns, invites or licensees, or due to any failure of the Tenant, its agents, employees, assignees, invites or licensees to comply with and perform any of the requirements and provisions of this Agreement on their part to be performed.

13. **PUBLIC LIABILITY INSURANCE**: Tenant agrees that it will, at its sole expense, maintain valid an enforceable policy issued by insurers of recognized responsibility, naming Landlord as an additional insured, a Renters' general liability insurance policy providing for claims for bodily injury or death and property damage occurring upon or about the demised premises and the adjoining streets and passageways, such insurance to afford protection to a limit of not less than Three Hundred Thousand ($300,000.00) Dollars with respect to bodily injury or death to any number of persons in any one accident, and not less than twenty-five Thousand ($25,000.00) Dollars with respect to damage of the property of any persons in any one accident.

14. **HOLDING OVER**: In the event Tenant remains in possession of the premises after the term of this Agreement has expired or is terminated, Tenant shall be deemed a month to month only tenant.

15. **WARRANT**:   Each Party, and each person signing on behalf of a Party, represents and warrants that they have the full legal capacity and authority to enter into and perform the obligations of this Agreement without any further approval.

16. **VENUE, SUCCESSORS & ASSIGNS**:   Both Parties agree that the venue for the terms, conditions and provisions of this Lease Agreement shall be the State of _____, and shall inure to the benefit of, and be binding upon heirs, successors and assigns of the Parties hereto.

17. **ADDITIONAL TERM AND CONDITIONS**:

a)_____

_____

_____

_____

IN WITNESS WHEREOF, Landlord and Tenant have executed this Agreement on the _____ day of _____, 20___.

TENANT

_____   _____
[Signature of authorized Signatory]   [Print Name]

LANDLORD

_____   _____
[Signature of authorized Signatory]   [Print Name]

LEASE WITH OPTION TO PURCHASE AGREEMENT

THIS LEASE AGREEMENT made by and between:

_____, whose address is

_____ (hereinafter called "Landlord")

and _____, whose address is

_____

(hereinafter called "Tenant"). The masculine singular pronoun shall be used throughout this Agreement, regardless of the sex or number of parties.

1. **LEASE PREMISES**: Landlord, in consideration of the rents to be paid and covenants to be performed by Tenant hereunder, hereby rents to Tenant for the Term and subject to the covenants and conditions hereinafter set forth, the following described premises lying and situated in the County of _____, in the State of _____, such real property having the street address of _____, together with all improvements thereon, all privileges, appurtenances, easements and all fixtures presently situated in said building, including appliances:

2. **TERM**: The term of this Agreement shall be twelve (12) months beginning on the _____ day of _____, 201__, and ending on the last day of _____, 201__. However, Landlord agrees that this Agreement may be extended at the option of the Tenant for two (2) additional terms of twelve (12) months each.

3. **RENT**: Tenant will pay Landlord each month during the term of this Agreement the sum of _____ ($_____) Dollars as rent for the premises, which payment shall be due on or before the first day of each month. If the payment is not received by the Landlord or their agent by 5:30 PM on the fourth day of the month a late charge of five percent five (5%) percent of the monthly payment shall also be due.

3.1.   **RENT CREDIT TOWARD AN OPTION TO PURCHASE (IF APPLICABLE):** Landlord agrees that whenever the monthly rent is paid on time, Landlord shall credit the sum of _____ ($_____) Dollars or _____ of the monthly rent per month towards the purchase price of the Property, should Tenant choose to exercise an option to purchase the Property during the term of the lease. Should Tenant **not choose** to exercise an Option to Purchase the Property; this credit shall be non-refundable and shall be considered as the sole and separate property of Landlord**.**

4. **SECURITY DEPOSIT**: Simultaneous with the execution of this Agreement, Tenant shall also deposit the sum of _____ ($_____) Dollars with Landlord as a security deposit. Said deposit shall serve as security for the faithful performance of this Agreement, including the repair and maintenance obligations set forth in Paragraph 7 herein, and all other obligations imposed on tenants by any applicable landlord-tenant legislation.

Within thirty (30) days after the termination of this Agreement, the security deposit or that portion thereof to which Tenant is entitled shall be returned to Tenant.

5. **USE OF THE PREMISES**: Tenant covenants that he/she/it shall not commit or suffer any waste in the premises, use the premises or permit them to be used for drugs or any unlawful purpose or any dangerous, noxious or offensive activity or cause or maintain any nuisance in the premises, nor operate a business for which the property is not zoned. At the end of the term of this Agreement, Tenant will deliver up the premises in as good an order and condition as they were received, reasonable use and ordinary wear and tear thereof and damage by fire or other casualty, excepted.

6. **UTILITIES**: Tenant is responsible for paying for all water, sewage, fuel, electric current and trash removal which may be charged against said premises during the term of this Agreement. Tenant further agrees to notify the appropriate utilities that he/she/it is occupying the property on the beginning date of this Agreement.

7. **REPAIRS AND MAINTENANCE**: Tenant agrees to maintain the lawn, remove snow, repair and/or replace any and all facilities related to the premises, to provide ordinary and customary preventive maintenance, and to maintain the property in good to excellent condition throughout the term of this Agreement. The costs of such maintenance and repairs shall be allocated as follows:

  7.1 The cost of repairs, maintenance and improvements, which are less than or equal to two hundred ($200.00) Dollars per repair shall be paid by Tenant.

  7.2 The cost of repairs and maintenance in excess of two hundred ($200.00) Dollars shall be paid by Landlord, provided that Landlord has approved of each expenditure in writing prior to the commencement of any work on the premises, and provided that the work is performed by a licensed contractor.

  7.3 Notwithstanding the above, the cost of all repairs required as a result of negligence by Tenant or his/her/its guests shall be paid in full by Tenant.

  7.4 Tenant may only make improvements or modifications to the property upon written approval of the Landlord. Any unapproved improvements or modifications to the property must be removed at Tenant's expense within seven (7) days of written notice to Tenant by Landlord.

8. **RIGHT TO INSPECT**: Landlord shall have the right to inspect the premises at any time upon a twenty four (24) hour notice to Tenant, unless such entry is required for emergency repairs in the absence of the Tenant.

9. PAYMENTS OF EXISTING LOANS, TAXES AND INSURANCE: Landlord shall be responsible for paying the taxes, loan payments and for keeping the property insured for its full replacement value during the term of this Agreement. In the event Landlord fails to make payments when due for taxes, insurance, or loan payments, Tenant may elect to make said payments and receive the amount paid as a full credit toward the next lease payment(s) due to be paid to Landlord.

10. LANDLORD'S REMEDIES ON DEFAULT: If default shall at any time be made by the Tenant in the performance of any of the covenants and duties articulated herein or otherwise imposed on tenants by any applicable landlord tenant legislation, or if Tenant shall be declared bankrupt or make a general assignment for the benefit of creditors, or have a receiver appointed for him/her/it, then in each and every such event, Landlord may, at his/her/its election (at any time thereafter), without any demand or notice and without declaring the said term ended as he/she/it may see fit, to re-enter the premises and each and every part thereof either with or without process of law, and to expel and remove Tenant and every other person occupying the Property. Further, Tenant agrees that all expense reasonably incurred in recovering possession of the demised premises, including all costs of attorneys' fees in connection with such terminating and recovering possession of the demised premises shall be paid by Tenant.

11. QUIET ENJOYMENT: Landlord agrees that if Tenant pays the rent on time and keeps and performs the covenants of this Agreement, Tenant will peaceably and quietly hold the premises during the term hereof without any hindrance, ejection or molestation by Landlord or any person lawfully claiming authority under Landlord.

12. LIABILITY: Tenant agrees that Landlord and its employees and agents shall not be liable to Tenant for any damage to or loss of personal property located in the premises or for injuries to persons occurring in the premises.

13. HOLD HARMLESS AGREEMENT: Tenant shall protect, save and keep the Landlord harmless and indemnified against any and all liability, loss, cost, damages, or expenses arising out of any accident or other occurrence on the demised premises, causing death, injury or damage to any person or property due to any act or neglect of the Tenant, its agents, employees, assigns, invites or licensees, or due to any failure of the Tenant, its agents, employees, assignees, invites or licensees to comply with and perform any of the requirements and provisions of this Agreement on their part to be performed.

14. PUBLIC LIABILITY INSURANCE: Tenant agrees that it will, at its sole expense, maintain valid an enforceable policy issued by insurers of recognized responsibility, naming Landlord as an additional insured, a Renters' general liability insurance policy providing for claims for bodily injury or death and property damage occurring upon or about the demised premises and the adjoining streets and passageways, such insurance to afford protection to a limit of not less than Three Hundred Thousand ($300,000.00) Dollars with respect to bodily injury or death to any number of persons in any one accident, and not less than twenty-five Thousand ($25,000.00) Dollars with respect to damage of the property of any persons in any one accident.

15. **HOLDING OVER**: In the event Tenant remains in possession of the premises after the term of this Agreement has expired or is terminated, Tenant shall be deemed a month to month only tenant.

16. **ASSIGNING THIS AGREEMENT**: Tenant hereby discloses and Landlord hereby understands and acknowledges that Tenant intends to assign its interest in this Lease Agreement and any other agreements that may result there from to a 3rd party assignee. Landlord further agrees that Tenant shall have the absolute un-contested right to assign his/her/its interest in these agreements.

16.1 **RIGHT TO RECEIVE AN ASSIGNMENT FEE**.   It is further agreed by the parties that Tenant shall have the absolute un-contested right to receive a fee for its assignment of the agreements contemplated herein. Said assignment fee shall be paid directly to Tenant.

17. **WARRANT**:   Each Party, and each person signing on behalf of a Party, represents and warrants that they have the full legal capacity and authority to enter into and perform the obligations of this Agreement without any further approval.

18. **VENUE, SUCCESSORS & ASSIGNS**:   Both Parties agree that the venue for the terms, conditions and provisions of this Lease Agreement shall be the State of _____, and shall inure to the benefit of, and be binding upon heirs, successors and assigns of the Parties hereto.

19. **ADDITIONAL TERM AND CONDITIONS**:

a) _____

_____

_____

_____

LEASE WITH OPTION TO PURCHASE AGREEMENT

IN WITNESS WHEREOF, Landlord and Tenant have executed this Agreement on the _____ day of _____, 20____.

TENANT

_____   _____
[Signature of authorized Signatory]   [Print Name]

LANDLORD

_____   _____
[Signature of authorized Signatory]   [Print Name]

LETTER TO DECLINING TENANT APPLICATION

Date: _____ / _____ / 20___

TO:	Potential Tenant
	Full address
FROM:	Your Name
RE:	Rental Application

Potential tenant name:

After having received and processed your rental application for the property at (address of property), we must regretfully inform you that your application has been declined at this time.

The reason(s) your application cannot be accepted at this time is/are:

_____

_____.

Thank you for submitting your rental application. We wish you the best.

Respectfully,

LETTER TO INSURANCE COMPANY
REGARDING TRANSFERRING TITLE

Your Personal Name
Your Personal Address

[DATE]
[NAME OF INSURANCE AGENT]
[ADDRESS OF INSURANCE AGENT]
Re: Policy #
Property Address:

Dear Sir or Madam:

Please be advised that I/we the undersigned are transferring title to the above referenced property into an entity that is wholly owned by me/us. The name of the entity is:

(Replace This With The Name Of Your Entity)
A *(Name of State) (Type of Entity)*

The business address of (*name of entity again*) is:

(Replace This With The Address Of Your Entity)

I/We wholly own this entity. (See the attached Declaration of Beneficial Interest)

(Attach a copy of your current Declaration of Beneficial Interest)

Please amend your policy to reflect the "loss payee" as stated above. Additionally, please also add the following parties as "additional insured's" for liability purposes:

(Put the names as they appear on the current insurance policy:)

_____

_____

Thank you for your consideration and assistance regarding this matter

Sincerely,

Your Name
(Entity Name)
(Your Title)

LETTER TO LENDER
REGARDING TRANSFERRED PROPERTY
INFORMATION AND CERTIFICATION

Lender: **(Lender)**

Borrower(s) Of Record: **(Names of Borrower)**
Loan #: **(Loan Number)**
Property Address: **(Property Address)**

Name Of Entity: **(Name Of Your Entity)**
Type Of Entity: **A (Name of State) (Type of Entity)**

The entity named above is owned as follows: **(If a Corporation)**

1. Borrower of Record: Borrowers of Record Owns 100% of the "C" Corporation stock.

The entity named above is owned as follows: **(If a Limited Liability Company)**

1. Borrower of Record: Directly holds 2% passive membership ownership interest in the LLC; and

2. NV "C" Corporation: Directly holds 98% membership ownership interest while the borrower's of Record Owns 100% of the "C" Corporation stock.

The entity named above is owned as follows: **(If a Limited Partnership)**

1. Borrower of Record: Directly holds 2% passive partnership ownership interest in the LP; and

2. NV "C" Corporation: Directly holds 98% general partnership ownership interest while the borrowers of Record Owns 100% of the "C" Corporation stock.

I/We, the undersigned state that the transfer of the above stated property into entities in which I/We own 100% of the beneficial interest qualifies for exemption from your right to accelerate my loan pursuant to the Garn-St. Germain Act (12 UCA 1701j-3), which imposed restrictions on the enforcement of the due-on-sale clauses.

Further, I/We, as the Borrower(s) of Record, state that I/we remain liable for the debt (mortgage) on the property and that I/we are only transferring the future income to the corporation (entity). I/we fully understand my/our legal rights and obligations in connection herewith and that having understood these rights and obligations, hereby certify that the entity named above is an entity wholly owned by me/us and that I/We will not alienate or transfer my/our interest in said entity at all times during the term of the loan identified above.

Signature: _____

Signature: _____

NOTARY ACKNOWLEDGEMENT

STATE OF _____)
) SS.

COUNTY OF _____)

On _____ before me, _____
                                                                (insert name and title of the officer)

personally appeared _____, who proved to me on the basis of satisfactory evidence to be the person(s) whose name(s) is are subscribed to the within instrument and acknowledged to me that he/she/they executed the same in his/her/their authorized capacity(ies), and that by his/her/their signature(s) on the instrument the person(s), or the entity upon behalf of which the person(s) acted, executed the instrument.

I certify under PENALTY OF PERJURY under the laws of the State of _____ that the foregoing paragraph is true and correct.

WITNESS my hand and official seal.

_____

Notary Public Signature

NOTICE TO LANDLORD
OF
TENANTS DESIRE TO RENEW LEASE TERM

To: _____ ("Landlord")

Reference is made to the Original Lease Agreement ("Lease") between Landlord and the undersigned as Tenant in respect to the premises to wit:

_____

_____

Therefore, please be advised that by this Renewal of Lease Document the undersigned is hereby exercising his/her/its right to renew the term of the Lease for a term of _____ Months(s), as specified in the Lease Agreement.

This Notice is given to you in accordance with paragraph _____ of said Lease that permits Tenant(s) to renew the term of the existing Lease.

IN WITNESS WHEREOF, Landlord and Tenant have executed this renewal of the term of the existing Lease on the _____ day of _____, 20___.

TENANT

_____
(Name of entity if any)

_____   _____
[Signature of authorized Signatory]   [Print Name]

_____
(Title of the authorized Signatory named above if an entity)

LANDLORD

Agreed to and accepted by the Landlord on the _____ day of _____, 20___

_____   _____
[Signature of authorized Signatory]   [Print Name]

NOTICE OF TENANT
TO EXERCISE OPTION TO PURCHASE

Date: _____ / _____ / 20____

To: _____

Address: _____

_____

VIA CERTIFIED MAIL
(Return Receipt Requested)

Dear: Sir or Madam,

I the undersigned hereby provide you with my/our notice that I/we the undersigned as Lessee(s) under a certain Lease dated the _____ day of _____, 20____, and Option to Purchase dated the _____ day of _____, 20____, do hereby desire to exercise my/our option under said Lease and option to purchase the property located at:

_____

_____

Enclosed is a deposit of _____ ($_____), dollars as required by paragraph 6 of the option to purchase agreement.

_____   _____
             Lessee   Lessee

NOTICE TO PAY RENT OR QUIT

NOTICE TO: _____,

[Tenant's Name(s)]

The premises referred to are commonly known as:

_____

_____

TENANT in possession and all others:

You are hereby required to pay the rent on the premises herein described, of which you now hold possession pursuant to a written lease, amounting to $_____, being the total rent including late fee(s) now due to me by you for the period from _____ / 20___ to _____ / 20___,

OR

You are hereby required to deliver up possession of the premises, within _____ days after service on you of this notice, to the undersigned or the undersigned will institute legal proceedings against you, to declare a forfeiture of the lease under which you occupy said premises and to recover possession thereof, including rents and damages.

The undersigned [ ] does or [ ] does not elect to terminate the lease if the rent is not paid within _____ days.

Signed on the _____ day of _____, 20___

_____

Landlord/Property Manager

OPTION TO PURCHASE AGREEMENT

A. PROPERTY: The real estate commonly known as:

_____

_____

together with all its improvements.

B. PARTIES: The parties to this Agreement (Option) are the owner of the Property, _____. (Seller), *hereby referred to as Optionor*

And

_____ (Buyer) *hereby referred to as Optionee and or assigns.*

C. OPTION TO PURCHASE: It is agreed that Optionee shall have the right (Option) to purchase said property from Optionor payable in cash or by third party financing or in any of the specified methods located in **SECTION H. FINANCING** at any time during the original term of the Option.

D. PERSONAL PROPERTY: Included by the exercising of this option but not limited by, will be all fixed equipment including attached lighting fixtures, mailboxes, hardware, attached mirrors, curtain rods, drapery, TV antennas and satellite dishes, attached grills, awnings, screens, garage door openers and all appliances minus these items:

_____

_____

E. TERM: The Option term shall begin on the _____ day of _____ 20____ and expire on the _____ day of _____ 20____ (original term).

F. CONSIDERATION EARNED TOWARD PURCHASE: If the Option is exercised during its term, the Option Fee paid by Optionee shall be applied towards the purchase price, Optionee's closing costs, and/or down payment at Optionee's choice. On the date herein stated, Optionor has been paid $_____ as Optionee's Option fee (consideration).

(Initials: Optionor _____ Optionee _____)

G. NOTICE TO EXERCISE THE OPTION: Optionee may exercise his/her/its Option by giving Optionor 3 days (or more) advanced written notice of Optionee's intent to do so.

H. FINANCING
This option may be exercised by any or all of the following INITIALED terms:

i) Cash or Third Party Financing: Buyer will pay cash or obtain third party financing such as a mortgage or other loan (s) in the amount of:

$_____

(Initials: Optionor _____ Optionee _____)

ii). Lease Purchase: Optionor will grant buyer the option to purchase the property in the amount of: $_____ while leasing the property for a _____ month period with payments of $_____ per month due and payable on the first day of each month and a $_____ non-refundable option fee consideration).

(Initials: Optionor _____ Optionee _____)

iii). Purchase Agreement: Buyer may purchase the said property by a purchase agreement in the amount of $_____ pursuant to terms acceptable to both parties at the time of executing said agreement:

(Initials: Optionor _____ Optionee _____)

iv) Subject to Existing Financing: Optionor will allow Optionee to take the property subject to existing financing for the amount of: $_____ Optionor understands that the underlining loan will stay in their (Optionor's) name until paid off by Optionee by an agreed upon time and written term, or within _____ months from the date of this Agreement. Optionee will be obligated to make all payments (loan, taxes, utilities etc) or any other payments agreed upon by Optionor and Optionee in writing.

(Initials: Optionor _____ Optionee _____)

I. EXTENTION OF OPTION: There shall be no extension of the Option unless in writing by all signing parties.

J. DEFAULT OF OPTION: If Optionee fails to exercise this option during its term or forfeits it due to default, all Option Fees shall be forfeited and shall be kept by Optionor as complete and liquidated damages. This option to purchase shall apply to and bind the heirs, executors, and administrators of the respective parties herein.

K. INSURANCE: Optionor agrees to maintain reasonable insurance on the property throughout the duration of this Agreement.

L. MAINTENANCE AND UPKEEP: Until Optionee exercises this option or title is delivered, Optionor agrees to maintain all utilities, appliances and the general good condition of the property subject to the lease agreement by and between the Parties hereto or unless otherwise stated in writing and signed by both Parties.

M. CLOSING: At closing (for cash purchase or 3rd party financing and Seller Financing):
    A) Seller shall deliver to Buyer a Grant Deed to the property.
    B) Seller's closing costs will be the cost of obtaining releases of liens and any outstanding utility depts.
    C) Buyer's closing costs will include all costs associated with new financing obtained by Buyer, costs associated with recording new loan and owner's title policy.
    D) Property taxes shall be prorated as of date of closing.
    E) Any rent payments, condo association fees and interest on loans may be prorated.
    F) Optionee shall pay for all closing costs if property is taken subject to the mortgage unless otherwise specified in writing.

N. GOVERNING LAW, JURISDICTION AND VENUE: This Agreement will be governed by and interpreted in accordance with the laws of the State of _____ without regard to conflict of laws provisions. Any action arising out of this Agreement or the relationship between the parties established herein shall be brought only in the courts of State of _____.

For and on behalf of Optionor - _____

_____   Date:_____/20_____
Optionor

For and on behalf of Optionee - _____

_____   Date:_____/20_____
Optionee

_____   Date:_____/20_____
Optionee

INVESTOR OPTION TO PURCHASE AGREEMENT

A. PROPERTY: The real estate commonly known as:

_____

_____

together with all its improvements.

B. PARTIES: The parties to this agreement (Option) are the owner of the Property, _____ (Seller), *hereby referred to as Optionor* and _____ (Buyer), *hereby referred to as Optionee and or assigns.*

C. OPTION TO PURCHASE: It is agreed that Optionee shall have the right (Option) to purchase said property from Optionor payable in cash or by third party financing or in any of the specified methods located in ***SECTION H. FINANCING*** at any time during the original term of the Option.

 D. PERSONAL PROPERTY: Included by the exercising of this option but not limited by, will be all fixed equipment including attached lighting fixtures, mailboxes, hardware, attached mirrors, curtain rods, drapery, TV antennas and satellite dishes, attached grills, awnings, screens, garage door openers and all appliances minus these items:

_____

_____

E. TERM: The Option term shall begin on the _____ day of _____ 20_____ and expire on the _____ day of _____ 20_____ (original term).

F. CONSIDERATION EARNED TOWARD PURCHASE: If the Option is exercised during its term, all Option Fees paid by Optionee shall be applied towards the purchase price, Optionee's closing costs, and/or down payment at Optionee's choice. Received today as Option consideration in the amount of: $_____

(Initials: Optionor _____   Optionee _____)

G. NOTICE TO EXERCISE THE OPTION: Optionee may exercise the Option by giving Optionor 3 days (or more) advanced written notice of Optionee's intent to do so.

H. FINANCING
This option may be exercised by any or all of the following INITIALED terms:

i) Cash or Third Party Financing: Buyer will pay cash or obtain third party financing such as a mortgage or other loan (s) in the amount of:
$_____

(Initials: Optionor _____   Optionee _____)

ii). Lease Purchase: Optionor will grant buyer the option to purchase the property in the amount of: $_____ while leasing the property for a _____ month

period with payments of $_____ per month due and payable on the first day of each month and a $_____ non-refundable option fee consideration).

(Initials: Optionor _____ Optionee _____)

iii). Purchase Agreement: Buyer may purchase the said property by a purchase agreement in the amount of $_____ pursuant to terms acceptable to both parties at the time of executing said agreement:

(Initials: Optionor _____ Optionee _____)

iv) Subject to Existing Financing: Optionor will allow Optionee to take the property subject to existing financing for the amount of: $_____ Optionor understands that the underlining loan will stay in their (Optionor's) name until paid off by Optionee by an agreed upon time and written term, or within _____ months from the date of this Agreement. Optionee will be obligated to make all payments (loan, taxes, utilities etc) or any other payments agreed upon by Optionor and Optionee in writing.

(Initials: Optionor _____ Optionee _____)

I. ASSIGNMENT

Optionee has full right to assign this agreement to anyone at any time. If Optionee does assign their interest, Optionor will sign a Release of Liability relieving the Optionee from any payments or any further liabilities whatsoever.

J. EXTENTION OF OPTION:

J. EXTENTION OF OPTION: There shall be no extension of the Option unless in writing by all signing parties.

K. DEFAULT OF OPTION:

K. DEFAULT OF OPTION: If Optionee fails to exercise this option during its term or forfeits it due to default, all Option Fees shall be forfeited and shall be kept by Optionor as complete and liquidated damages. This option to purchase shall apply to and bind the heirs, executors, and administrators of the respective parties herein.

L. INSURANCE: Optionor agrees to maintain reasonable insurance on the property throughout the duration of this Agreement.

M. MAINTENANCE AND UPKEEP: Until Optionee exercises this option or title is delivered, Optionor agrees to maintain all utilities, appliances and the general good condition of the property subject to the lease agreement by and between the Parties hereto or unless otherwise stated in writing and signed by both Parties.

N. ACCESS: Optionor grants optionee access to the above property for showing to prospective buyers, contractors, or appraisers. Optionor must maintain proper insurance on the property throughout the duration of this agreement.

O. MAINTENANCE AND UPKEEP: Until Optionee exercises this option or title is delivered, Optionor agrees to maintain all utilities, appliances and the general good condition of the property unless otherwise in writing and signed by both parties.

P. CLOSING: At closing (for cash purchase or 3rd party financing and Seller Financing):

    A) Seller shall deliver to Buyer a general warranty deed to the property.

    B) Seller's closing costs will be the cost of obtaining releases of liens and any outstanding utility depts.

    C) Buyer's closing costs will include all costs associated with new financing obtained by Buyer, costs associated with recording new loan and owner's title policy.

    D) Property taxes shall be prorated as of date of closing.

    E) Any rent payments, condo association fees and interest on loans may be prorated.

    F) Optionee shall pay for all closing costs if property is taken subject to unless specified in writing.

Q. NON-COMPETE: If Optionor should sell said property during the Option term to any other person, such person shall be furnished with the copies of this Agreement and shall agree in writing to be fully bound by the terms with regard to the Buyer's rights under this Agreement. Both parties hereby agree that the optionor, nor any corporation and/or its subdivisions, employees, agents or consultants with whom he/she is associated, will not initiate any actions to circumvent the terms of this agreement, deal with or otherwise become involved in any transaction with persons either (1) revealed to him or her by the other party hereto or (2) introduced to him or her through the other party's contacts during the course of business being transacted (specifically including, but not limited to, roll-overs, transfers, extensions, and revisions of any agreements or contracts); without discussing the pertinent details of such transactions with the other party hereto and without paying such appropriate fees as have been agreed to the other party hereto, either verbally or otherwise.

R. DISCLOSURE OF INTENT TO PROFIT: Optionor hereby understands that optionee has full intention of making a profit on this transaction by either assigning or releasing their interest of this option, or by purchasing and selling the property.

S. GOVERNING LAW, JURISDICTION AND VENUE: This Agreement will be governed by and interpreted in accordance with the laws of the State of _____ without regard to conflict of laws provisions. Any action arising out of this Agreement or the relationship between the parties established herein shall be brought only in the courts of State of

_____.

For and on behalf of Optionor - _____

_____   Date:_____/20_____
Optionor

For and on behalf of Optionee - _____

_____   Date:_____/20_____
Optionee

WHEN RECORDED RETURN TO: _____

_____

_____

MEMORANDUM
OF
INVESTOR OPTION TO PURCHASE AGREEMENT

THIS MEMORANDUM is made by and between _____,
whose address is _____ (hereinafter referred to
as the "Grantor") and _____, whose address is
_____ (hereinafter referred to as the "Grantee").

WITNESSETH

Grantor owns that certain real property described on Exhibit "A" attached hereto (hereinafter referred to as the "Property"), whose street address is:

_____

_____

Further, Grantor has granted Grantee an option to purchase the Property on such terms as have been agreed upon by Grantor and Grantee (the "Option"). Grantor and Grantee hereby give actual and constructive notice to all persons dealing with the Property of the existence of the Option and that the rights of Grantor and the Property are subject to the Option.

IN WITNESS WHEREOF, Grantor and Grantee have executed this Memorandum on the _____ day of _____, 20___.

GRANTEE

_____
(Name of entity if any)

_____   _____
[Signature of authorized Signatory]   [Print Name]

_____
(Title of the authorized Signatory named above, if an entity)

GRANTOR

_____   _____
[Signature of authorized Signatory]   [Print Name]

PROMISSORY NOTE
WITHOUT FULL ASSIGNMENT
(Without full Assignment fee being paid to Optionor)

Amount of Note: _____ ($_____) **Dollars**

This promissory note has been undertaken by the undersigned maker(s) in order for the maker(s) to pay the unpaid balance stated herein from the total Assignment Fee of _____ _____ ($_____.00) Dollars.

1.   The undersigned jointly and severally promise(s) to pay to the order of the holder of this note the sum of _____ ($_____.00) Dollars. Said amount being payable on or before the fifteenth (15th) day of each and every month in US Dollars starting on the fifteenth (15th) day of _____, 20___, in monthly installments of _____ ($_____.00) Dollars, and continuing thereafter until _____ day of _____, 20___, or until said principal has been paid in full to the holder at such place as the holder hereof may designate in writing from time to time. The parties agree that all payments shall be made by "direct payment" from the maker's/co-maker's bank account to the holder's bank account.

2.   Each maker and endorser severally waives demand, protest, and notice of maturity, non-payment, and all requirements necessary to hold each of them liable as makers and endorsers and, should litigation be necessary to enforce this note, each maker and endorser waives trail by jury and consents to the personal jurisdiction and venue of a court of subject matter jurisdiction located in the State of _____ and in the County of _____.

3.   Each maker and endorser further agrees, jointly and severally, to pay all costs of collection, including a reasonable attorney's fee in case the principal of this note or any payment is not paid at the respective maturity thereof, or in case it becomes necessary to protect the security hereof, whether suit be brought or not.

4.   This note is to be construed and enforced according to the law of the State of _____; upon default in the payment of principal when due, the whole sum of principal then remaining unpaid shall, at the option of the holder, become immediately due and payable without notice to maker and/or endorser.

5.   Installments not paid within five (5) days of their due date shall incur a late fee of ten (10%) percent of the installment amount (but not less than ten ($10.00 Dollars). The Holder shall be entitled to all costs of collection should this Note, or any part of the indebtedness evidenced hereby, be accelerated and not paid. Should this note be collected at law or by an attorney at law, an Attorney/Collection Fee of fifteen (15%) percent of the balance due (but not less than one hundred ($100.00 Dollars), plus any costs and administration fees, shall be added.

6.   Unless specifically disallowed by law, should litigation arise hereunder, service of process therefore may be obtained through certified mail, return receipt requested; the parties hereto waiving any and all rights they may have to object to the method by which service was perfected.

IN WITNESS WHEREOF: On this the _____ day of _____, 20___, the undersigned acknowledge(s) that they have read and understand this Agreement and agree to all of the terms and conditions contained herein, and that they have been given a copy of this Agreement.

HOLDER PAYMENT SCHEDULE

Total Amount Due: $_____

Number Of Payments: _____ (max 12 payments)

Amount Due Each Payment: $_____

Date Due:	Amount	Date Due:	Amount
____/____/20___	$_____.00	____/____/20___	$_____.00
____/____/20___	$_____.00	____/____/20___	$_____.00
____/____/20___	$_____.00	____/____/20___	$_____.00
____/____/20___	$_____.00	____/____/20___	$_____.00
____/____/20___	$_____.00	____/____/20___	$_____.00
____/____/20___	$_____.00	____/____/20___	$_____.00

_____ _____ _____ - ____ - _____
Debtor/Maker   Printed Name   Social Security #

_____ _____ _____ - ____ - _____
Debtor/Maker   Printed Name   Social Security #

PROMISSORY NOTE
WITHOUT FULL ASSIGNMENT OR FULL DOWN PAYMENT
(For use without full option fee or full down payment being paid to Seller)

Amount of Note: _____ $_____ **Dollars**

FOR VALUE RECEIVED the undersigned jointly and severally promise(s) to pay to the order of _____ the principal sum of _____ Dollars ($_____.00) from date until maturity, said principal being payable monthly on or before the tenth (10th) day of each and every month in US Dollars on the Tenth (10th) day of _____, 20___, in monthly installments of _____ Dollars ($_____.00), and continuing thereafter until _____, 20___, or until said principal have been paid in full, to _____ whose address is _____ or at such other place as the holder hereof may designate in writing from time to time.

Each maker and endorser severally waives demand, protest, and notice of maturity, non-payment, and all requirements necessary to hold each of them liable as makers and endorsers and, should litigation be necessary to enforce this note, each maker and endorser waives trail by jury and consents to the personal jurisdiction and venue of a court of subject matter jurisdiction located in the State of _____ and in the County of _____.

Each maker and endorser further agrees, jointly and severally, to pay all costs of collection, including a reasonable attorney's fee in case the principal of this note or any payment is not paid at the respective maturity thereof, or in case it becomes necessary to protect the security hereof, whether suit be brought or not.

This note is to be construed and enforced according to the law of the State of _____ upon default in the payment of principal when due, the whole sum of principal then remaining unpaid shall, at the option of the holder, become immediately due and payable without notice to maker and/or endorser.

Installments, or payment (*if single payment Note*), not paid within 5 days of due date shall incur a fee of 15% of the installment or payment, but not less than $10.00. The Holder shall be entitled to all costs of collection should this Note, or any part of the indebtedness evidenced hereby, be accelerated and not paid. Should this note be collected at law or by an attorney at law, an Attorney/Collection Fee of 15% of the balance due, but not less than $100.00, plus any costs and administration fees, shall be added.

Unless specifically disallowed by law, should litigation arise hereunder, service of process therefore may be obtained through certified mail, return receipt requested; the parties hereto waiving any and all rights they may have to object to the method by which service was perfected.

IN WITNESS WHEREOF: On this the _____ day of _____, 20___, the undersigned acknowledge(s) that they have read and understand this Agreement and agree to all of the terms and conditions contained herein, and that they have been given a copy of this agreement.

PAYMENT SCHEDULE

Total Amount Due: $_____

Number Of Payments: _____ (Max 12 Payments)

Amount Due Each Payment: $_____

Date Due:	Amount	Date Due:	Amount
____/____/20___	$_____.00	____/____/20___	$_____.00
____/____/20___	$_____.00	____/____/20___	$_____.00
____/____/20___	$_____.00	____/____/20___	$_____.00
____/____/20___	$_____.00	____/____/20___	$_____.00
____/____/20___	$_____.00	____/____/20___	$_____.00
____/____/20___	$_____.00	____/____/20___	$_____.00

_____   _____   _____ - ____ - _____
Debtor/Maker   Printed Name   Social Security #

_____   _____   _____ - ____ - _____
Debtor/Co-Maker   Printed Name   Social Security #

_____   _____   _____
Note Holder/Agent   Printed Name   Title, if any

RELEASE OF PROMISSORY NOTE AGREEMENT

This Release has been executed on the _____ day of _____, 20___, by
_____ (hereinafter Releasor) to _____ (hereinafter Releasee).

In consideration of _____ ($_____) dollars, receipt of which is acknowledged, Releasor voluntarily and knowingly executes this release with the express intention of effecting the extinguishment of any and all obligations created by or arising out of:

1.   The option to purchase agreement dated on the _____ day of _____, 20___, between _____(Seller) and _____.

2.   Promissory Note Dated _____/_____/20___, ___, between _____(Seller) and _____.

Releasor, with the intention of binding itself, its spouse, heirs, legal representatives, and assigns, expressly releases and discharges Releasee and its heirs and legal representatives from all claims, demands, actions, judgments, and executions that Releasor ever had, or now has, or may have, known or unknown, against Releasee or its heirs or legal representatives created by or arising out of said claim.

IN WITNESS WHEREOF, Releasor has executed this release on the day and year first above written.

This Release Agreement is subject to seller successfully closing with Tenant / Buyer (Buyer). If such closing does not take place, then the aforementioned Agreements shall still be completely and fully in effect.

_____   _____

[Releasor Authorized Signature]   Date

_____   _____

[Releasee Authorized Signature]   Date

PROPERTY BUYING WORKSHEET

Date: _____ / _____ /20___

Owners Name: _____

Address: _____ City _____

State _____ Zip Code _____

Phones: Day (_____) _____ - _____   Evening Day (_____) _____ - _____

E-Mail: _____

Property Address: _____

          City _____ State _____ Zip Code_____

Asking Price: $ _____

Estimated Value: $ _____

How was the Property Value Determined: _____

Bedrooms / Baths _____ / _____

Lot Size _____   Square Feet _____

Year Built _____   Date Purchased _____ / _____ / 20___

Does the home need repairs?   [ ] **Yes**   [ ] **No**

If yes, what repairs are needed? _____ $ _____

Amount currently owed on the property (in total)? $ _____

1ˢᵗ **Mortgage** Lender: _____ $ _____

What is your monthly payment: $ _____

Does this include Principle, Interest, Taxes and Insurance (PITI)?   [ ] **Yes**   [ ] **No**

2ⁿᵈ **Mortgage** Lender: _____ $ _____

What is your monthly payment: $ _____

Does this include Principle, Interest, Taxes and Insurance (PITI)?   [ ] **Yes**   [ ] **No**

Are the Payments Current?   [ ] **Yes**   [ ] **No**
If "No," how much behind? $_____

Are the Property Taxes Current?   [ ] **Yes**   [ ] **No**
If "No," how much behind? $_____

Any other liens on the house?   [ ] **Yes**   [ ] **No**
If yes, explain:_____

Reason for selling: _____

When do you want / need to move?_____

Why are you moving? _____

What are you immediate cash needs? $ _____

Would you sell your house for what you owe on it?   [ ] **Yes**   [ ] **No**

If I can get you the same amount of money that you would walk away with if you listed, and sold your home through a Realtor®, would you be open to that type of an offer?

                                                                 [ ] **Yes**   [ ] **No**

What's the least amount you would take if you got cash for your equity and I took over your payments? $ _____

- - - - - - - - - - - - - - - - - - Internal Use Only -

Comps #1: $_____   Comps #2: $_____   Comps #3: $_____

Comps #4: $_____   Comps #5: $_____   Market Rent: $_____

Tax Value: $_____   FMV: $ _____   Max Offer: $_____

Notes: _____

PROPERTY
MANAGEMENT AGREEMENT

This Agreement dated on this the _____ day of _____, 20___ is made by and between _____, (hereinafter "Owner"), and _____, (hereinafter "Agent").

1. <u>Agency</u>. The Owner hereby employs the Agent to lease and manage the Owner's property (hereinafter referred to as "Property") located and described as follows:

2. <u>Duties of Agent</u>. In order to properly manage and lease the property, the Agent shall have the following duties and responsibilities:

A. <u>Best Efforts</u>. The Agent shall use its best effort to attract and retain tenants for the property.

B. <u>Lease Negotiations</u>. The Agent shall handle all negotiations with tenants with respect to leases. All such agreements are subject to the approval of the Owner. However, the Owner may provide the Agent with authorization to lease under certain specified terms and conditions.

C. <u>Repairs and Maintenance</u>. The Agent shall contract for or undertake the making of all necessary repairs and the performance of all other necessary work for the benefit of the property including all required alterations to properly carry out this contract.

D. <u>Mortgages and Other Expenses</u>. From the rents received the Agent shall pay all operating expenses and such other expenses as requested by the Owner. This may include the payment of mortgages or taxes.

E. <u>Collection of Rents</u>. The Agent shall collect the rents and other income from the property promptly when such amounts come due taking all necessary steps to collect same and performing all reasonable acts on behalf of the Owner for the protection of the Owner in collection of such amounts. The Agent will make payments to the Owner or such other individual or entity directed by the Owner from time to time from the funds being held the Agent.

F. <u>Representation in Court</u>. The Agent may served all legal notices required by lease or law to the tenants and may maintain any appropriate eviction proceeding in court in its own name.

3. <u>Compensation of Agent</u>. The Owner shall pay the Agent as full compensation for the services of the Agent the sum of _____ ($ _____) Dollars per month. These amounts shall be payable to the Agent when such funds become available from the amounts collected by the Agent according to this contract.

4. <u>Term of Contract</u>. This contract shall continue for a period of one year from the date hereof, and shall be automatically renewed from year to year unless terminated by either party upon written notice sent to the other party not less than fifteen (15) days before any expiration date.

5. <u>Termination of Contract</u>. This contract may be terminated at any time by the Owner upon giving the Agent thirty (30) days written notice in the vent of a bona fide sale of the property, and without notice in the vent the Agent fails to discharge the duties of the Agent faithfully in the manner herein provided.

_____
Owner

_____
Agent

PURCHASE AND SALE AGREEMENT
(Which Favors the Buyer)

THIS AGREEMENT dated this _____/_____/20____ is by and between:
_____ (hereinafter "Seller")
whose address is _____

and

_____ (hereinafter "Buyer")
whose address is _____

1. The Property. The parties hereby agree that Seller will sell and Buyer will buy the following property, located in the County of _____, State of _____, known by street and address as

_____
_____

The sale shall also include all personal property and fixtures, except:

_____
_____

Unless specifically excluded, all other items will be included, whether or not affixed to the property or structures. Seller expressly warrants that property, improvements, building or structures, the appliances, roof, plumbing, heating and/or ventilation systems are in good and working order. This clause shall survive closing of title.

2. Purchase Price. The total purchase price to be paid by Buyer is _____
($_____) payable as follows:

Nonrefundable earnest money deposit (see below) $_____
Balance due at closing in cash or certified funds $_____

3. Earnest Money. Agent of buyer's choice shall hold the buyer's earnest money in escrow. Upon default of this agreement, seller shall retain earnest money as his sole remedy without further recourse between the parties.

4. Mortgage or Third Party Financing. It is agreed that buyer may require a new mortgage loan to finance this purchase. The application for this loan will be made with a lender acceptable to Buyer, and unless a mortgage loan acceptable to buyer is approved without contingencies other than those specified in this contract within 15 (fifteen) days from the date of acceptance of this contract, buyer shall have the right to terminate this contract. Buyer shall return any surveys and copies of leases received from seller. Seller acknowledges that there may be a new institutional mortgage being placed on the property and closing may be extended a reasonable amount of time to accommodate the mortgage financing process.

5. Closing. Closing will held be on or about _____, 20___ at a time and place designated by buyer. Buyer shall choose the escrow, title and/or closing agent. Seller agrees to convey clear title by a general warranty deed, free of any liens, judgments or any other encumbrances. Taxes will be prorated at closing.

At closing, Buyer shall pay the following costs in transferring title:

_____

_____

At closing, Seller shall pay the following costs in transferring title:

_____

_____

Seller agrees to provide possession of the property free of all debris and in "broom clean" condition at closing. Buyer reserves the right to do a final "walk through" the day of closing.

6. Execution in Counterparts. This Agreement may be executed in counterparts and by facsimile signatures. This agreement shall become effective as of the date of signature(s).

7. Inspection. This Agreement is subject to the final inspection and approval of the property by the buyer in writing on or before _____, 20___.

8. Access. Buyer shall be entitled a key and be entitled to access to show partners, lenders, inspectors and/or contractors prior to closing. Buyer may place an appropriate sign on the property prior to closing for prospective tenants and/or assigns.

9. Additional Terms (if any):

_____

_____

_____   _____

Seller   Date

_____   _____

Buyer   Date

PURCHASE AND SALE AGREEMENT
(Which Favors the Seller)

THIS AGREEMENT dated this _____ day of _____, 20____ is by and between:

_____ (hereinafter "Seller")

whose address is _____

and

_____ (hereinafter "Buyer")

whose address is _____.

1. THE PROPERTY. The parties hereby agree that Seller will sell and Buyer will buy the following property, located in the County of _____, State of _____, known by street and address as

_____

_____

Seller makes no warranties, expressed, implied or for any particular purpose about the property, improvements, building or structures, the neighborhood, the appliances, roof, plumbing, heating and/or ventilation systems. Buyer takes the property and everything in or on it in its present 'as is' condition."

2. PURCHASE PRICE. The total purchase price to be paid by Buyer is _____ ($_____) payable as follows:

Nonrefundable earnest money deposit (see below)	$_____
Additional earnest money due on _____, 20__	$_____
Balance due at closing in cash or certified funds	$_____
Owner financing from seller (see below)	$_____
New loan (see below)	$_____

In the event that buyer is required to obtain a new loan from a lending institution, seller shall not be obligated to reduce the purchase price if said lending institution does not appraise the property In an amount equal to the purchase price.

3. EARNEST MONEY. Earnest money must be paid in cash or certified funds and shall be held in escrow by seller or escrow agent of seller's choice. Upon default of this Agreement, seller shall retain all earnest money as liquidated damages and not as a penalty.

4. NEW LOAN. This Agreement is contingent upon buyer's ability to obtain a new loan in the amount of _____ ($_____). Buyer shall make diligent application for a loan new in the amount described above with at least three lending institutions. Buyer is required to accept any loan with reasonable interest rates, terms and closing costs or points offered by lending institution. Buyer shall provide seller with written proof of a firm loan commitment on or before _____, 20___.

Within 48 hours of the execution of this Agreement, buyer shall provide seller with buyer's complete financial and credit information for seller's approval. Within 72 hours after receipt of such information, Seller may terminate this contract and refund buyer's earnest money if, in seller's sole opinion, buyer does not have the creditworthiness to qualify for a loan from a third party. Seller's decision and opinion shall be final in this regard, and buyer shall have no further recourse after return of his earnest money deposit.

In the event that Seller approves of buyer's financial ability to qualify for a loan, buyer hereby gives his/her/its express permission to all parties, including lenders, employers, financial institutions, credit agencies, mortgage brokers and real estate agents to release any appropriate financial information to the seller. Seller shall not be obligated to complete any repairs, improvements or upgrades required by buyer's lending institution.

6. SELLER FINANCING. In the event part of the purchase price is to be satisfied by seller financing, buyer shall provide seller with buyer's complete financial and credit information for seller's approval. Within 72 hours after receipt of such information, Seller may terminate this contract and refund buyer's earnest money if, in seller's sole opinion, buyer's creditworthiness and/or financial ability are not sufficient. Buyer agrees to execute a "Fannie Mae" style promissory note and mortgage prepared by seller to secure performance of payment. Such mortgage shall be drafted by the seller and shall contain a strict "due-on-sale" provision.

8. CLOSING. Closing will held be on _____, 20___ at a time and place designated by seller. Seller shall choose the escrow, title and/or closing agent.

At closing, buyer shall pay the following costs in transferring title:
    [ ] title insurance policy
    [ ] loan assumption
    [ ] transfer fee
    [ ] transfer taxes
    [ ] recording fees
    [ ] title company closing, escrow and delivery charges
    [ ] hazard insurance premium
    [ ] mortgage insurance premium
    [ ] survey
    [ ] credit application
    [ ] Other _____

The following Items will be prorated at closing:

[ ] Mortgage insurance
[ ] Property taxes
[ ] PMI Insurance
[ ] Hazard insurance
[ ] Homeowner's association dues
[ ] Rents
[ ] Other _____

Seller agrees to convey title by a special warranty deed. In the event that an abstract of title issued by a reputable title company reveals defects in title, seller shall have the option of curing said title or canceling this Agreement. Upon cancellation, seller shall return buyer's deposit. Seller agrees to deliver possession of the property within five (5) working days of closing.

9. NOT ASSIGNABLE. This Agreement is not assignable by the buyer.

10. EXECUTION IN COUNTERPARTS. This Agreement may be executed in counterparts and by facsimile signatures. This Agreement shall become effective as of the date of the last signature.

11. LEAD INSPECTION. Buyer shall be permitted an opportunity to inspect the premises solely for the purposes of the presence of lead-based paint hazards on or before _____, 20___. Lead addendum required? [ ] **Yes**   [ ] **No**

12. TIME IS OF THE ESSENCE. All parties agree that time is of the essence in this Agreement.

_____   Date:_____
Seller

_____   Date:_____
Buyer

SECURITY DEPOSIT AGREEMENT

The undersigned Tenant(s) have paid to Landlord the sum of $_____ as a security deposit for the premises located at:

_____

_____

Tenant may not, without Landlord's prior written consent, apply this security deposit to the last month's rent or to any other sum due under this Agreement. Landlord, may, in his/her/its sole discretion, apply part or all of this security towards unpaid rents, late charges or any other charges due on the annexed lease agreement.

Within 30 days after Tenant has vacated the premises in "broom clean" condition, removed all personal effects and rubbish, returned keys and provided Landlord with a forwarding address, Landlord will provide Tenant with an itemized written statement of the reasons for, and the dollar amount of, any of the security deposit retained by the Landlord, along with a check for any balance remaining.

_____   Date:_____
Tenant

_____   Date:_____
Tenant

_____   Date:_____
Landlord

SELLER'S DISCLOSURE STATEMENT

PROPERTY ADDRESS: _____

Purpose of Statement: This statement is a disclosure of the condition of the property in compliance with the Sellers Disclosure Act. This statement is a disclosure of the condition and information concerning the property, known by the Seller(s). Unless otherwise advised, the Seller(s) do not/does not possess any expertise in construction, architecture, engineering, or any other specific area related to the construction or condition of the improvements on the property or the land. Also, unless otherwise advised, the Seller(s) has not conducted any inspection of generally inaccessible areas such as the foundation or roof. This statement is not a warranty of any kind by the Seller(s) or by any agent representing the Seller(s) in this transaction, and is not a substitute for any inspections or warranties the buyer may wish to obtain.

Seller(s)'s Disclosure: The Seller(s) disclose(s) the following information with the knowledge that even though this is not a warranty, the Seller(s) specifically makes the following representations based on the Seller(s) knowledge at the signing of this document. Upon receiving this statement from the Seller(s), the Seller(s)'s agent is required to provide a copy to the buyer or the agent of the buyer. The Seller(s) authorizes its/their agent(s) to provide a copy of this statement to any prospective buyer in connection with any actual or anticipated sale of property. The following are representations made solely by the Seller(s)and are not the representations of the Seller(s)'s agent(s), if any.

This information is a disclosure only and is not intended to be a part of any contract between buyer and Seller(s).

Instructions to the Seller(s): (1) Answer ALL questions. (2) Report known conditions affecting the property. (3) Attach additional pages with your signature if additional space is required. (4) Complete this form yourself. (5) If some items do not apply to your property, check NOT AVAILABLE. If you do not know the facts, check UNKNOWN.

Failure To Provide A Purchaser With A Signed Disclosure Statement Will Enable A Purchaser To Terminate An Otherwise Binding Purchase Agreement.

Appliances / Services / Systems

The items below are in working order and are included in the sale of the property – if the purchase agreement so provides:

	Yes	No	Unknown
Attic Fan	_____	_____	_____
Ceiling Fan(s)	_____	_____	_____
Central Air Conditioning	_____	_____	_____
Central Heating System	_____	_____	_____
City Sewer System	_____	_____	_____
City Water System	_____	_____	_____
Dishwasher	_____	_____	_____
Dryer	_____	_____	_____
Electrical System	_____	_____	_____
Fireplace & Chimney	_____	_____	_____
Garage Door Opener & Remote Control	_____	_____	_____
Hood/Fan	_____	_____	_____
Lawn Sprinkler System	_____	_____	_____
Microwave	_____	_____	_____
Pool Heater, Wall Liner & Equipment	_____	_____	_____
Plumbing System	_____	_____	_____
Range/Oven	_____	_____	_____
Refrigerator	_____	_____	_____
Sauna/Hot Tub	_____	_____	_____
Septic Tank & Drain Field	_____	_____	_____
Sump Pump	_____	_____	_____
Trash Compactor	_____	_____	_____
TV Antenna, Controls and Rotor	_____	_____	_____
Washer	_____	_____	_____
Water Heater	_____	_____	_____
Water Softener/Conditioner	_____	_____	_____
Wall Furnace	_____	_____	_____
Well & Pump	_____	_____	_____

Comments:

_____

_____

_____

Unless otherwise agreed, all household appliances are sold in working order except as noted, without warranty beyond date of closing.

Property Conditions, Improvements & Additional Information

1. Basement / Crawl Space: Has there been evidence of water?   [ ] **Yes**   [ ] **No**
   If yes, explain:

_____

_____

_____

2. Insulation: Is there any?   [ ] **Yes**   [ ] **No**
   If known, describe:

_____

_____

   Urea Formaldehyde Foam Insulation (UFFI) installed?   [ ] **UnKnown** [ ] **Yes**   [ ] **No**

3. Roof: Are there any leaks?   [ ] **Yes**   [ ] **No**
   If yes, explain:

_____

_____

   If known, approximate age _____

4. Well: Is there a well on the property?   [ ] **Yes**   [ ] **No**
   If yes, what type of well if known: (i.e. depth, diameter, age, repair history, etc)

_____

_____

   Has the water been tested?   [ ] **Yes**   [ ] **No**

5. Septic Tanks / Drain Fields: Are they included with the property?   [ ] **Yes**   [ ] **No**
   If known, describe:

_____

_____

_____

6. Heating System: Is a heating system included?   [ ] **Yes**   [ ] **No**
   If yes, what type and of what approximate age if known:

_____

_____

_____

7. Plumbing System: Is one included with the property?　　　[ ] **Yes**　　[ ] **No**
　　Type: _____ Copper _____ Galvanized _____ Other: _____
　　Are there are any known problems, explain:

_____
_____
_____

8. Electrical System: Are there any known problems?　　　[ ] **Yes**　　[ ] **No**
　　If yes, explain:

_____
_____
_____

9. History of Infestations: Are there any known problems?　　[ ] **Yes**　　[ ] **No**
　　If yes, explain: (i.e. carpenter ants, cockroaches, termites, etc)

_____
_____
_____

10. Environmental Problems: Are you aware of any substances, materials or products that may be an environmental hazard such as, but not limited to, asbestos, radon gas, formaldehyde, lead-based paint, fuel or chemical storage tanks and contaminated soil on the property?　　　　　[ ] **UnKnown**　　[ ] **Yes**　　[ ] **No**

If yes, explain:

_____
_____
_____
_____
_____
_____

11. Flood Insurance:
　　Do you have flood insurance on the property?　　　　[ ] **Yes**　　[ ] **No**

12. Mineral Rights:
　　Do you own any mineral rights?　　　　[ ] **UnKnown**　　[ ] **Yes**　　[ ] **No**

Miscellaneous
Are you aware of any of the following items:

1. Any encroachments, easements, zoning violations, or nonconforming uses?

[ ] **UnKnown**   [ ] **Yes**   [ ] **No**

2. Any 'common area' facilities such as pools, tennis courts, walkways or other co-owned or homeowners association areas that have authority over the property?

[ ] **UnKnown**   [ ] **Yes**   [ ] **No**

3. Structural modifications, alterations, or repairs made without necessary permits or licensed contractors?

[ ] **UnKnown**   [ ] **Yes**   [ ] **No**

4. Settling, flooding, drainage, structural, or grading problems?

[ ] **UnKnown**   [ ] **Yes**   [ ] **No**

5. Major damage to the property from fire, wind, floods, or landslides?

[ ] **UnKnown**   [ ] **Yes**   [ ] **No**

6. Any underground storage tanks?

[ ] **UnKnown**   [ ] **Yes**   [ ] **No**

7. Any outstanding utility assessments or fees, including any natural gas main extension surcharge?

[ ] **UnKnown**   [ ] **Yes**   [ ] **No**

8. Any outstanding municipal assessments of fees?

[ ] **UnKnown**   [ ] **Yes**   [ ] **No**

9. Any pending litigation that could affect the property or the Seller (s)'s right to convey the property?

[ ] **UnKnown**   [ ] **Yes**   [ ] **No**

If the answer to any of these questions is yes, explain and use additional sheets if necessary:

_____
_____
_____
_____
_____
_____
_____
_____
_____
_____
_____

The Seller(s) has/have lived in the residence on the property from _____ (date) to _____ (date). The Seller(s) has/have owned the property since _____ (date). The Seller(s) has indicated above the condition of all the items based on information known to the Seller(s). If any changes occur in the structural / mechanical / appliance / services / systems of this property from the date of this form to the date of closing, Seller(s) will immediately disclose the changes to buyer. In no event shall the parties hold the broker liable for any representations not directly made by the broker or broker's agent.

Seller(s) certifies that the information in this statement is true and correct to the best of Seller(s)'s knowledge as of the date of Seller(s)'s signature.

Buyer should obtain professional advice and inspections of the property to more fully determine the condition of the property. Buyers are advised that certain information compiled pursuant to the sex offenders registration act, 1994 pa 295, mcl 28.721 to 28.732, is available to the public. Buyers seeking that information should contact the appropriate local law enforcement agency or sheriff's department directly.

Buyer is advised that the state equalized value of the property, homestead exemption information and other real property tax information is available from the appropriate local assessor's office. Buyer should not assume that buyer's future tax bills on the property will be the same as the seller(s)'s present tax bills. Under some state laws, real property tax obligations can change significantly when property is transferred.

By signing below I/we acknowledge to have filled out and completed this form in its entirety.

_____	_____	_____
Seller	Printed Name	Date
_____	_____	_____
Seller	Printed Name	Date

Buyer has read and acknowledges receipt of this statement in its entirety.

_____	_____	_____
Buyer	Printed Name	Date
_____	_____	_____
Buyer	Printed Name	Date

SELLER'S DISCLOSURE STATEMENT FOR INVESTORS

PROPERTY ADDRESS: _____

NOTICE TO BUYER(S):   This is a disclosure of Seller's knowledge of the condition of the property as of the date signed by Seller(s) and is not a substitute for any inspections or warranties that Buyer(s) may wish to obtain. It is not a warranty of any kind by Seller(s) or a warranty or representation by anyone involved in the sale of this property.

1.   Seller(s)s have owned the property for _____ less (or) ___ more than one year.
2.   Seller(s) have never lived in the property.
3.   Buyer(s) acknowledge(s) Seller(s) is/are Investor(s) and reselling for profit.
4.   Seller(s) can make no warranties or guarantees of any kind as to any aspect of the property's condition or contents. Buyer(s) acknowledge(s) receipt of copy of previous Seller's Property Disclosures if available.

_____   _____   _____
Seller   Printed Name   Date

_____   _____   _____
Seller   Printed Name   Date

RECEIPT AND ACKNOWLEDGMENT BY BUYER

I have inspected the property and the surrounding neighborhood or area and have been advised to seek professional help for an inspection should I so desire. I acknowledge that the Seller(s) is (are) not an expert(s) in detecting or repairing any defects to the property.

I understand that unless otherwise stated in the contract and sales agreement with Seller(s), the property is being conveyed in its current "As-Is"/"Where-Is" condition, with NO warranties or guarantees of any kind by the Seller(s). By affixing my signature below, I acknowledge that NO representations concerning the property are being relied on by me (us) except those disclosed above and/or those in the contract and sales agreement.

I have been informed to seek legal advice should it be desired.

_____   _____   _____
Buyer   Printed Name   Date

_____   _____   _____
Buyer   Printed Name   Date

TENANT / BUYER APPLICATION FEE RECEIPT
(*Required of each adult that will reside in the property*)

This Receipt is provided to: _____ who
tendered an application fee of $25.00 on _____ day of _____, 20___.

Said application fee has been charged each prospective tenant wanting to complete a rental / option to purchase application. This fee is to cover the cost of processing and initiating a credit check.

NOTE: **The $_____ application fee is non-refundable**.

_____
Landlord
(Authorized Signature)

TENANT / BUYER INFORMATION

Date: _____/_____/20____

Which property are you calling about? _____

Prospective Buyer Name: _____

Contact Phone: (_____) _____ - _____   E-Mail: _____

1. How would you rate your credit?   [ ] **Excellent** [ ] **Good** [ ] **Fair** [ ] **Poor**

2. Do you have any problems with us running your credit?   [ ] **Yes**   [ ] **No**

3. Within the last 7 years have you had a foreclosure or bankruptcy?   [ ] **Yes**   [ ] **No**

4. Have you have a loan application turned down in the past?   [ ] **Yes**   [ ] **No**

5. Do you currently rent or own?   [ ] **Rent** [ ] **Own**

6. What is your current rent/mortgage payment per month? $_____

7. How quickly do you need a home?   [ ] **Within 30 days**
                                           [ ] **Within 90 days**
                                           [ ] **Open**

8. Employment?   [ ] **Employed**
                       [ ] **Self-Employed**
                       [ ] **Retired**

9. What is your present gross monthly income? $_____
     ("Take-home" income equal to at least two times the monthly lease payment)

10. How much cash do you have to put down? $_____

Comments or Questions: _____

_____

_____

www.ingramcontent.com/pod-product-compliance
Lightning Source LLC
Chambersburg PA
CBHW050827220326
41598CB00006B/331